FINAL RESTING PLACES

ORANGE COUNTY'S DEAD AND FAMOUS

FAIRHAVEN MAUSOLEUM
A.D. 1916

Michael Thomas Barry

Schiffer Publishing Ltd

4880 Lower Valley Road, Atglen, Pennsylvania 19310

Copyright © 2010 by Michael Thomas Barry
Text and photos courtesy of author
Library of Congress Control Number: 2009937638

Designed by Stephanie Daugherty
Type set in Trajan/New Baskerville BT

ISBN: 978-0-7643-3421-4
Printed in The United States of America

DEDICATION

To my wife, Christyn, I owe more than I can ever express. This book is a tribute to you, an amazing woman who can do almost anything she puts her mind to. You have been with me every step of the way and have been an inspiration. Any success I have is due to your unconditional love and commonsense critiques. This book could not have been written without you; thank you from the bottom of my heart—I love you.

It is with a heavy heart and with great emotion that I also want to dedicate this book to the memory of my father, Thomas F. Barry. He was a man of great integrity, who over came many adversities in life but never complained. He was a mentor and friend, who is missed everyday. I hope that I have made you proud; I love you; rest in peace.

ACKNOWLEDGMENTS

Writing a book is an adventure. To begin with, it is a toy and an amusement; then it becomes a mistress, then it becomes a master, and then a tyrant. In the last phase is that just as you are about to be reconciled to your servitude, you kill the monster, and fling him out to the public.

~ *Winston Churchill*
Prime Minister of Great Britain (1874 to 1965)

I wish to express my sincere thanks to all those who helped support me through this exhaustive writing process. There have been so many kind and caring people that have helped write this book. To those I inadvertently fail to acknowledge, a sincere thank you. I am especially grateful to Kimberly Eazell, whose knowledge of famous graves in Orange County is unequalled, and without whose help, large portions of this book could not have been written.

I also received valuable assistance from numerous cemetery employees, especially Jerry Neiblas (Mission San Juan Capistrano), Lou Carlson (Fairhaven Memorial Park), Julio Amarillas, (Santa Ana Cemetery), and Bill Steiner, (Anaheim Cemetery). They went the extra mile to provide me with inside information that otherwise would have been impossible to uncover.

To Gene Ellis and Mark Traversino, whose relatives are mentioned in this book, the information you provided was priceless, and without such would have made a complete evaluation of their loved ones lives incomplete.

I have been very fortunate to have been guided in my research by many thoughtful and intuitive individuals. I want to especially thank Deb McGrath for her friendship and guidance. Without her unique insight and intuitive nature, this book would have been difficult to write.

It is hard to properly find the words to acknowledge family members who have been most supportive during this writing process. To my in-laws, Phyllis and Steve Nelson, and my sister Laura Barry, thanks for supporting my dreams. My deep love and appreciation goes out to my stepdaughters, Kate and Allyson Triglia, for their encouragement and support. To my daughter Ashley Barry, who helped edit and kept me company on numerous cemetery expeditions, all my love and thanks. To my mother, Dolores Barry, I extend special gratitude. Over the years, your sacrifices have been unparalleled, your love has been unconditional, and you are irreplaceable. I do not know where I would be without you—all my love and thanks.

I want to extend my special gratitude to those important people who have passed on from this life. To my grandparents, you taught me how to love, educated me on the importance of family values, gave me wisdom, and provided financial security— you are missed. Without them this book could never have been written.

To the staff at Schiffer Books; thanks for giving me the chance of a lifetime. To all the other amazing people that I met on this wondrous journey, and have failed to acknowledge, I apologize for not including you, but you know who you are, thank you from the bottom of my heart.

CONTENTS

INTRODUCTION

On a bright sunny afternoon in March, I walked the steep, wind-swept slope down to the holy grail of Orange County gravesites. Pacific View Memorial Park in Newport Beach, California, with its panoramic views of the Pacific Ocean, and its quiet, park like atmosphere hold the mortal remains of one of Hollywood's true iconic legends. The gravesite of John Wayne is the most well-known burial place in the county. To the chagrin of cemetery personnel, it is also the world's worst-kept secret. Wayne's simple bronze grave marker is underwhelming at first, but as one stands and contemplates the accomplishments of this humble and legendary figure, it is hard not to celebrate his life.

Then looking out at the beauty of the bright blue Pacific Ocean in the distance, you can not help but think of your own mortality. What have I accomplished in this life, have I been a good person, and will I be remembered? These are simple questions that enter your mind in places such as this. These questions are not easily answered, but what is certain is that our destinies in the end are all the same.

My thoughts then drifted to an epitaph I came across while touring another cemetery in researching this book; the grave was of no one of great importance but its message was profound. It read "from where you stand now, I once stood, and from where I am now, you will one day be." Those are powerful and thought-provoking words. In our busy lives, we don't often take the time to sit and enjoy life.

Orange County is a land of many faces. It is where summer never ends and one can see endless miles of white sandy beaches meeting the bright blue Pacific Ocean. It's where scantly clad sun worshippers mingle with fanny pack wearing, camera touting tourists. It is where the "Happiest Place on Earth" meets the "Real House Wives of Orange County." It's about gated communities, strip malls, and the movie mega-plex. Orange County is all of these things and more.

The historical roots of the county run much deeper than anyone has been led to believe. It is hard to imagine what the county looked like 200 years ago; the landscape has changed dramatically. The low rolling hills laden with wild flowers, the canyons covered in dry scrub brush, and abundant forms of wild life everywhere have been replaced by super highways, Olive Garden Restaurants, and Wal-Marts. The casual observer has to look really deep to find the cultural and historical heritage of the region.

My intention in writing this book is to celebrate the history and culture of Orange County. In this book are the stories of the famous people, whose lives contributed to the historical and cultural growth of this county. This book is not just about death, dying, and cemeteries. Although, that does take up a good portion of the manuscript, its main function is to celebrate and memorialize the lives of these noteworthy people. Orange County has always played second fiddle to its more populous neighbor to the north, Los Angeles. The cemeteries and graveyards of Los Angles are teaming with a host of well-known celebrities. But Orange County is also fertile soil for the rich, famous, and infamous. Since the late 1700s, Orange County has been a lure for those seeking fame, wealth, and opportunity. Explorers, fortune seekers, scalawags, entertainers, and sports stars, all alike have been drawn to its golden shores.

I have attempted to find and include as many of the famous graves as possible. The sheer volume has unfortunately led me to make some drastic cuts, and I apologize to those people who have not been included. The three criteria used to determine whether a person was to be included are as follows: one, they must be dead; two, they must be buried within the boundaries of Orange County; and three, they must have contributed something of importance or have been involved in some kind of important historical or cultural event. Numerous celebrities and other noteworthy people have had their ashes scattered at sea near the Orange County coastline and I have chosen not to include them in this book.

I must explain that I have an immense love and respect for the game of baseball. It is my belief that baseball is America, and its history is our history; baseball marks the passage of time. I have chosen to include every professional baseball player that I could find who is buried within the boundaries of Orange County—no matter if the person played one game or just one inning.

We all have a story to tell, and the people I have chosen to write about, all lived as we live, and their stories have needed to be told for a long time. This book is a celebration of life, not of death. I also wanted to explore the forces that draw us to the graves of famous people. Why are their lives and deaths fascinating to us? Is it that their joys, loves, triumphs, defeats, last moments, and final resting places, all encompass a life we do not have? In other words, are these people more than the granite, the marble, and the bronze markers that mark their graves? I think the answer is simply yes; they are more, and in the end, all any of us really wants is to be remembered. Writing this book has been a great labor of love. Its incarnation has evolved over my entire lifetime. Through personal experiences, educational training, and professional opportunities, all have led me to write this volume.

In conclusion, the cult of celebrity in which many people propel themselves today, has become a new form of religion. The searching out and visitation of the graves of famous people has become a growing pastime for a large number of fans. Whatever the reason for visiting the graves of the rich, famous, infamous, and noteworthy, the main enjoyment is being as close to our heroes as possible. Our presence in these cemeteries and mausoleums announces that there is an unbroken chain that stretches back to the roots of our county, state, and nation; and by extension, this links us to the future.

~ Michael T. Barry
Anaheim Hills, California

1

HISTORIC GRAVEYARDS

History is the version of past events
that people have decided to agree upon.

~Napoleon Bonaparte
Emperor of France (1769-1821)

I n the busy urban sprawl of today's Orange County, it is hard to imagine the old days of the missions and ranchos. It was a time when there were no freeways, strip malls, or Disneyland. Orange County's historical past is often difficult to locate, but not impossible to find. Interspersed between the planned communities and movie megaplexes are deep historical roots. Those roots are just as old, if not older, than the East Coast. Our preservation of important landmarks has been lagging. This chapter will discuss the historic cemeteries in which are interred many founding fathers and historically significant people. These individuals laid the groundwork for the modern county we see today. They shaped the history of the region, state, country and world.

THE RICHARD M. NIXON PRESIDENTIAL LIBRARY, MUSEUM, AND BIRTHPLACE

18001 Yorba Linda Boulevard
Yorba Linda, California 92886
Telephone: 714-983-9120

Open daily 10 a.m. to 5 p.m., Sundays 11 a.m to 5 p.m.

RICHARD MILHOUS NIXON

No discussion of famous final resting places in Orange County can begin without telling the story of the county's most illustrious resident and native son, Richard Milhous Nixon (January 9, 1913 to April 22, 1994). Nixon was the 37th President of the United States (1969-1974), 36th Vice-President of the

United States (1953-1961), United States Senator (1950-1953), and United States Congressman (1947-1950).

In July of 1990, the Richard Nixon Library and Birthplace was opened in Yorba Linda, California. It was originally a private institution that was run on donations. It was built around land that was once owned by the Nixon family. The centerpiece of the library would be the restored house in which Nixon had been born. The library was officially brought into the system of federally funded Presidential libraries on 2007. Today, the library is also the repository for the President's records and archives.

Nixon was born in Yorba Linda, California, in a house built by his father. He attended Fullerton and Whittier High Schools, was a graduate of Whittier College, and the Duke University School of Law. In 1938, he met his future bride and first lady, Pat Ryan. The two were married on June 21, 1940. During World War II, he rose through the ranks of the Navy to become a lieutenant commander. He was assigned to the Pacific Combat Air Transport Command, which supported the southwest Pacific theater during the war. He was discharged from military service in 1946.[1]

Nixon's foray into politics took place in 1946, when he was elected to the United States House of Representatives from California's 12th District. He gained national attention during the Alger Hiss Spy case, as an ardent anti-communist. In 1950, he ran for the United States Senate against Democrat Helen Douglas. It was Douglas who nicknamed him "tricky Dick," for his unsavory campaign techniques. Nixon won the election in a landslide. In the Senate, he was known as a critic of President Harry Truman, and for his anti-communist stance. In 1953, he was selected by Republican Presidential candidate Dwight D. Eisenhower as his Vice-Presidential running mate. The Eisenhower/Nixon ticket defeated Democrat Adali Stevenson in a landslide. During the Eisenhower administration, Nixon transformed the office of Vice-President from a figurehead into a powerful and important position. In 1959, he was sent by President Eisenhower to the Soviet Union to meet with Soviet Premier Nikita Khruchev. Their meeting was a rousing success, and the debates that occurred between Nixon and the Soviet leader became legendary. The two debated the merits of Capitalism and Communism in what became known as the "kitchen debates."[2]

In 1960, Nixon launched a campaign for president against Democrat John F. Kennedy. Nixon lost the election by a very narrow margin. The loss was blamed on Nixon's lack of physical appeal and his perceived mediocre performance on several nationally televised debates. This was the first major political set back for Nixon and he retreated to his home in California to assess his future. The next few years Nixon wrote several books and practiced law. In 1962, encouraged by state Republicans, he ran for Governor of California against Democrat Pat Brown. The campaign was clouded with controversy and Nixon again lost by a narrow margin.

This could have spelled the end of Nixon's political career. The next six years were spent waging war against social ills of the country and trying to resurrect his political image. In 1968, he again ran for president. Nixon appeared to be the calming factor in a time of extreme upheaval, with the assassinations of Martin Luther King, and Robert F. Kennedy, the country was on the brink and needed change. His campaign slogan, "Nixon's the One," was a success, and he handily defeated Democrat Hubert Humphrey in a landslide.[3]

President Richard M. Nixon and Pat Nixon's burial site.

In Nixon's first term as president, he set out to restore relations with allies, putting an end to the arms race with the Soviets and Chinese. He also ramped up military operations in Southeast Asia, approving more troops and the bombing of North Vietnam. In 1972, he ran for a second term as president. The campaign against George McGovern was easy, and he again won by a landslide. Nixon's second term was filled political scandal. Paranoia in the administration led to a cover-up of a break-in at the Democratic National Headquarters at the Watergate office complex in Washington. Implication of improper actions led all the way back to the office of the president. Nixon was implicated in the cover-up and was forced to resign the presidency.

On the evening of August 8, 1974, before a nationally televised audience, Richard Nixon became the first president in United States history to resign. The next day, Vice-President Gerald R. Ford took the oath of office and succeeded Richard Nixon as the 38th President of the United States. Nixon returned to his San Clemente home in disgrace. On September 8, 1974, he was pardoned by President Ford for any and all involvement in the Watergate scandal. Over the next few decades, Nixon attempted to rehabilitate his tarnished image. To a great extent his was successful; he authored numerous books on world affairs, and gained support as an elder statesman.[4]

PAT NIXON

On June 22, 1993, Pat Nixon died from complications of emphysema and lung cancer. Her funeral services and burial were held at the Nixon Library. She was laid to rest in a simple grave in the rose garden of the library. Richard Nixon was distraught and retreated to his home in New Jersey to write. Eight months later on April 18, 1994, he suffered a severe stroke, and fell into a deep coma from which he never recovered. The 37th President of the United States died on April 22, 1994, at age eighty-one. His funeral was held five days later at the Nixon Library. It was his express wish not to have a state funeral. Speaking at the funeral service were President Bill Clinton, Henry Kissenger, Senator Bob Dole, California Governor Pete Wilson, and the reverend Billy Graham. Also in attendance were four former Presidents; Ford, Carter, Reagan, and Bush. Richard Nixon was laid to rest next to his wife, Pat, in the rose garden of the library, just yards from the home in which he was born.[5]

Nixon's legacy today was primarily in foreign policy. He was an idiosyncratic President with brilliant ideas, but lacked moral fortitude. He had a practical approach to relations with the Soviet Union and China. His escalation and continuation of the Vietnam War was a part of his downfall. A CSPAN 2009 poll ranked the former president 27th among the 44 men who have held the office.[6] It is apparent that history is treating Nixon better than his contemporaries did. He had again arisen from the ashes, a true survivor. Will the second half of the twentieth century be known as the "age of Nixon," as Senator Bob Dole stated in his eulogy?[7] Only time will tell.

MISSION SAN JUAN CAPISTRANO

26801 Ortega Highway
San Juan Capistrano, California
Telephone: 926-234-1300

The old cemetery on the grounds of Mission San Juan Capistrano is the oldest graveyard in Orange County. Actually, the mission cemetery is divided into two separate places. The oldest cemetery on the actual grounds of the mission, next to the Serra Chapel was established in 1781. A newer burial ground was established in the mid-1800s, off the grounds of the mission, on a hill, near the present day intersection of the Ortega Highway and interstate 5 freeway.

The Mission San Juan Capistrano was actually founded twice, first in 1775 by father Francisco de Lausen, and in 1776 by father Junipero Serra. The first recorded burial at the mission occurred in 1781. In the years leading up to the establishment of the new mission cemetery, nearly 4,000 Native Americans and early settlers of San Juan Capistrano were buried on the grounds. At the time, it was the custom to dig up the remains after a few years and transfer the bones to a common grave within the cemetery. This allowed for new burials. Bones were relocated numerous times, so that a small space like the mission cemetery could hold many thousands of remains.

Unfortunately, no one knows exactly where any given grave is located in the cemetery. Most of the graves within the cemetery are unmarked with a few exceptions. A large memorial, dedicated in 1924, stands in the middle of the cemetery and it honors the Native Americans interred within the grounds who helped build and establish the mission. Also interred below the Serra Chapel alter floor are many priests who called the mission home. Many visitors to Mission San Juan Capistrano ask where Father Junipero Serra is buried.

✤ He died on August 28, 1784, at his beloved Mission San Carlos Borromeo in Carmel, and he is interred beneath the sanctuary floor there.

JOSE ANTONIO YORBA I

There are two famous burials on the grounds. First is Jose Antonio Yorba I (July 20, 1743 to January 16, 1825). Yorba was a Spanish soldier, and early settler of Alta California. He was born in Catalonia, Spain, and came to America for adventure and wealth. Yorba was a corporal in explorer Gaspar de Portola's expedition to map Alta California in 1769. In the following decades, he was stationed throughout different outposts of the Alta California frontier. By 1797, Yorba had retired from the military and settled down to a quiet, private life. In 1810, he was granted lands by the King of Spain for services rendered to the crown. Yorba was the grantee of Rancho Santiago de Santa Ana. This land was immense and today consists of almost the entire County of Orange. Yorba and his wife had many children, several of whom went on to fame and fortune of their own.

The history of the Yorba family is the history of Orange County. Jose Antonio Yorba I died at his rancho on January 16, 1825 at age eighty-two.[8] He was buried at the mission cemetery in an unmarked grave (at his request). The location of the grave was lost to time, and it was only in recent years that a cenotaph marker was placed near what is believed to be Yorba's final resting place. The headstone is hard to miss. There are only a few markers in the cemetery, and Yorba's is near the center path sidewalk.

The original Spanish grantee of the Rancho Santiago de Santa Ana, Jose Antonio Yorba's grave at the Mission San Juan Capistrano.

MONSIGNOR JOHN O'SULLIVAN

The other notable burial on the cemetery grounds is that of Monsignor John O'Sullivan (March 19, 1874 to July 22, 1933). Father O'Sullivan is best known as the restorer of the old mission. He was placed in charge of the mission ruins in 1910. His dream was to restore the mission buildings to their former glory. Slowly the old mission was restored. It was an arduous task. By 1918, the job had been completed and Father O'Sullivan was appointed the first modern pastor of the church. O'Sullivan died on July 22, 1933 in Orange, California.[9] He was originally buried at the Calvary Chapel in Los Angeles but his remains were moved to the Mission cemetery at a later date.[10] Today, Father O'Sullivan's tomb is found between the Serra Chapel he helped to restore and the cemetery memorial he helped to build.

THE OLD MISSION CEMETERY

Ortega Highway, east of Interstate 5

When the burial grounds of the mission were filled in the early 1860s, a new mission cemetery was established on a nearby hill. The land on which the cemetery was established has always been a burial site. Since the early 1800s, local Native Americans buried their dead in and around the present day location. The land was originally owned by James Sheehan (d. October 8, 1888). He donated the one-acre parcel to the mission in 1870. Sheehan is also interred within the grounds.

Today, the cemetery is overseen by mission personnel in cooperation with the Diocese of Orange. Burials are limited to those who can prove direct lineage to area pioneers. Like Yorba Cemetery (which will be discussed later), this cemetery was vandalized and in disrepair for many years. Most of the original grave markers have been destroyed. The cemetery records are sketchy and incomplete; actual burial locations are almost impossible to find. The grounds have been left in a natural state, out of respect for the Native American interments. Buried within the grounds are numerous pioneers of the area, as well as their descendants. Also interred within the grounds are several prominent participants of the infamous Juan Flores raid, which will be discussed in Chapter Eight.

The cemetery is located just east of interstate five, on the Ortega Highway. Turn left at the Shell gas station, park along the frontage road (limited spaces); the cemetery is on the right, at the top of a small hill, a one-lane access road (no cars allowed) leads to the gates. The cemetery has very limited public access and visitation is guarded and granted in very limited numbers by special request.[11]

JOHN FORSTER

The most famous burial at this cemetery is John Forster (1815 to 1882). Forster, known as "Don Juan," was one of the largest landowners in California. He married Ysidora Pico in 1837; she was the sister of the last Mexican Governor of California, Pio Pico. With this family connection, Forster was able to acquire

The Forster family vault at the Old Mission Cemetery.

vast tracts of land that today includes parts of Camp Pendleton, Mission Viejo, Rancho Santa Margareta, and Trabuco Canyon that encompassed nearly 200,000 acres of land. In 1844, he purchased the ruins of the old mission—it was there that he made his home until 1864—at that point, the property was deeded back to the Catholic Church. After his death in 1882, the rancho Trabuco and Mission Viejo were sold to James Flood.[12] Don Juan Forster is buried on the grounds of the Old Mission Cemetery. His small above-ground family burial vault in the center of the grounds is the only such edifice in the cemetery.

THE YORBA CEMETERY

Woodgate Park
Yorba Linda, California 92886
Telephone: 714-973-3190

It is open for public tours on the first Saturday of each month from 11:30 a.m. to 12:30 p.m. (based on staff availability).

The Yorba Cemetery is the oldest private cemetery in Orange County. In 1858, Don Bernardo Yorba deeded one acre of land for a cemetery to the Catholic Church, on a hill, one-quarter mile west of his rancho in Yorba Linda. Only the Mission Cemetery at San Juan Capistrano predates this cemetery in its age. Interred within the grounds are many members of the Yorba family (including Bernardo Yorba) as well as other prominent citizens of the Santa Ana Canyon area. The cemetery was closed to new burials in 1939; it then became neglected and was desecrated by vandals. Many of the original headstones and grave markers were stolen or destroyed. In 1967, the Orange County Board of Supervisors was deeded the land by the Catholic Archdiocese and began to restore the historical cemetery to its original look. Today, the tiny cemetery is tucked between housing developments, and is difficult to find.

BERNARDO YORBA

The most famous burial within the graveyard is that of Bernardo Yorba (August 4, 1801 to October 21, 1858). Bernardo was the tenth of fourteen children of Jose Antonio Yorba I. Bernardo was one of the largest landholders of early Orange County. In 1834, he was granted land by the Mexican government. The Rancho Canon de Santa Ana encompassed nearly 13,000 acres of modern day Yorba Linda, Anaheim, Brea, and Placentia.[13]

Bernardo Yorba built a huge adobe hacienda on the land that was the center of social life in the Santa Ana Valley. During his lifetime Yorba was married three times, with two of his wives dying in childbirth. He fathered twenty children.

He died on October 21, 1858 at the rancho, and in his last will and testament stipulated that a small portion of the rancho be made into a cemetery.

The Mexican land grant owner of the Rancho Canon de Santa Ana, Don Bernardo Yorba's grave site, Yorba Cemetery.

Temporarily, his body was to be interred at the old Calvary Church cemetery in Los Angeles until the land was ready for burials.

The Yorba cemetery was not ready for internments until 1862, and for unknown reasons, his remains were left in Los Angeles. The remains of Yorba and other deceased family members remained "temporarily" buried Calvary Cemetery for sixty-four years. Finally, in 1923, Yorba descendants had his remains (along with nine other deceased family members) returned home to the beloved Rancho Canon de Santa Ana.[14]

Today, Bernardo Yorba's burial plot holds a place of honor in the center of the cemetery that he bequeathed.

MARIA DE JESUS ALVARADO YORBA
FELIPE DOMINQUES YORBA
ANDREA ELIZALDE YORBA
JOSE ANTONIO YORBA II
TOMAS ANTONIO YORBA
TEODOCIO YORBA
ALVINA DE LOS REYES

Also interred within the historic grounds of the Yorba Cemetery are many members of the Yorba family including all three of Bernardo's wives, Maria de Jesus Alvarado Yorba (1796 to 1828), Felipe Dominques Yorba (1833 to September 7, 1851), and Andrea Elizalde Yorba. Also buried on the grounds are Bernardo's brother's Jose Antonio Yorba II, Tomas Antonio Yorba (see Dona Vicente Sepulveda Yorba y Carrillo in Anaheim Cemetery), and Teodocio Yorba, the later was the original grantee of the Rancho Lomas de Santiago (present day Silverado Canyon area). Teodocio's involvement with the Juan Flores gang raid on San Juan Capistrano will be discussed in Chapter Eight.

The final noteworthy burial at the Yorba cemetery is Alvina De Los Reyes (d. December 2, 1910), the alleged pink lady ghost. Folklore states that Alvina was killed in a buggy accident on her way home from a dance and that her ghost has been seen wondering the Yorba cemetery in a pink evening gown. The story had become so popular that hundreds of people turn out every June 15th (erroneously thought to be her death date) to watch for the ghostly figure to materialize. Apparently, though, a local librarian, who pieced together other ghost stories and applied them to the local area, made up the whole tale.

El Toro Memorial Park had the blue lady, the old mission cemetery in San Juan Capistrano has the white lady, and Yorba cemetery now has the pink lady. A search of burial records shows that Alvina De Los Reyes died of pneumonia and not a buggy accident. Despite the evidence, ghost hunters still gather at the old cemetery every other year hopeful of catching a glimpse of her restless spirit.[15]

🌺 Her grave is found in the southeast section of the grounds, near a large oleander bush.

2

PUBLIC CEMETERIES

History is indeed little more than the register
of the crimes, follies and misfortunes of mankind.

~Edward Gibbon
English historian (1737 to 1794)

The first public cemeteries in Orange County started out as privately owned and operated graveyards. All were administered by either private entities or individual cities. As administrative costs began to climb, there arose a need for a more uniform system of public burials. In 1926, Anaheim, Santa Ana, and the El Toro cemeteries joined together with the approval of the Orange County Board of Supervisors. A central administrative agency was established (today, located at El Toro) and the Orange County Cemetery District began operation.

ANAHEIM CEMETERY

For Information: Orange County Cemetery District
1400 East Sycamore Street
Anaheim, California 92805
Telephone: 714-535-4928

Anaheim is a city steeped in history, being one of Orange County's earliest settlements. Founded in 1857 by German immigrants, the city's name was derived from its proximity to the Santa Ana River, "Ana," and "heim," German for home. Early pioneers considered this their home by the river.

Orange County in the mid-1800s was a rural area—the population was small; illness and tragedy were common. In the late 1860s, there were only two established cemeteries in the county, and both were for Catholics; one belonged to the Church at the Mission San Juan Capistrano, and the other to the Yorba family in Santa Ana Canyon. During this period, the Anaheim colony witnessed a handful of deaths, and had no public place for burial. The leaders of the colony realized there was a need for a public cemetery.

The Pioneer gate was the original entrance to the Anaheim Cemetery.

In 1866, the Anaheim Cemetery Association was established. This organization secured five acres of land east of the colony from Phillip Siechel. The colonists gave their little cemetery the name "Gotte's Acker" (God's acre). By 1893, the cemetery had grown to encompass over seventeen acres; improvements included the first public mausoleum built on the West Coast (which opened in 1914),[1] and a beautiful entrance arch that was dedicated in 1917 to the early pioneers.[2] Interred within the grounds are many of the early settlers of Anaheim, and other Orange County cities. It is also the final resting place for dozens of Civil War veterans.

Anaheim Cemetery also holds the remains of an unknown and undocumented number of Chinese laborers. They helped build the Southern Pacific Railroad (whose western terminus ended in Orange County). Upon completion of the railroad, these laborers were released to find whatever employment they could obtain. Many went to work in the fledgling agricultural industry; while others started small businesses.[3] Their mass, unmarked graves are located in the southeast corner of the grounds.

The cemetery has a tranquil feel that blends the old with the new. It is small by modern standards and is well maintained. Navigating the cemetery is fairly easy. One road traverses the grounds in a U-shape, but that is where simplicity ends, and confusion begins. The cemetery is laid out in a haphazard manner and has limited section markers. The oldest graves are easiest to locate due to their ornate tombstones. The newer sections of the cemetery primarily use flush to the ground markers and are harder to locate. As a general rule, most of the important graves are located near the rear of the cemetery and are clustered near the pioneer memorial, in lawn section AOC.

A walk through this cemetery is a stroll through local history. The grounds are dotted with ornate headstones that herald an earlier era in Orange County. Today, the Anaheim Cemetery is cared for by the Orange County Cemetery District. It is the oldest public graveyard in Orange County.

MARIA "PETRA" JESUS ONTIVEROS-LANGENBERGER

The cemetery's first notable burial took place on September 8, 1867: Maria "Petra" Jesus Ontiveros-Langenberger (1832 to September 7, 1867) was the daughter of Juan Pacifico Ontiveros, the original grantee of the 35,790-acre Rancho San Juan Cajon de Santa Ana.[4] In 1857, her father Juan Ontiveros sold 1,165 acres of the rancho to George Hansen and John Frohling. This land purchase was fondly known as the "Mother Colony," which later became the city of Anaheim. Petra was seen as a devoted wife and mother.[5] She died early on September 7, 1867, from complications due to childbirth and tuberculosis.[6]

AUGUSTUS LANGENBERGER

Petra was the first wife of Augustus Langenberger (1849 to April 3, 1895), prominent citizen and Anaheim's first merchant. He was born in Studhagen, Germany, and immigrated to California in the late 1840s. He was a leading member of the committee that chose Anaheim as the site for the "Mother Colony." He served the city and county in every capacity from town trustee, to director of the Water Company, and as a county supervisor.[7]

Following Petra's untimely death, Augustus became entangled in a scandalous love affair with Clementine Schmidt, the wife of Theodore E. Schmidt, a vineyard owner, and a prominent citizen of Anaheim. Allegedly, Langenberger was so enamored by Clementine's beauty that he pursued her by purchasing, and naming a plot of land in her honor. Ironically, this land was located adjacent to property already owned by Theodore. Augustus and Clementine carried on their torrid affair for sometime, and this eventually led to the Schmidt's divorce.[8] On April 15, 1874, Augustus and Clementine were married, and they lived a long, happy life togther.[9] Augustus died on April 10, 1895 at his residence of heart failure[10] and Clementine died on October 8, 1913, in San Francisco, at the home of her son.[11] Although, Theodore Schmidt was an original trustee of the Anaheim Cemetery, and remained in the city his entire life, in the end, he refused to be buried at the cemetery.

The Langenberger's final resting places are found in lawn section AOC. Locate the ornate Langenberger mausoleum; it is southeast of the pioneer memorial. Interred within the mausoleum are Augustus and Clementine (lot 12, crypt 7 and 8) and other members of the family. Petra's original wooden grave marker was destroyed and the spot went unmarked for many years. Eventually, the Anaheim Historical Commission placed a commemorative plaque on her grave. Her marker reads; in memory of Petra Ontiveras, daughter of Juan Pacifico and Martina Ontiveras, wife of August Langenberger, member of Anaheim's first pioneer family, 1832-1867.

An early Anaheim area pioneer, August Langenberger's mausoleum with his first wife, Petra's grave in the foreground.

❧ This marker is found in lawn AOC, lot 12, space 2, and is directly in front of the Langenberger mausoleum.

PHILIPP GEORGE HAMMES
AMELIA HAMMES-FROHLING

The first colonist to arrive in Anaheim was Philipp George Hammes (1803 to April 15, 1881), businessman and watchmaker. It is in his unfinished home, where Anaheim's first marriage ceremony was held. The nuptials took place between Hammes' daughter Amelia, and Anaheim colony founder, John Frohling.[12] Philipp Hammes and Amelia Hammes-Frohling (d. February 23, 1923) are buried in lawn AOC, lot 50, space 2 and 3.

❧ The Hammes family plot is just four sections north of the Langenberger mausoleum. Locate the large tree on the curb, five rows to the east is the Hammes family plot. Phillip is the only family member memorialized on the tombstone, and Amelia's grave is unmarked.

JOHN AUGUST F. HEYERMANN

Anaheim's first physician was John August F. Heyermann (December 11, 1818 to February 1, 1888). On his way to Anaheim in 1862, Apache Indians attacked his wagon train, and many in the expedition were killed. Heyermann was lucky to survive the ordeal.[13] This was very fortunate for Anaheim, because his arrival in 1862, helped ease suffering caused by a county wide epidemic of smallpox.[14]

❧ His burial plot in lawn F, lot 8, space 7, locate the grave marker of Eleanor and Charles Wheaton on the west curb, and four rows east is Doctor Heyermann's final resting place.

WILLIAM N. HARDIN

Interred within the grounds of Anaheim Cemetery are several pioneers of Orange County's citrus industry. The first orange tree was planted by William N. Hardin (September 16, 1826 to November 11, 1887). Hardin purchased two barrels of decayed Tahiti oranges in 1870, and used the seeds to plant the first orchard in Orange County.[15]

❧ His grave is marked by a large upright, white marble stone. It is located north east of the Hartmann mausoleum, in lawn AOC, lot 110, space 1.

SHELDON LITTLEFIELD

Another giant of the early citrus industry was Sheldon Littlefield (February 18, 1834 to July 27, 1909). In the early 1870s, he planted the first commercial groves of Valencia Oranges in Fullerton.[16] On July 17, 1889, he was elected to the first Orange County Board of Supervisors.[17] Littlefield is buried in lawn AAD, section 1, lot 35, space 6. Locate the Boyd-Scott monument near the curb on the east side of the lawn.

❧ The Littlefield family plot is located on the backside of the Boyd-Scott's monument.

DANIEL KRAEMER

Other notable burials at the cemetery include Daniel Kraemer (d. February 6, 1882), the founder of the city of Placentia. In 1865, Kraemer acquired four thousand acres of land from Juan Pacifico Ontiveros in the former rancho San Juan Cajon de Santa Ana. This land had been dubbed useless "peor es nada" or (nothing is worse) by Ontiveros but this could not have been farther from the truth. The land was fertile and proved to be agriculturally viable for the citrus industry. It also proved to be a profit windfall when oil was discovered.[18]

Present day Kraemer Boulevard, which traverses the cities of Yorba Linda, Placentia, and Anaheim, is named in honor of Daniel Kraemer. He died on February 6, 1882 from pleurisy, a painful infection of the lungs.

His burial plot is located in lawn AOC, lot 16, space 1. Kraemer's cylindrical up right marble marker is found southwest of the Pioneer memorial, in the center of the lawn.

REVEREND LEMUEL P. WEBBER

The founder of Westminster, Reverend Lemuel P. Webber (June 8, 1832 to September 25, 1874) was Anaheim's first Presbyterian minister. Reverend Webber had a dream of establishing a temperance colony. He purchased seven thousand acres of land from the Stearns Ranchos Company in what would become the city of Westminster.[19] Webber's plan included the following: "settlement of persons whose religious faith, notions of morals, and education, should be nearly alike, that they might cordially cooperate from the first in the maintenance of a Christian Church and a superior school." Lots in the new colony sold for thirteen dollars an acre, and citizens were instructed not to buy or sell alcohol.[20]

In 1874, as the Westminster colony had just began to prosper, tragedy struck, their leader, Reverend Webber died of consumption.[21] The town had been thriving until this tragedy, but rapidly fell apart. It was not until after World War One, that the city saw resurgence and growth.[22]

Lemuel Webber's upright marble marker is hard to miss, and is found on the north curb, in lawn section AOC, lot 29, space 1.

ADDISON PRATT

One of the most historically important, and little-known residents at Anaheim Cemetery is Addison Pratt (February 21, 1802 to October 14, 1872). He was an adventurer, Mormon missionary, and California gold rush pioneer. Addison Pratt was born in Winchester, New Hampshire, the fourth son of famous New England organ builder Henry Pratt.[23] Addison's life is divided into four major epochs; as a sailor on whaling vessels (1821-1831), as a farmer and early convert to Mormonism (1831-1841), as a missionary to the French Polynesian Islands, traveler in the western United States, and as a California gold rush pioneer (1841-1858), and finally, as a community leader in Southern California following separation from the Mormon church (1858-1872).

For eight years, Addison sailed the seven seas as a merchant sailor aboard the whaling ship "Rambler," and other vessels. He visited many exotic lands, but his love for the South Pacific Islands, would bring him life long adventure.[24]

While visiting home, he became acquainted with a young woman named Louisa Barnes (she would go on to fame of her own, as an early feminist writer).

They married April 3, 1831, and settled into a farming life at Ripley, New York. In the early years of marriage, the Pratt's became members of the Church of Latter-day Saints and on June 18, 1838, Addison was baptized into the new Mormon faith.[25]

In the fall of 1841, the Pratt's were invited to move to Nauvoo, Illinois, a colony run by church prophet and leader Joseph Smith. It is during this time that Addison became close friends of Smith and rose quickly in the ranks of the church hierarchy. Due to Pratt's experience as a seaman and his knowledge of the South Pacific, it was agreed upon that Pratt, along with three other Mormon men, Benjamin Grouard (see Santa Ana Cemetery), Noah Rogers, and Knowlton Hanks, would travel to French Polynesia. There, they would preach to the natives, teaching the tenets of the church. These men became the first recognized foreign missionaries of the Mormon church.[26]

On June 1, 1843, the four men left Illinois on their mission. In Boston, they boarded the whaling ship Timoleon, and on October 6, 1843, set sail for the South Pacific.[27] During the six-month voyage, Knowlton Hanks died, and he was buried at sea. Addison Pratt and the others suffered many hardships during the voyage, and encountered severe opposition during their time in the South Pacific islands. Courageously, they continued their mission, and were successful in baptizing and converting hundreds of islanders. In May 1852, the French government began to resist the Mormon missionaries. Pratt and the others missionaries were expelled from the islands.[28]

Addison returned to the United States, and came home to a changed Mormon church. Joseph Smith, the founder, prophet, and close personal friend had been murdered. The Mormon colony had moved from Illinois to Utah. Plural marriage became common practice and all these changes came under the leadership of Brigham Young. Pratt did not believe in many of the new tenants of the church, especially plural marriage. He fought with the church hierarchy over these issues; this resulted in Pratt's disillusionment and subsequent departure from the church. As a byproduct of this action, the Pratt's marriage dissolved and the family was

Early Mormon missionary and western adventurer, Addison Pratt grave, Anaheim Cemetery.

fractured. Some of the family ventured with Addison to Southern California, while others stayed with Louisa in Utah.[29]

In 1848, Pratt left Utah for California and was present at Sutter's Mill when gold was discovered.[30] Having traveled throughout the western states, Pratt settled into Southern California and became involved in the "Spiritualist" movement.[31] Late in life, Addison Pratt lived with his daughter Frances and her husband Jones Dyer. He suffered hearing loss, dropsy (edema), and congestive heart failure, dying in his sleep on October 14, 1872, at Anaheim California.[32] His legacy today can be seen in his descendants many of whom are noteworthy politicians in Arizona and Oregon.[33]

❧ Pratt's obelisk-style monument is located about twenty feet southwest of the Pioneer memorial, in the old section of the cemetery, lawn AOC, lot 19, space 5.

THOMAS HENRY KUCHEL

After leaving nineteenth-century America, and Orange County pioneers behind, we venture into twentieth century political history. Thomas Henry Kuchel (August 15, 1910 to November 21, 1994) was a moderate Republican United States Senator from California. He was born in Anaheim, and his father, Henry, was editor of the *Anaheim Gazette*.

Thomas Kuchel's political career started at the age of twenty-six. He was elected to public office as a representative in the California State Assembly representing Orange County's 75th District from 1937 to 1941. Subsequently, he was elected to the state Senate for one term 1941 to 1945 and as state Controller from 1946 to 1953.[34]

In 1953, Senator Richard Nixon was elected Vice-President of the United States; this left Nixon's senate seat vacant. Kuchel was appointed by California Governor Earl Warren to serve out the remainder of Nixon's term and was subsequently elected to two senatorial terms from 1953 to 1969.

Kuchel was known as a moderate Republican and supported the Desegregation and Civil Rights Acts of the 1960s. He was labeled a maverick and outsider by the conservative wing of the Republican Party because of his refusal to endorse several leading Republican candidates during the 1964 and 1966 elections. Among them were Barry Goldwater (President) and Richard Nixon (Governor), and George Murphy (Senate) in 1964 and Ronald Reagan (Governor) in 1966. Without party support, he lost his bid for re-election in 1968. After his defeat in the 1968 election, Kuchel engaged in the private practice of law in Los Angeles. He never again entered the political arena.[35]

An interesting side note, while attending Anaheim High School, Kuchel was a member of the school debate team. It is alleged that his team debated a team from rival Whittier High School. In this debate Kuchel is said to have personally debated, and handily defeated a young Richard Nixon.[36]

Thomas Kuchel died on November 21, 1994 in Beverly Hills, California, due to complications from lung cancer.[37] He is buried in lawn AAD, section B3, lot 45, space 7. The grave is located in the center of lawn, four rows from the curb.

❧ Find the grave of Mary R. Maas on the western curb. Kuchel's final resting place is due east, and is marked by a flat head stone. His marker is non-descript and fails to represent his political contributions or achievements.

CHARLES HITCHCOCK & LOIS HITCHCOCK

Charles Hitchcock (1852 to January 23, 1888) and Lois Hitchcock (1853 to January 23, 1888) were murder victims. The Hitchcocks were early settlers in Garden Grove. They owned substantial property in the area and farmed the land. John Henrich Fredrick Anschlag was a penniless drifter and petty swindler. He had approached Mr. Hitchcock about selling his ranch. The two parties agreed to a selling price of eight thousand dollars in cash.[38] Anschlag had no way of obtaining such a sum and concocted a scheme in which he would murder the Hitchcock's, dispose of their bodies, and take over the ranch.

On January 23, 1888, Anschlag met with the Hitchcocks and killed them both in their own home. He disposed of their bodies, hiding them in a secluded place, where he thought they would not be discovered. He thought that no one would suspect any wrong doing, because he was supposed to purchase the property. Anschlag was wrong on all counts; the neighbors began to wonder why the Hitchcocks had left with out a word. They were well liked, and to leave in such a clandestine manner was very suspicious.

Law enforcement authorities put the heat on Anschlag and several weeks after the crime, he cracked under pressure, confessing to murdering the Hitchcocks.[39] He was arrested in early February 1888, had a speedy trial in which he was found guilty of the murders, and was sentenced to death by hanging.[40]

Anschlag was supposed to have been executed on November 16, 1888 in Los Angeles, but this did not occur. Just two days prior to his scheduled date with the hangman, Anschlag was able to obtain some poison and killed himself.[41]

⚘ The Hitchcocks large upright grave marker is located on the north side of lawn AOC, lot 91, space 1 and 2, four rows from the western curb.

Murder victims Charles and Lois Hitchcock's grave site.

DONA VINCENTA SEPULVEDA & YORBA Y CARRILLO

Buried a few yards away is a member of one of Southern California's most esteemed Spanish pioneer families. Dona Vincenta Sepulveda Yorba y Carrillo was born into the famous Sepulveda family and was the sister of Jose Andres Sepulveda. In 1834, she married Tomas Yorba (buried at Yorba Cemetery), son of Jose Antonio Yorba I (buried at the Mission San Juan Capistrano burial ground). Tomas was shot to death in 1845, and Vincenta took over operations of the family rancho. For several years, she ran the rancho by herself, until she met and married Jose Ramon Carrillo (buried at Yorba Cemetery). In May of 1864, tragedy again struck her second husband, Jose, was murdered—shot in the back. He had been outspoken and an active resister to the United States' take-over of Alta California after the Mexican-American War. Dona Carrillo was no stranger to heartbreak; her son was also shot, and killed.

In 1872, Vincenta sold the rancho, and moved to Anaheim. She purchased the Mother Colony House from August Langenberger and lived out the rest of her life.[42] Her final resting place lay unmarked, and was lost for many years. Through the hard work of the "Anaheim Cemetery Angels," Dona Vincenta's grave is now marked and it reads; Vincenta Sepulveda Yorba y Carrillo, 1818-1907, Southern California Spanish pioneer who lived during rule of Spain, Mexico, and America, first woman to obtain Spanish land grant La Sierra Sepulveda, mother of twelve, as widow managed two ranchos, Santa Ana Viejo and Valle De San Jose, honored for her perseverance and independence, rest in peace.

🔑 It is found in lawn AOC's northwest section, across the road from the Schumacher mausoleum, two rows from the western curb. It is also rumored that she is interred at the Yorba Cemetery. This unsubstantiated claim is based on the plaque at the entranceway to the Yorba Cemetery, which lists her as being buried at the site.

JOHN RAITT

Also rumored to be buried within the grounds is actor John Raitt (January 19, 1917 to February 20, 2005). Born in Santa Ana, California, his family was original pioneer settlers in the area. John was a star of television, film, and stage but is best known for his stage performances in musicals such as:

🔑 *Carousel*

🔑 *Oklahoma!*

🔑 *The Pajama Game*

🔑 *Three Wishes for Jamie*

🔑 *A Joyful Noise*

In 1945, he was the recipient of the first Theatre World Award for his role in *Carousel*. Notable television roles included appearances on the *Bell Telephone Hour*. He is the father of famed country-rock singer Bonnie Raitt. He died on February 20, 2005, at his home in Pacific Palisades, California, from pneumonia.[43] The death certificate describes Anaheim Cemetery, as the place of final disposition but a search of cemetery records shows no such burial.[44] Further research showed that his parents, grandparents, and extended family are buried at Fairhaven Memorial Park in the Raitt family burial plot. A search of cemetery records there, also failed to find John Raitt. Other sources such as newspapers were also unsuccessful in substantiating his actual burial location. It is interesting to note that his wife, Rosemary's maiden name is Kraemer. The Kraemers are a very prominent family in Orange County, and their large burial plot is at Anaheim Cemetery. It is possible that Rosemary decided to keep John's ashes with her until she passes, and at which point they would be interred together at the cemetery. It is also possible that the remains were interred under an assumed name, buried else where, or scattered at an unknown location at sea. All these scenarios are conjecture.

CHARLES F. LEHMAN
DAVID S. DAVIS

Other notable internees such as Charles F. Lehman and David S. Davis, will be discussed in Chapter Eight, "Murder and Mayhem."

SANTA ANA CEMETERY

1919 E. Santa Clara Avenue
Santa Ana, California 92705
Telephone (714) 953-2959

The office is open Monday through Friday, with the general grounds open every day from dawn to dusk.

This cemetery is the second oldest public graveyard in Orange County. It was established in 1870 by Jacob Ross Sr., and was originally located at Eighth and Ross Streets. The cemetery was moved to its present location on Santa Clara Avenue in 1878. The land for the cemetery was purchased from A.B. Chapman, and has been administered by the Orange County Cemetery District since 1926. The grounds are comprised of twenty-nine acres of monuments, green lawns, and majestic trees. It is a historic site that, like the Anaheim Cemetery, blends the old with the new.

Numerous Orange County pioneers are buried here, along with several hundred Civil War veterans, both Union and Confederate. Many veterans went on to become political and business leaders in the county. The cemetery is easy to maneuver with both upright and ground-level grave markers. The lawn sections are laid out in grids that are in alphabetical order, with each section clearly marked on the curb.

The two sections flanking the cemetery office are lawns H and SG. In the old days, these areas were called Potter's Fields, and were reserved for unknowns, vagrants, paupers, criminals, and other indigent people. Grave locations are scattered, with few markers. The records that are available are scarce, haphazard, and unreliable. Burials within in these sections were often done quickly, with no regard to uniformity. Over time the exact burial locations were lost. It is within these two sections where the mortal remains of several of Orange County's most heinous criminals and their victims are interred.

WILLIAM MCKELVEY
FRANCISCO TORRES

The following is the tragic story of William McKelvey (1841 to July 31, 1892) and Francisco Torres (1867 to August 20, 1892), two people who are forever connected to the first and only incidence of vigilante mob violence in Orange County. In the late 1800s, Orange County was a quiet and mostly peaceful community of rural farmers and small businesses. Violence was not unheard of but was certainly not commonplace. William McKelvey was the much-admired and adored foreman at famed Polish actress Madame Helena Modjeska's ranch in rural Santiago Canyon, a position he had held for several years.[45] Francisco Torres, who often went by the nickname "Poncho" was a twenty-five year old Mexican drifter and migrant worker who was occasionally employed at the Modjeska ranch.[46]

At the Modjeska ranch and throughout the county it was customary to withhold $2.50 from laborers wages as a poll tax at the end of each month. Torres took exception to this and angrily sought out McKelvey on the early morning of Sunday, July 31, 1892. Torres found McKelvey at the ranch attending to the morning rituals. Torres confronted him, and demanded to have his $2.50 returned. McKelvey refused, explaining that this was not his decision but was an order from the tax collector. This explanation did not satisfy Torres and angry words were exchanged. Torres continued to fume, stalking McKelvey throughout the ranch. Eventually, things came to boiling point. McKelvey entered a feed barn, Torres followed, picked up a pickaxe, and hit McKelvey in the head, crushing his skull. In this frenzy of rage, Torres pulled out a knife and plunged it into the chest of his stricken victim. Believing McKelvey was dead, Torres then fled the scene.[47]

An intensive manhunt for Torres ensued. Dozens of law enforcement officers were on his trail. A 200 dollar reward was issued by the Orange County Board of Supervisors for Torres' capture, but even with this bounty on his head, he was able to elude capture for ten days.[48] On August 10, 1892, Francisco was apprehended in the town of Rancheria in rural San Diego County. He was taken into custody by constables A. L. Wood and D.M. Knowles of Mesa Grande. Orange County Sheriff Theo Lacy was dispatched to Mesa Grande, and Torres was extradited back to Santa Ana to stand trial.[49]

Francisco Torres was arraigned in Santa Ana Superior court on August 12, 1892, and charged with William McKelvey's murder.[50] As the trial proceedings commenced, tensions began to run high in the community. Whispers of secret meetings and the possible lynching of Torres began to circulate throughout the city. On the early morning of Saturday, August 20, 1892, a masked group of men stormed the Santa Ana jail, subdued the jail guard, and forcibly extracted Torres from his jail cell, dragging him to the corner of Fourth and Sycamore Streets. Not a word was spoken between the masked men, only the sobs of Torres could be heard. There they bound Torres hand and foot. Tied a noose around his neck and hung him to the corner telephone pole. The body was discovered later that morning, attached was a note that read "change of venue."[51] The identities of the vigilantes were never uncovered and no one was ever prosecuted for Torres' death. This was the first and only known lynching to occur in Orange County, and it was also the last in the state of California.[52]

It must be noted that the descriptions and accounts of the aforementioned events of July and August of 1892, were reported through newspaper accounts of the day. These primary sources did not always use fair and balanced reporting techniques. They were often prejudiced, with unbalanced approaches to the facts. The racist attitudes of the time period were often an extension of the popular views of many. Although this attitude is unthinkable today, the reader must understand the events from a historical context.

The tragic tale of Francisco Torres and the murder of William McKelvey were reported in great detail in these sources. The newspaper industry during this time was very competitive and most used a brand of news reporting known as "yellow" journalism. This style of newspaper writing used bold, eye catching, and titillating headlines to grab the attention of potential readers. Torres was tried in these newspapers before he got a fair trial; he was convicted, and executed by the court of public opinion before having the opportunity to defend himself. With that said, even if the case had gone to a full trial, the outcome may already have been a forgone conclusion. The late eighteenth century was a time fraught with racial bigotry, hatred, and fear of minorities. Due to this attitude, a man like Torres, had little chance of receiving a fair trial. The authorities were quick to point the finger of guilt at a person who could not defend himself. The question is: Did Francisco Torres murder William McKelvey? The evidence as presented in the newspapers and the preliminary trial proceedings, all point to his guilt. In reality, there are only two people who know what happened on that early July morning in 1892; and neither is talking.

🐝 William McKelvey's is buried in lawn H, block 7, lot 17, space 1, and his grave is unmarked. Francisco Torres is also buried within the grounds, in lawn SG, block 7, lot 9, space 1, and his grave is also unmarked. Lawn sections SG and H flank the cemetery office building to the north and south.

EFFIE SCHOLL

Also interred in lawn H is Effie Scholl (July 1861 to November 2, 1889); she is infamously known for murdering her two young children, John (3 years old) and Eva (5 years old). In the fall of 1889, a recent divorcee, Effie was struggling to hold her life together. She lived in an age of religious repression and intolerance, in a society that frowned upon and ostracized divorce.

The Scholl's had been married for seven years, but those years were filled with great unhappiness. Their divorce was granted by default and Mr. Scholl left the county. Effie was left destitute with no income, and with no place to turn, she filed for public assistance. Mr. Scholl hearing of this, returned to California. He was not fond of the idea of his children being raised in such squalid conditions, and immediately proceeded to gain custody of the children. He believed Effie was an unfit mother and was in the process of having these papers drawn up when the horrific events of October 16, 1889 took place. Throughout the process, Effie had threatened to kill the children should Mr. Scholl ever get guardianship, and no one took her dramatic ranting seriously.[53]

On the morning of October 16, 1889, Effie Scholl was very disturbed, and not in her right mind. She rationalized that there was no other course; preferring the children and herself to be dead, rather than suffer the humiliation of her ex-husband gaining custody of the children. Effie reasoned that she and the children would be meeting their maker and would be in a much better place. As the tragic event unfolded, Effie used chloroform to subdue the children; she placed them in their beds, and cut their throats. Then, in an attempt to kill herself, she ingested a large quantity of poison, a mixture of muriatic and carbolic acids. Fearing that this would not accomplish the deed; she took a knife, and cut her own throat. Effie lost consciousness, due to loss of blood but did not die. It was not until sometime later that she gained awareness of the events. Several notes were left at the scene; one of which was addressed to her mother, Mary Goodwin.[54] It reads in part;

"this is this last blow of that cruel thing that calls himself a man. He can never have my sweet little ones to bring up in wickedness. I can say that he is a vile, wicked, depraved, devilish liar. My little ones will be in the arms of Jesus. I give up life everlasting that my little ones may gain it."[55]

Reports of the crime scene were gruesome, the children were found in their beds soaked in blood, while Mrs. Scholl was found laying in her own vomit,

covered in blood and unconscious. The planned effects of the poison were not immediately successful. Effie lingered in and out of a coma for two weeks.[56] In lucid moments she was quite repentant of her evil act, and had a desire to reconcile with her maker. Effie finally succumbed to the effects of the poison, dying on the evening of November 2, 1889; having lingered near death for eleven days.[57] The Scholl murder's shocked the tiny hamlet of Tustin. Never before had the citizens of this small town witnessed such a heinous act of savagery.

❦ Effie Scholl's final resting place is found on the east side of lawn H, block 8, lot 10, space 2. The white unassuming marble

Effie Scholl who murdered her two small children and then committed suicide is buried at Santa Ana Cemetery.

tombstone is located two rows from the curb, near an old oak tree, between the graves of her mother and sister. This simple head stone underplays the unnecessary savagery that played out that fall morning, one hundred and eighteen years ago.

As for the final resting places of the children, John and Eva, newspapers of the day, point to Santa Ana Cemetery, as their place of burial. Cemetery records show no such burial ever taking place. This is not uncommon; cemetery records of the late nineteenth century are often incomplete and unreliable.

RICHARD CROMWELL

Two sections to the right of the office are lawn P is the final resting place of legendary Hollywood actor Richard Cromwell (January 8, 1910 to October 10, 1960). Cromwell appeared in over forty films during the 1930's and 1940's. Born Roy M. Radabaugh, Harry Cohn gave him his stage name, and launched his career in show business.[58] Cromwell's film credits include The Lives of a Bengal Lancer, which was nominated for an Academy award for best picture of 1935, and starred Gary Cooper, Jezebel (1938) with Bette Davis and Henry Fonda and Young Mr. Lincoln (1939).[59]

Cromwell was married briefly to actress Angela Lansbury (who was only nineteen) in 1945. Lansbury attributed the demise of the marriage to Cromwell's alleged bisexuality.[60] In later years Cromwell gained a reputation as an artist, his oil paintings and clay masks of film personalities were highly sought out. He died on October 10, 1960 in Hollywood, California, of cancer at the age of fifty.[61]

❧ Cromwell's cremated remains are found near his parents, beneath an unassuming flat marker in lawn P, block 7, lot 17, space 2. The marker bears his given name of Roy M. Radabaugh, and is located two rows from the curb, near two giant trees on the west side of the lawn.

JUSTIN MATTHEW CARMACK

Directly across the street to the west is lawn section O, here is the grave of Justin Matthew Carmack (1981 to July 28, 2000). Carmack was a young, up-and-coming actor who had appeared in several episodes of the television series, Full House (1994), in which he played the role of Scott. He also appeared in the 1993 independent film Delivering.[62]

As a young child, Justin was enrolled in the South Coast Repertory Youth Theater group and appeared in a production of Macbeth at the Grove Theater in Anaheim, California. On July 20, 2000, he was tragically killed in an automobile accident at the age of nineteen; it was alleged that alcohol or drug use was a contributing factor in the crash.[63]

❧ Carmack's grave is found in section O, block 14, lot 10, space 1. Locate the grave of Etta Riggs on the east side of the lawn; Mathew's final resting place is six rows from the curb.

JACOB ROSS SR.
ELIZABETH "BETSY" THOMPSON ROSS

The first pioneer family to settle in the Santa Ana area was that of Jacob Ross Sr. (August 12, 1813 to December 7, 1870) and Elizabeth "Betsy" Thompson Ross (June 3, 1815 to October 26, 1895). The Ross's were prominent farmers and mill operators in central Illinois and founded the town of Rossville. The Homestead Act of 1862 and the promise of free land in the west enticed Ross to make the move. In April of 1865, the Ross family left Illinois for California. The journey west to California was arduous but uneventful. The Ross' at first settled in Castroville in Northern California but found land in the area very expensive. Traveling south Jacob Ross learned that there was land for sale in the Anaheim area. In September of 1868, he struck a bargain with Prudencia Yorba an heir to the Rancho Santiago de Santa and purchased one hundred plus acres. Over the next year, Jacob continued to purchase land, amassing a total of 575 acres by 1869. In late 1869, William Spurgeon (see Fairhaven) and Ward Bradford offered to buy 75 acres of Ross' land to start the city of Santa Ana. Jacob was reluctant at first to selling the land, seeing no point in establishing a new town. Eventually, he did sell the property to Spurgeon for eight dollars an acre.[64]

Part of Ross' land was used to build Santa Ana's first cemetery, which was located at the corner of Eighth and Ross Streets. The Ross' young grandson William Jacob Ross died on October 20, 1870, (at the age of one year and three months) and was the first burial. This graveyard existed until 1878 when present day Santa Ana Cemetery was established. Young William's remains were removed from the old graveyard and were the first to be reinterred in the new location.[65]

William Jacob Ross' grave is located in lawn section I, block 8, lot 3, space 8, his upright tombstone is not far from his grandparents on the curb.

Jacob Ross Sr., died on December 7, 1870, his wife Elizabeth joined him twenty-five years later. The Ross' graves can be found in lawn section I, block 8, lot 2, spaces 7 and 8. Their graves are in the northwest section of the lawn on the curb. Jacob's marker is adorned with two hands that are clasp together in embrace, the markers inscription reads:

> *"farewell my wife and children all, from you a father Christ doth call, morn not for me, it is in vain, to call me to your sight again."*

JACOB ROSS JR.

Their son Jacob Ross Jr. (August 7, 1845 to November 3, 1919) was a civic leader and active in local politics. He was member of the first Orange County Board of Supervisors, and also served as the county assessor.[66]

Ross Jr. died on November 3, 1919, and his plain grave marker is located within the Ross family plot, lawn I, block 8, lot two, space 8, four rows from the curb.

SAMUEL DUNGAN

Samuel Morrison "Sam" Dungan (January 29, 1866 to March 16, 1939) was a professional baseball player. Dungan played outfield and first base for the Chicago Colts (Cubs) 1892 to 1894, he was a teammate of Harry DeMiller in 1892 (see Fairhaven), the Louisville Colonels 1894, and in 1900 for the Chicago Orphans (who had changed their name from the Colts and would soon become the Cubs). Dungan also played for the Washington Senators 1900 to 1901. In 1900, he won the American League batting title.[67] His career statistics are 382 games played, 1543 at bats, 464 base hits, with a career batting average of .301. Dungan died in Santa Ana, California on March 16, 1939.[68]

❧ His grave is found in section X, block 19, lot 1, space 2. On the south side of the lawn on the curb locate the gravestone of Jay A. Stone, seven markers to the north is Dungan's grave.

JAMES BOYD UTT

The mortal remains of United States Congressman James Boyd Utt (March 11, 1899 to March 1, 1970) can be found in section M. James Utt was an outspoken and controversial conservative Republican politician. He represented Orange County in the 35th Congressional District of California from 1953 to 1970. As a senior member of the Ways and Means committee, he voted against the Civil Rights Acts of 1960, 1964, and 1968, and the Voting Rights Act of 1965.[69] He served in the California State Assembly from 1932 to 1936 and as the inheritance tax appraiser with the California State Controllers office from 1936 to 1952. James Utt died on March 1, 1970 of a heart attack in Bethesda, Maryland.[70]

❧ His grave can be found in section M, block 19, row 4, space 5. On the east side of the lawn, find the Steskal monument. From the monument, Utt's grave is six rows to the west.

MARY J. "MOLLIE" ARBUCKLE

Mary J. "Mollie" Arbuckle (d. February 20, 1899) was the mother of famed silent film actor Roscoe Conklin "Fatty" Arbuckle. The Arbuckles lived in Santa Ana for several years in a home at 826 North Birch Street. Young Roscoe worked at the local opera house for fifty cents a night as an extra, and it is there that he gained the nickname "Fatty." Following his mother's death, Roscoe and his father left Orange County. In the years following his mother's death, Roscoe seldom visited her grave. For many years the plot lay over run with weeds, and the original wooden marker disappeared. At some unknown point, the headstone was replaced by a marble marker but it too has faded with time, and is hard to read.[71] While it is certain that Mollie is buried at this cemetery, it is important to note that there is a decrepancy in death date and the tombstone inscription. This might be explained by shoddy record keeping at the cemetery.

❧ Mollie Arbuckle's grave can be found in lawn K, block 8, row 1, space 1. It is located in the center of the lawn, three rows from the west curb.

Molly Arbuckle's alleged faded grave marker, she was silent screen actor, Fatty Arbuckle's mother.

ROBERT MCFADDEN

Lawn J is the final resting place of Orange County pioneer, city founder, and businessman Robert McFadden (August 25, 1845 to May 8, 1923). McFadden was born in Delaware County, New York, and as a young man moved to Sacramento. In 1870, he, along with his brothers James and John (both buried at Fairhaven), moved to Santa Ana and purchased large tracts of land. The McFadden brothers spent time developing and selling property to early settlers in the county. He and his brother established the Newport Wharf and Lumber Company in 1874, which shipped goods from San Francisco to Newport. He was also instrumental in developing and establishing the Santa Ana and Newport Railway. McFadden died on May 8, 1923 at the age of seventy-seven due to complications from influenza.[72]

❧ The McFadden family plot is located in the center of section J, block 4, lot 4, space 8 and is marked with a large upright marble marker.

Henry W. Head, M.D.

Henry W. Head, M.D. (January 1, 1840 to December 5, 1919) was an early Orange County settler, physician, and state politician. A veteran of the Civil War, Head enlisted in the Confederate army in 1861, and was assigned to the 9th Tennessee Infantry, where he rose in rank from a private to captain. Head and the 9th Tennessee participated in the battles of Shiloh, Perryville, Chickamauga, Missionary Ridge, Atlanta, Franklin, and Nashville. After the war, he graduated from the Nashville Medical College, and in 1876, moved to what is now Garden Grove. There he became the city's first practicing physician.[73] He served in the California State Assembly from 1883 until 1885. Dr. Head, along with other prominent citizens, lobbied the State government at Sacramento for Orange County's succession from Los Angeles. Dr. Henry Head died on December 5, 1919 in Santa Ana at the age of seventy-nine of pneumonia.[74]

His grave is located in the center of section D, block 14, lot 2, space 7.

Columbus Tustin

Columbus Tustin (1826 to 1883) was the founder of the city of Tustin. In the late 1840s, Tustin came to California to strike it rich in the gold fields. Later he came to Orange County and bought land from Nelson Stafford who was partitioning the old Rancho Santiago de Santa Ana. Columbus laid out Tustin City on the eastern tracts of this land. Tustin had high ideals, was a generous man, and invited many people to the area. In 1870, he announced that lots would be given away to anyone who would make improvements to the land. He also gave blocks of land away to families that had four or more children. Tustin City's hope of becoming a large city was dashed when Santa Ana won rights to the extension of the railroad. Even with this setback, the city prospered with the influx of citrus farming.[75] Tustin was appointed postmaster for the city and served in that function until his death.

He is buried in lawn F, block 7, lot 1. Locate the flat Tustin family marker on the north curb, Columbus' grave is the second from the curb.

Josiah Clay Joplin

Lawn OO is the final resting place of another Orange County pioneer, local politician, Civil War veteran, and businessman Josiah Clay Joplin (September 15, 1844 to June 19, 1933). In 1862, at the age of seventeen and at the outset of the Civil War, he enlisted in the Confederate cavalry. While attached to the 2nd Virginia, Joplin saw action in all the major battles of the eastern campaign including 2nd Manassas, Antietam, Gettysburg, The Wilderness, Petersburg, and Appomattox. He was wounded three times throughout the course of the war.[76]

In 1876, he moved to Santa Ana, purchased over 600 acres of land, and became a very successful rancher. Joplin got involved in Orange County politics in the 1880s and was instrumental in the county's succession from

Los Angeles. In 1898, he was elected as County Treasurer, a post he held for twenty-five years.[77]

Among his many other accomplishments, Joplin is credited with being the first person to successfully develop a chemical process for preserving and exhibiting of local fruits. In 1893, he represented Orange County at the Columbian Exposition in Chicago, where he managed an exhibition of county agricultural products. Two years later, he reprised this exhibit at the Louisiana Purchase Exposition at St. Louis.[78]

※ Josiah Joplin died on June 19, 1933, and is buried in the center of lawn OOE, block 11, lot 4, space 10, near the Wentz monument.

BENJAMIN F. GROUARD

Benjamin F. Grouard (1819 to March 28, 1894) was an early Mormon missionary. In 1843, Grouard, Addison Pratt (see Anaheim Cemetery), Noah Rogers, and Knowlton Hanks were sent by Mormon prophet and leader Joseph Smith to the South Pacific Islands as missionaries of the Church of Latter-day Saints.[79] They were successful in converting many natives. These men are credited by the Church of Latter-day Saints as the first missionaries to preach in a language other than English. It was during this time that Grouard married the daughter of the chief of the Island of Anaa, she bore three children [80], one son, Frank Grouard, would became a famous U.S. Army scout and was present at the Battle of the Rosebud June 17, 1876. At this battle, General George Crook's 2nd and 3rd Calvary were tactically victorious, but strategically defeated by Lakota Sioux, Cheyenne, Crow, and Shoshone Indians under the leadership of Crazy Horse. This "tactical victory" slowed down and subsequently prevented Crook's forces from joining up with General George A. Custer's 7th Calvary, this ultimately led to Custer's demise at the Battle of the Little Big Horn June, 25-26 1876.[81]

In 1852, Benjamin Grouard returned to the United States, traveling throughout the west, finally settling in Southern California. At some point, he had a falling out with the Mormon Church hierarchy and this lead directly to his exploration and involvement in the "Spiritualist" movement. Spiritualism was a quasi-religion founded on the writing of Swedish born mystic Emanuel Swedborg. The premise of the movement was the belief that spirits of the dead could be contacted through mediums, and that these spirits could relay information to the living. The movement first appeared in up state New York in the 1840's and spread through the United States and the world, reaching a peak of eight million believers in 1897.[82]

Benjamin suffered a small stroke in the spring of 1893, while visiting his son, Frank, in Wyoming. Upon his return to Santa Ana, California, ill health plagued him and on the afternoon of March 28, 1894, he suffered a fatal heart attack while walking in his yard.[83] All printed newspaper records of Benjamin F. Grourad's death point to burial at Santa Ana Cemetery. Although a personal search of cemetery records showed no such interment. It must be noted that cemetery records of the nineteenth and early twentieth century are inconsistent; there are numerous errors in spelling, burial records have been lost, misplaced, and are incomplete.

❦ Graveyard administrators of the time did not believe that anyone in the future would need this information. Thus it is highly likely that Grouard is indeed interred with the grounds of Santa Ana Cemetery but his actual grave is likely only to be discovered by chance.

EDWARD H. PERLEY AKA CHARLES G. PERLEY

Silent film actor Edward H. Perley aka Charles G. Perley (August 14, 1885 to February 10, 1933) is also buried in lawn J. Perley's film career from 1909 to 1918 includes:

> ⚜ *The Mexican Sweethearts* (1909), starring Mary Pickford (in one of her first screen roles), and was directed by D.W. Griffith

Other notable screen roles include:

> ⚜ *The Emerald Pin* (1916), starring Eileen Sedgwick
>
> ⚜ *The Girl and the Crisis* (1917), starring Dorothy Davenport

Perley appeared in over seventy-seven films primarily for Biograph Studios from 1909 to 1918.[84] He died on February 10, 1933, at the age of forty-eight from influenza.[85]

❦ His death certificate, and newspaper stories place his burial at Santa Ana Cemetery but a search of cemetery records was unsuccessful in locating his actual grave. Like other questionable burials at this cemetery, it is highly likely that he is indeed interred within the grounds; recording keeping at this location is highly suspect.

JAMES F. STACY,
CAPTAIN NATHAN ULM
THEO LACY
JOE MATLOCK

Also interred at Santa Cemetery are James F. Stacy, Captain Nathan Ulm, Theo Lacy, and Joe Matlock whose claim to fame will be discussed later in the Chapter Eight, "Murder and Mayhem."

EL TORO MEMORIAL PARK

25751 Trabuco Road
Lake Forest, California 92630
Telephone: 949-951-8244

This cemetery, originally known as El Toro Cemetery, is the only public graveyard in south Orange County. It was established in 1896, as an enterprise of the El Toro Land and Water Company. To attract prospective buyers to purchase stock in the company, they began to sell cemetery plots at El Toro Cemetery for one dollar to each shareholder. The first burial in the cemetery was Maude Simmons. In 1926, the cemetery was incorporated into the Orange County Cemetery District. The name of the cemetery was officially changed to El Toro Memorial Park in 1985. Interred within its grounds are numerous people who shaped early Orange County history. There are political leaders, entertainment personalities, businessmen, and sports legends. The cemetery encompasses over twenty-five acres of gentle rolling hills, and is set in a tranquil park-like setting.

Throughout the year the cemetery hosts a variety of events, including veteran and other patriotic programs. The cemetery is easy to navigate, and lawn markings are clearly visible on the curbs. Like the Anaheim and Santa Ana cemeteries, a stroll through El Toro Memorial Park is a peaceful walk back in time.

FLORENCE GRIFFITH-JOYNER

The most famous internment at El Toro Memorial Park is legendary Olympic track star Florence Griffith-Joyner (December 21, 1959 to September 21, 1998). Joyner whose nickname was Flo-Jo was born in Los Angeles, California. Flo-Jo was an athlete who was known for her speed, flashy style, and long painted fingernails. She attended the University of California, Los Angeles where her track career blossomed, winning the 1980, NCAA 200- and 400-meter titles. At the 1984 Los Angeles Olympics, she won the silver medal in the 200-meter race. At the 1987 World Championships in Rome, she won a silver medal in the 200-meter and

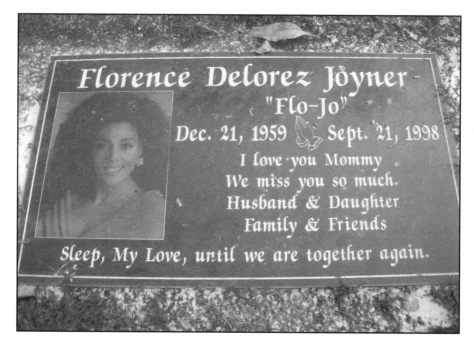

gold medal in the 4x100 meter relay. Determined to do better at the 1988 Seoul Olympics, Joyner won three gold medals in the 100, and 200-meter races, and the 4x400 meter relay. In the 100-meter contest she set a new world record of 10.49 seconds. Controversy soon dogged Joyner, whispers of wind gauge malfunctions, and the use of a performance enhancing drug began to circulate.[86]

Following the 1988 Olympics and at the apex of her career, Joyner abruptly retired from completive athletics. This lead to more speculation, as mandatory drug testing of Olympic athletes was set to begin in 1989. The rumors that Joyner used steroids and other drugs during her record-breaking track career were never proven or disproven. Soon after leaving the track world Florence and her husband Al Joyner (the brother of fellow track runner Jackie Joyner-Kersee) settled into a quiet family life in Mission Viejo, California.

In the early morning hours of September 21, 1998, Florence died; she had suffered a massive epileptic seizure, and while lying on her stomach suffocated in a pillow, and died. There was a massive outpouring of grief and disbelief at the sudden death of such a young and powerful woman. On September 25, 1998, a memorial service was held in west Los Angeles. The Olympic sprinter's flower-draped casket lay in the chapel of a local funeral home, where hundreds of mourners waited in long lines to pay their final respects.[87]

❧ Florence Griffith Joyner's final resting place is located in the Los Alisos lawn, block 34, lot 4, space 4; it is near the rose garden area, in the first row closest to the southeast perimeter the cemetery. Her simple black marker is adorned with a picture and is inscribed "I love you mommy, we miss you so much, husband, and daughter, family, and friends, sleep, my love until we are together again."

LEONARD EARL FRIBOURG

Not far from Flo-Jo is the grave of Brigadier General Leonard Earl Fribourg (December 31, 1921 to August 14, 1993). Fribourg was born in Shaker Heights, Ohio, and in 1942, while attending Fenn College, enlisted in the Marine Corp Reserve. Commissioned a second lieutenant in 1943, he was present at the battles of Guam and Okinawa. For valor in combat, he was awarded the Bronze Star and Purple Heart. Fribourg took part in the famous "Mosquito Bowl," football game as member of the fourth Marine Regiment. The game took place on Christmas Eve, December 24, 1944, on the island of Guadalcanal. An estimated 10,000 soldiers watched this game, and bet hundreds of thousands of dollars on its outcome.[88]

Fribourg tried his hand in Hollywood in 1949, as the technical advisor for the World War II film, *The Sands of Iwo Jima*, starring John Wayne (see Pacific View Memorial Park), John Agar, and Forrest Tucker. To help the actors get a feel for what the Marine Corp and combat was all about, Fribourg put the actors through a mini boot camp at Camp Pendleton.[89]

In 1969, Fribourg was promoted to brigadier general and named commander of the Marine Corp Reserve. His final military assignment came as the commanding officer at Camp Pendleton. General Fribourg, a veteran and hero of three wars (World War Two, Korea, and Vietnam), died on August 14, 1993, from kidney failure.[90]

❧ His grave is found in Los Alisos, block 34, lot 23, space 3. Locate a small olive tree, and a white marble memorial bench, three rows northeast of Joyner's grave. Four markers southwest of the bench is the simple grave marker of General Fribourg.

JOHN BECK III

Also buried at El Toro is film writer and producer John Beck III, (October 24, 1909 to July 18, 1993). Beck wrote and produced several award-winning movies from the 1940s through the 1960s. His film credits include:

- *One Touch of Venus* (1948), starring Ava Gardner

- *The Countess of Monte Cristo* (1948), starring Sonja Henie

- *Family Honeymoon* (1949), starring Claudette Colbert

- *Kill the Umpire* (1950)

- *Harvey* (1950), starring Jimmy Stewart and Josephine Hull (garnered an Academy Award for Hull as best actress, and a Golden Globe nomination for best picture)

- *Fury at Showdown* (1957)

- *King Kong vs. Godzilla* (1962)—he was the writer and producer

- *The Singing Nun* (1966), starring Debbie Reynolds and Ricardo Montalban (this film was nominated for a best music Academy Award)

- *The Private Navy of Sgt. O'Farrell* (1968), starring Bob Hope and Phyllis Diller

❧ Beck died in Woodland Hills, California, on July 18, 1993.[91] His remains were cremated and scattered in the rose garden area (Los Alisos, block 33, lot 211, space 1); there is no marker. The garden is south of the flagpole, and on the eastern perimeter of the cemetery.

JOSEPH FRANCIS BIROC

Also interred within the rose garden area is award-winning cinematographer Joseph Francis Biroc (February 12, 1903 to September 7, 1996). Biroc was born in New York City. He was a very talented cameraman, whose career as a cinematographer began while assigned to the Army Signal Corp and his filming of the liberation of Paris during World War II. An accomplished director of photography, one of Biroc's early accomplishments in Hollywood was the first 3-D movie, Bwana Devil, in 1952. He was director Robert Aldrich's favorite cameraman. Biroc was nominated for a best cinematographer Academy Award three times, finally winning the honor in 1974 for The Towering Inferno. In 1989, he received the Society of American Cinematographers life-time achievement award.[92] Biroc's film and television career spanned four decades beginning in 1929, and he has over 100 film credits, highlights include:

- *It's a Wonderful Life* (1946) starring Jimmy Stewart
- *Hush, Hush Sweet Charlotte* (1964), starring Bette Davis and Joan Crawford
- *The Russians are Coming, the Russians are Coming* (1965)
- *Escape from the Planet of the* Apes (1970)
- *Cahill, U.S. Marshall* (1972), starring John Wayne
- *Blazing Saddles* (1973), directed by Mel Brookes
- *The Longest Yard* (1973), starring Burt Reynolds
- *The Towering Inferno* (1974), starring Paul Newman and Steve McQueen
- *Airplane* (1979)[93]

His numerous television credits consist of:

- *The Adventures of Superman* (various episodes, 1955 and 1956)
- *Brian's Song, (1971)* the made-for-television movie, starring James Caan and Billy Dee Williams (Biroc won the Emmy Award for cinematography)
- *Wonder Woman* (1973)
- *Casablanca* (He won an Emmy Award for the episode entitled "The Master Builder's Woman" in 1982).[94]

Joseph Biroc died on September 7, 1996, in Woodland Hills, California. His remains were cremated and scattered in the rose garden of the cemetery, (Los Alisos, block 33, lot 542, space 1); there is no marker. The rose garden is on the east perimeter of the cemetery, south of the flagpole area.

GEORGE "CATFISH" METKOVICH

From Hollywood to the world of sports and buried in the southeast lawn area is professional baseball player and actor George "Catfish" Metkovich (October 8, 1921 to May 17, 1995). Metkovich played outfield and first base for the Boston

Red Sox, Cleveland Indians, Chicago White Sox, Pittsburgh Pirates, Chicago Cubs, and the Milwaukee Braves. His ten-year playing career began in 1943 and ended in 1954. A light hitting outfielder that amassed a career record of 1055 games played, 3,585 at bats, 934 hits, 373 runs batted in, with a batting average of .261.[95]

He got his nickname "catfish" from Casey Stengel, when he hurt himself fishing. During the 1944 season, while with the Boston Red Sox, Metkovich capably replaced Ted Williams in right field while the future Hall of Famer was away in the army. During that season, Catfish had a twenty-five game hit streak.[96] As a player for the Red Sox, he also participated in the 1946 World Series versus the St. Louis Cardinals. He had two pitch hit appearances, with one double and one run scored.[97] On June 4, 1953, Metkovich was involved in a blockbuster trade that sent himself, as well future Hall of Famer Ralph Kiner from the Pittsburgh Pirates, to the Chicago Cubs.[98]

Metkovich also appeared in several films as an actor. His film credits include:

+—❧ *The Stratton Story* (1949)

+—❧ *Three Little Words* (1950)

+—❧ *Love is Better Than Ever* (1952)

+—❧ *The Winning Team* (1952)[99]

❧ George Metkovich died on May 17, 1995, in Costa Mesa, California, due to complications from Alzheimer's disease.[100] His grave is located in the southeast section, block 21, lot 9, space 10. Find the grave of Margaret Seligman on the east curb, seven rows west is the grave of Metkovich. His flat black grave marker is adorned in the upper left corner with a baseball player.

WILLIAM HENRY KEATING

Buried within the old section of the cemetery is William Henry Keating (September 26, 1807 to October 21, 1898). Keating was born in Nottingham, England. He was the Deputy Provincial Secretary of the Executive Council in Nova Scotia, Canada, in the mid-nineteenth century. It was a prestigious position that was equivalent to the office of secretary of state in which duties included running the treasury, official correspondence with the colonial office in London, handling ceremonial tasks pertaining to visits of dignitaries, and he also served as records administrator in the province. The position was usually the most senior member of the provincial cabinet outside of the premier.[101] After Canada gained its independence from Great Britain in 1867, Keating and his wife moved to Southern California. William died on October 21, 1898, in Los Angeles, California. He is buried with his wife, Elizabeth, beneath a very large cross-like monument at the top of the hill on the northeast side of the old lawn section in block 11.

The Keating Memorial at El Toro Memorial Park.

WARREN FOSTER

Warren Foster (October 24, 1904 to December 13, 1971) was a writer, cartoonist, and songwriter. Foster is best known for his work as a writer at Warner Bros., and the Hanna-Barbera animation studios from 1938 to 1986. At Warner Bros., he was the guy who knew all the gags, and his prolific career started with Porky Pig in Porky in Wackyland (1938).[102] Foster was a writer, and story line developer for many of the greatest cartoons of all time, including the legendary Looney Tune characters of Bugs Bunny, Daffy Duck, Tweety Bird, and others. He wrote the theme song for Tweety, "I Taut I Taw a Puddy Tat."[103]

In the early 1960s, he left Warner Bros. Studios for Hanna-Barbera, where he collaborated and wrote story lines for numerous famous cartoons such as *The Yogi Bear Show*, *The Jetsons*, and *The Flintstones*. Warren Foster died in San Clemente, California, on December 13, 1971.[104]

His grave is situated on the north side of the old section, block 12, lot 1, space 4. Find the grave of Bill Rohlffs on the north curb, five markers south is Foster's flat grave marker.

RALPH REED FREETO

Also interred within the ground of El Toro Memorial Park is child actor Ralph Reed Freeto (August 12, 1931 to January 21, 1997). Freeto appeared in several films as a teenager actor, his film credits include:

- *Sing Your Way Home* (1945), starring Jack Haley
- *Calendar Girl* (1947)
- *Louisiana* (1947)
- *The Gangster* (1947)

Ralph Freeto died in El Toro, California, on January 21, 1997.[105] His grave is located in Live Oak, block 13, lot 4, space 9. Find the grave of Clayborne Reynolds on the south curb (near a small cement waste receptacle), five rows north is the burial place of Fretto.

CHRISTIAN K. NELSON

Christian K. Nelson (March 11, 1893 to March 8, 1992), was the inventor of the "Eskimo Pie." Nelson was born in Denmark and immigrated to the United States in 1893 with his parents. The Nelsons settled in Iowa and Christian attended the University of Nebraska intent on becoming a teacher. After returning from military service in 1919, he taught school by day and ran a local ice cream shop in the evenings.[106]

Legend states that in 1919, a young customer by the name of Douglas Ressender came into Nelson's ice cream shop one day; the boy could not decide whether to buy a chocolate candy bar, or an ice cream sandwich. Nelson had an idea, why not combine the two? He tinkered with many different concoctions, and finally found a mixture of coca butter and chocolate that clung to the ice cream. This was the beginning of the Eskimo Pie, but early versions of the product were hard to market, and Nelson found few companies willing to develop it. On his own he began to sell the product calling it the "I-scream bar." In 1921, he patented his product with the help of Russell Stover. Together the two businessmen launched an ice cream frenzy. Stover is credited with changing the name of the ice cream bar to "Eskimo Pie." The product was very successful and in 1923, Stover left the Eskimo Pie Corporation to embark on other endeavors, which included founding Russell Stover Candies. Nelson on the other hand, held out for a time, and then finally sold his interest to the R.S. Reynold's Foil Company. The Reynold's Company would be the parent company for Eskimo Pies until 1992. After selling his interest in the company, Nelson was a wealthy man and retired. In 1935, out of boredom, Nelson joined the Reynold's Company as a consultant and embarked on new manufacturing and marketing ideas for the Eskimo Bar.[107]

Nelson and his wife, Myrtle, moved to Leisure World in Laguna Hills, California, in 1979. There they lived a peaceful life until October 1991, when Myrtle died. Christian followed her in death several months later; he died on March 8, 1992.[108]

🎗 Christian Nelson's grave is located in the live oak section, block 27, lot 26, space 3. Locate the gravestone of Jesus Ruiz on the south curb, twelve markers north is the Nelson's burial plot.

GORDON JUMP

A noteworthy interment at El Toro Memorial Park belongs to veteran television actor Gordon Jump (April 1, 1932 to September 22, 2003). Jump was a prolific character actor best known for playing Arthur Carlson, the bewildered radio station manager on the television program WKRP in Cincinnati from 1978-1982. In 1989, he became the spokesman for the Maytag Corporation, where he played the role of the lonely repairman in their commercials, a character he played until his death in 1993. Jump appeared in numerous well-known television series from 1965 until 2003. The more famous included:

+🎗 *Get Smart* (1966-67)

+🎗 *Green Acres* (1967-69

+🎗 *The Partridge Family* (1970-73)

+🎗 *The Love Boat* (1980-86)

+🎗 *Growing Pains* (1986-91)

Gordon Jump, a long time resident of Coto de Caza, died at his home on September 22, 2003 from pulmonary fibrosis (a scarring of the lungs that causes heart or respiratory failure).[109]

The lonely Maytag repairman's final repose, actor Gordon Jump's grave at El Toro Memorial Park.

He is buried in the Centennial lawn area, block 90, lot 5 (ECS). Look for a small tree and white marble memorial bench in the middle of the lawn at the top of the hill. The memorial bench is in honor of Jump, on one side is inscribed, "You are my sunshine," and the other side displays his name. His flat grave marker is adorned with the inscription, "loved and respected by all who knew him, God takes our loved ones from our homes, but never from our hearts."

MANUELA WITTHUHN

Also buried at El Toro is a victim of the original night stalker unsolved murder case from the early 1980s, Manuela Witthuhn. Her story along with other victims in the case will be told in Chapter Eight, "Murder and Mayhem."

3

FAIRHAVEN MEMORIAL PARK

It is not length of life but depth of life.

~ Ralph Waldo Emerson
American essayist and philosopher (1803 to 1882)

1702 Fairhaven Avenue
Santa Ana, California 92705
Telephone: (714) 633-1442

Hours of operation are 6 a.m. until dusk, Monday through Friday, 8 a.m. to 6 p.m., Saturdays, and Sundays 9 a.m. to 6 p.m.

On August 28, 1911, Fairhaven Memorial Park was opened to the public. Founded by local businessman Oliver Halsall, he created a beautiful modern cemetery for the rapidly growing Orange County metropolitan area. Situated on seventy-three acres of lush manicured lawns, this cemetery stands apart from others in the area with its large expanse of exotic trees (nearly 1,000) from around the world. This has allowed the cemetery to become a member of the American Association of Botanical gardens and Arboreta.

In 1916, the historic mausoleum was open to the public, being one of the first buildings of its kind in California. It was built of the finest marble and includes many imported handmade, stained glass windows. The windows are distinctive in that they do not depict religious icons, but rather poets and literature legends. An interesting fact about the historic mausoleum is that because of the chapel's unique echo, it was used by director Cecille B. DeMille for recording the voice of "God" in the 1956 film, *The Ten Commandments*, which starred Charlton Heston. Like most cemeteries in Southern California, Fairhaven has its share of movie stars, and other celebrities, but the majority of its famous residents made their claim to fame in slightly different ways.

Locating graves within this cemetery can be a daunting task due to flat gravestones, limited lawn markers, few landmarks, and unmarked interior roads. The cemetery is laid out in haphazard fashion with lawn sections designated by alphabetic listing, with lot and space enumerations for each individual grave.

The historic mausoleum at Fairhaven Memorial Park was built in 1916.

This is a rather large cemetery, so make sure that ample time is set aside to tour the grounds, two hours or more is adequate.

CLYDE A. BRUCKMAN

Located in section AG in the southern most section of the cemetery, are the remains of several noteworthy individuals. First, Clyde A. Bruckman, (September 20, 1894 to January 4, 1955) was a writer and director, best known for directing films such as The General, (1926) starring Buster Keaton and The Fatal Glass of Beer (1933), starring W.C. Fields. He also wrote, directed, and collaborated with other legendary comedians such as Laurel and Hardy, The Three Stooges, Abbott and Costello, and Harold Lloyd.[1]

On January 4, 1955, Bruckman was out of work and out of money. He borrowed a gun from actor Buster Keaton and drove to a restaurant in Santa Monica. After eating a dinner he could not pay for, he entered the restroom and killed himself. When interviewed later, Keaton told police that Bruckman had asked to borrow the hand gun for a hunting trip.[2]

✿ Clyde Bruckman's grave can be found in lot 1610, space one, which is located in the southeast corner of section AG. Along the fence is a white marble bench, located three rows directly north of the bench is late directors grave.

WILLIAM H. MORTENSEN

Not very far from Bruckman's final repose and only seven grave markers to the right in lot 1587, space one is the final resting place of pioneering American art photographer, William H. Mortensen (January 27, 1897 to August 12, 1965). He is considered to be one of the most enigmatic figures of twentieth-century American photography. During the 1920s and 1930s, he was a photographer to

Hollywood's most popular movie stars such as Marlene Dietrich, Jean Harlow, and Fay Wray. His "pictorialist" style of photography, which used a soft focus and pioneering darkroom techniques, produced finely toned and finished prints. In 1926, he worked for Cecille B. DeMille, shooting all the still photography for the movie King of Kings. Leaving Hollywood in the late 1930s, he opened the Mortensen School of Photography in Laguna Beach. He published several books of photography, including: Monsters and Madonnas and The Command To Look.[3]

❧ Mortensen died of leukemia on August 12, 1965.[4] He is buried next to his wife, Myrdith Mortensen, who was a frequent model for many of his photographs.

ARTHUR E. BEAUMONT

Across the street, and northeast of lawn AG is lawn AL. Interred here is famed naval artist Arthur E. Beaumont (March 25, 1890 to January 24, 1978). Beaumont was born in England and immigrated to the United States in 1908. He was professionally trained at the San Francisco School of Art, Chouinard School of Art, Los Angeles, and the Slade School of Art at the University of London. He opened his first commercial art studio in 1917. Throughout the 1920s into the early 1930s, Beaumont was primarily an impressionist painter, with oil on canvas landscapes. In 1931, he won first place at the Long Beach Art Association Show for his work The Little Mother. His focus changed from landscape oil paintings to portraiture, and maritime art with an emphasis on watercolors.

In 1932, he began a life long association with the United States Navy. As a civilian, he was commissioned to paint the portraits of several naval officers, including Admiral William Leahy. Leahy was impressed with Beaumont's talent, and offered him the opportunity to paint the fleet as a commissioned naval reserve officer. Beaumont accepted the offer, and his first official art commission was of thirty-nine warships entitle Our Glorious Fleet. His prolific career as official naval artist took him to the decks of warships during naval battles of World War II, to both the north and south poles, and also to the south Pacific during the atomic bomb testing.

In early 1941, he was commissioned by the National Geographic magazine to paint eight battleships, such as the U.S.S. Arizona, U.S.S. Oklahoma, and U.S.S. Utah; these ships would be destroyed later in the year in the surprise attack on Pearl Harbor, December 7, 1941.

In 1946, while painting the sinking of the Japanese battleship, Nagato, during the atomic testing, he was left adrift and rescued several days later. In the years following the war, he continued to paint naval vessels, but his interest turned to historic ships such as the U.S.S. Constellation, and U.S.S. Constitution.

Beaumont had a prolific career, and many of his paintings hang in art galleries around the world including the National Museum of Art, the White House, the Pentagon, and the U.S. Naval Academy. He was personally awarded the Meritorious Service Citation from President Franklin D. Roosevelt, for his contributions during the war. He rose to the rank of lieutenant commander in the Navy, refusing the offer of honorary rear admiral because he wanted to be able to walk on any ship without ceremony or fanfare. On January 24, 1978, the famed artist died in Laguna Hills, California, of heart failure at eighty-seven.[5]

❧ His final resting place is in lawn AL, lot 116, space 1, and is found on the south curb where the road slightly bends, in the first row.

William R. Hughes

To the west of lawn AL is section AE; here is the final resting place of professional baseball player William R. Hughes (November 25, 1866 to August 25, 1943). Hughes played first base and outfield for the Washington Nationals (1884) and Philadelphia Athletics (1885). He appeared in eighteen games, had sixty-five at bats, with nine base hits for a career batting average of .138. Hughes pitched two games for the Athletics in 1885 but lost both games.[6]

William Hughes' burial spot is in section AE, lot 270, space 1, located in the northwest corner of the lawn, three rows from the curb, and not far from a large oak tree.

Chester Milton "Chick" Brandom

After viewing Hughes' grave, move to lawn Z. Interred here are two noteworthy people. First is professional baseball player Chester Milton "Chick" Brandom (March 31, 1887 to October 7, 1958). Brandom was a pitcher for the Pittsburgh Pirates 1908 to 1909 and the Newark Peppers of the Federal League in 1915. He pitched in thirty-two games, winning three and losing one with an earned run average of 2.08.[7]

❧ His grave is located in lawn section Z, lot 688, space C. Located in the northeast sector of Z, seven rows from the road.

Evylena Nunn Miller

Next is international famed artist Evylena Nunn Miller (July 4, 1888 to February 26, 1966). Miller was a noted artist who is best known for her historical paintings of Southwest and Indian scenes. She studied under Anna Hills and Hannah Tempest Jenkins at the Art Students League in New York City in the early 1920s. The Bowers Museum in Santa Ana has in its permanent collection many of her Pueblo Indian paintings, and other works of art. In 1933, she won a gold medal at the Los Angeles Museum of Art's annual Gold Medal Exhibition for her oil on canvas painting entitled Chicago, 1933. She also has a painting on display at the Smithsonian Museum of American Art in Washington D.C., entitled Where Desert and Mountain Meet. Miller served as the "artist in residence" at Pomona College in 1945, was the director of the Bowers Museum in 1956, was the past president of the Woman Painters of the West, and was a founding member of the Laguna Beach Art Association. Nunn-Miller died on February 26, 1966 at seventy-seven.[8]

❦ Her grave is located in lawn Z, lot 752, space H, find the grave marker of Clara Orme on the east curb of the lawn, nine rows west is the artists final resting place.

MARY ESTHER DENVER

Another area of interest is lawn AB, located in the southwest corner, three rows from the curb in lot 229, space 1A is character actress Mary Esther Denver (May 10, 1918 to June 3, 1980). She made numerous film and television appearances from the late 1950s to the mid-1970s, primarily as a character actress. Denver's film credits include:

↠ *Born to be Loved* (1959)

↠ *The Fortune Cookie* (1966)

↠ *Wicked, Wicked* (1971)

↠ *Frasier the Sensuous Lion* (1973)

Her television career included roles in such iconic programs as:

↠ *Ben Casey* (1964)

↠ *Star Trek* (1967)

↠ *Bewitched* (1971)

↠ *Columbo* (1974)[9]

❦ Mary Esther Denver died on June 3, 1980 in Hollywood, California.[10] Her cremated remains are found buried with her parents Dr. Vaughn and Anna Wood.

JOHN SIMON FLUOR SR.

Also interred in this section is pioneering businessman and founder of the Fluor Corporation John Simon Fluor Sr. (March 4, 1867 to July 29, 1944). Fluor was born in Switzerland and immigrated to the United States with his two brothers in 1888. The Fluors first settled in Wisconsin and established a paper mill. A carpenter by trade, John soon became the mill's manager. In the early 1900s, John branched out on his own, moving to Southern California. There he started a general construction business; by the 1920s, John began to tailor his construction business to accommodate the new and burgeoning petroleum, and natural gas industry. The Fluor Construction Company was incorporated in 1924, and expanded its endeavors to include engineering along with construction.

In 1929, due to the stock market crash, the company was under great financial strains. To infuse capital, the company re-incorporated under a new name the Fluor Corporation. By the 1940s, the company again saw change. The pressures of World War II created an energy crisis, which led to Fluor's development and design of high-octane gasoline and synthetic rubber products. All of these changes and innovations came under the leadership of John S. Fluor Sr.

On July 29, 1944, Fluor died from heart and kidney failure.[11] He is buried in lawn AB, lot 123, space 1; the grave is found on the east side of the lawn towards the center. Locate the large cement waste receptacle and the grave of Ralph Crane near the curb, two rows from here to the west is Fluor's grave.

JOHN SIMON FLUOR, JR.

Also interred within the grounds of Fairhaven is John Simon Fluor, Jr. (April 22, 1902 to September 13, 1974), the son of John Fluor Sr.; he, along with his brother, Peter, took control of the Fluor Corporation following their father's death. In 1947, Peter Fluor died unexpectedly, leaving John Jr. as sole leader of the company. John Fluor Jr. held the title of Chief Executive Officer and Chairman of the Board, until his retirement in 1962. He was also a trustee of Chapman University, the California Institute of Technology, and the Los Angeles Church of Religious Science. The latter granted him an honorary doctorate. Fluor was also actively involved in the YMCA and was vice-chairman of the Southern California United Way.[12]

John Simon Fluor Jr. died on September 10, 1974, due to complications following open-heart surgery. His crypt is found in the main mausoleum in the east alcove, tier D, very near the crypt of Glenn L. Martin.

HARRY DeMILLER

Moving on to lawn section X, and the final resting place of Harry DeMiller (November 12, 1867 to October 19, 1928) professional baseball player. He pitched for the Chicago Colts (Cubs) in 1892, appearing in four games, winning one, losing one, with two no decisions.

Harry DeMiller died in Santa Ana, California on October 19, 1928.[13] His grave marker is located in the western sector of lawn X, lot 831, space D, and is two rows from the west wall.

GLENN LUTHER MARTIN

Located in the center of the grounds is the massive historic mausoleum; interred within its corridors are numerous noteworthy individuals. First is one of Orange County's most famous residents, pioneering aviator Glenn Luther Martin (January 11, 1886 to December 4, 1955). He was born on January 11, 1886, in the small town of Macksburg, Iowa.[14] The Martin family relocated several times during Glenn's early childhood.[15] Near the turn of the nineteenth century, as Glenn was entering his teen years, the Martin family finally found a permanent home in Santa Ana, California.[16]

At an early age Martin was fascinated with flight and the Wright brothers. In 1909, at the age of twenty-three, he built a flimsy airplane, made out of bamboo and other wood. The frame was covered in sailcloth, and powered by a Ford Model N engine. On August 1, 1909, he and this aircraft took flight in a vacant field just inside the Santa Ana city limits. The plane was destroyed on the first attempt, Martin was uninjured but his ego was bruised. Undaunted by

The Martin family crypt, which is located in the historic mausoleum. Famed aviator Glenn L. Martin's crypt is in the center between his parents.

this failure, he repaired the aircraft and attempted another flight; this time he was successful. The aircraft flew for twelve seconds, rising to a height of 100 feet. For this, Martin has been credited with building the first airplane of its kind, to fly that distance, at that height, under its own power.[17]

In 1912, Martin formed the Glenn L. Martin Company, which built training aircraft for the United States military. During this same period, Glenn barnstormed throughout the west coast, attending county fairs, giving rides on his plane. One of his first passengers was his mother Minta, another was famed actress Mary Pickford.[18] Pickford and Martin became good friends, and in 1915, she offered him a supporting role in her movie *The Girl of Yesterday*, in which Martin played the villain.[19]

Martin's first corporate success came during World War I with production of the MB-1 bomber. Unfortunately, for Glenn the war ended before full production of the bomber could begin. Throughout the decades of the 1920s, 1930s, and 1940s, the Martin Company was at the vanguard of military aircraft design with such aircraft as the SC-1 scout bomber, B-10 bomber, and the *China Clipper* flying boat. The Martin Company's most successful designs came during World War II with the B-26 Marauder, the A-22 Maryland, and the B-29 Super fortress bombers. After the war, the Martin Company continued its successes with production of the Vanguard rocket, which was used in the early days of N.A.S.A. and the United States space program.[20]

During Martin's long and illustrious career, he was credited with several aeronautical firsts, he was the pilot for the first woman parachutist on June 21, 1913[21] and on May 10, 1910, he made the first extended flight over ocean water (Newport Beach to Catalina Island) which covered approximately sixty six miles.[22]

In 1949, Glenn L. Martin stepped down as Chairman of the Martin Aviation Company but remained a principal stockholder in the company.[23] He retired to his country home on the Maryland shore along the Chesapeake Bay. On December 4, 1955, Glenn L. Martin died from a cerebral hemorrhage at his home; he was sixty-nine.[24]

Funeral services were held on December 6, 1955, at the First Presbyterian Church of Santa Ana, the same church where he worshiped as a boy. The funeral was officiated by the Reverend O. Scott McFarland. There were over

300 mourners in attendance; many were prominent aerospace industry founders, legends, and leaders. A special guest was Glenn's old friend, actress Mary Pickford. Honorary pallbearers included a mix of celebrities, politicians, and early aerospace pioneers such as Lawrence Bell, Donald Douglas, James McDonnell, actor Joe E. Brown, former Ohio Governor Thomas Herbert, and Kansas Senator Frank Carlson. Following the funeral service, in a light rain shower, a procession of cars made its way from the church to Fairhaven Memorial Park.[25] Martin's remains were entombed in the historic mausoleum with his mother, Minta and his father, Clarence.

❧ The Martin family crypt is located in the east corridor, room C, tier 2. As you enter the building, walk toward the chapel; as you pass under the cupola turn left, at the first hall, make a quick right. The second private alcove on the right is the Martin Family crypt.

LINDA CORDOVA

There are also two noteworthy actresses entombed in the historic mausoleum. Linda Cordova (March 19, 1926 to May 21, 1994) was a character actress during the late 1950s and early 1960s; she played small roles in movies and television, appearing mostly in westerns. Linda's movie credits include:

     ↦ *Virgin Sacrifice (1959)*

     ↦ *The Long Rope (1961)*

     ↦ *Hombre (1967) starring Paul Newman*

Her television career included several episodes of:

     ↦ *Have Gun Will Travel* (1962)

     ↦ *Wanted: Dead or Alive* (1961) starring Steve McQueen[26]

❧ Cordova died on May 21, 1994 in Los Angeles; her cremated remains are interred in the Alcove of Remembrance, N-8. It can be found in the second hall way on the right, first alcove. Her urn reads: "In your death you will be spoken of as those in the sky, like the stars, in loving memory, Linda Cordova Flores, 1926-1994, beloved Mom, Grandma, and Great-Grandma." The urn is also adorned with a youthful picture of Cordova.

MARGARET FIELDER IRVING-JAMES

Margaret Fielder Irving-James (January 18, 1898 to March 5, 1988), was an actress whose prolific career spanned four decades from the 1920s to the 1960s, and included numerous roles on stage, film, and television. Irving's show business career began in 1919 with the Ziegfeld Follies. It was during this time that she met composer Irving Berlin. He was so smitten with her beauty that it is alleged that she was the inspiration for his song A Pretty Girl is like a Melody, first performed in 1919 by the Ziegfeld Follies.[27]

Margaret's noteworthy stage roles included the Broadway production of *The Desert Song* in which she played the Spanish siren. Her film credits include:

- *Animal Crackers* (1935) with the Marx Brothers
- *Thanks a Million* (1935) with Dick Powell
- *Wife vs. Secretary* and *San Francisco* (1936) both starring Clark Gable

In one of her final movie appearances, Irving starred alongside the iconic comedic duo of Bud Abbott and Lou Costello in 1944's, *Abbott and Costello in Society*.[28] Her numerous television credits include:

- *The Peoples Choice* (1955)
- *My Little Margie* (1955)
- *77 Sunset Strip* (1960)[29]

Margaret Irving died of cancer on March 5, 1988, in Westminster, California.[30] Her cremated remains can be found next to her husband, William James, in columbarium 3, niche 101. As you enter the mausoleum take the first hall way left and to the end; on the left there is a small alcove, which contains the remains of Irving.

LEWIS FENNO MOULTON
NELLIE GAIL MOULTON

Lewis Fenno Moulton (1854 to 1938) and Nellie Gail Moulton (1878 to 1972) were prominent Orange County pioneering ranchers. Lewis came to California in 1874, becoming a sheep rancher on the Irvine ranch. He, along with partner Jean Pierre Duguerre, purchased and restored 26,000 acres of land that was originally part of the Avila land grant. This ranch became known as the Moulton Ranch. It remained in operation until 1960, after which the land was sold and developed. The old Moulton Ranch would become the new communities of Laguna Hills and Leisure World. Nellie Gail Moulton was a school teacher at the El Toro school before she met and married Lewis Moulton. She was well thought of in the county and her philanthropic contributions to local charities and education advocacy were monumental.[31]

The Moultons are interred in the main mausoleum. Their crypts are found in the west alcove room. It can be found to the right of the rotunda.

JAMES IRVINE III

Also entombed within the mausoleum is a prominent member of the Irvine family. James Irvine III (June 11, 1893 to June 23, 1935) was the grandson of James Irvine I, who was an early settler, and founded the Irvine Ranch in the 1860s, and son of James Irvine II, who took over management of the ranch following James Irvine Sr.'s death in 1890. He was the brother of Myford Irvine (see Pacific View Memorial Park).

Irvine III, led an active social and civic life outside of the activities of the Irvine Ranch. He was director of the Santa Ana Valley Hospital and director of the First National Bank. Irvine suffered for sixteen years from the side effects of influenza, which he had contracted while in the armed forces during World War I. These viral side effects held on for many years, and he was forced to undergo nine heart operations.

⚜ The strain on his health finally took its toll, and on June 23, 1935, at the age of forty-two, James Irvine III died.[32] His cremated remains can be found near the rotunda in room one, niche 351. Upon entering the main rotunda, room one is to the left. Once in the room, to the right and in the center of the wall is a glass case, which holds the urn with James' remains. The gold metallic urn reads, "James Irvine, Jr., June 11, 1893 June 23, 1935, To live in the hearts of those you love, is not to die."

BOYD ELLIS

Before exiting the main mausoleum there is one more prominent burial to note—Boyd Ellis (December 26, 1884 to July 11, 1974). Ellis was a pioneer racecar driver and boxing promoter. He and his brother, Henley, were teammates in several Los Angeles to Phoenix road races in the early twentieth century. These early races were precursors to today's Baja 500 and were filled with thrills and daring. In the early days of automobile racing, the drivers also built their own cars, and the Buick that the Ellis' assembled, attained high speed records for the period. The Ellis racing brothers were contemporaries of early racecar legends such as Barney Oldfield, Teddy Tetzlaf, Joe Nikrant, and Earl Cooper.[33]

Boyd was a boxer of note in his early days and was a conditioning partner of Oscar "Battling" Nelson (the two-time lightweight boxing champion 1905-1906 and 1908-1910). Prior to Nelson's title fight (July 13, 1909) versus Adolph Wolgast (lightweight boxing champion 1910-1912) at Los Angeles, he conditioned and sparred with Ellis at a training facility in Orange County. The Nelson/ Wolgast fight ended in a ten-round no-decision contest with Nelson retaining the championship. During the 1920s and 1930s, this boxing background influenced Ellis to promote four-round boxing matches in Orange County at the Delhi Athletic Club, in Santa Ana.[34]

Following his boxing career, Ellis purchased 110 acres of ranch land in what is now Fountain Valley, farming lima beans and raising dairy cows. The Ellis ranch was one of the first operating dairies in Orange County. In addition, present day Ellis Avenue in Fountain Valley is named in his honor. Boyd was also inducted into the Orange County Sports Hall of Fame in the early 1970s.[35] Sports pioneer Boyd Ellis passed away on July 11, 1974 at the home of his son, Gene Ellis, from a stroke.[36]

⚜ His crypt is found in the north hall, tier C. Upon entering the main mausoleum, turn left at the first hallway; Boyd's final resting place is located in the first row of crypts, third from the bottom. His epitaph reads, "Boyd Ellis 1884-1974, Sports Pioneer."

ROLLIN RAYMOND REES

Leaving the mausoleum, head to lawn Q. Buried here is United States Congressman Rollin Raymond Rees (January 10, 1865 to May 30, 1935). Rees served as prosecuting attorney in Ottawa County, Kansas, from 1895 to 1899, was a member of the Kansas State House of Representatives from 1899 to 1903, and judge of the Thirtieth Judicial District 1903 to 1910. He was elected to represent Kansas as a Republican to the Sixty-second Congress March 4, 1911 to March 3, 1913.37 Rollin R. Rees died at his ranch in Anaheim, California, May 30, 1935, of an apparent heart attack.[38]

❧ Rees' grave, lot 320, space one is in the southwest corner, two rows from the curb; he is buried next to his wife Hattie.

MARY MCCREA-CULTER

Across the street and to the west is lawn section P. Interred here is author Mary McCrea-Culter (April 12, 1858 to November 14, 1940). She penned six books from 1897 to 1917, that include:

+➾ *What the Railroad Brought to Timkin and other Short Stories* (1897)

+➾ *Four Roads to Happiness* (1900)

+➾ *The Girl Who Kept Up* (1902)

+➾ *A Prodigal Daughter* (1908)

+➾ *A Jolly Half Dozen* (1910)

+➾ *A Real Aristocrat* (1917)

She also wrote seventy-five serials and more than one thousand poems.[39]

❧ Culter's grave is found in the northwest sector of lawn P, lot 66, space two. Locate the grave of Mary H. Thomas on the curb, two rows to the east is Mary's marker that she shares with her husband John E. McCrae.

ERNEST RUDOLPH JOHNSON

Moving west from lawn P to lawn O is the final resting place of Ernest Rudolph Johnson (April 29, 1888 to May 1, 1952), professional baseball player. Johnson played for the Chicago White Sox, St. Louis Browns, and New York Yankees from 1912 to 1925. He is best known for replacing Swede Risberg as the starting short stop on the 1921 White Sox. Risberg had been banned from playing by Commissioner Kenesaw Mountain Landis for his involvement in the 1919 Black Sox scandal and the fixing of the World Series.[40]

Johnson played in 809 games, had 2,629 at bats, with 697 hits, and had a career batting average of .265. He appeared in the 1923 World Series with the

New York Yankees and played alongside teammate George Herman "Babe" Ruth; this was the Yankees' first World Series championship team.[41]

❦ Johnson is buried in section O, lot 328, space 1; locate the grave of H. C. Martens on the curb, five rows east is Johnson's marker.

ROSS W. CORTESE

Ross W. Cortese (1916 to October 1991) was a businessman, land developer and founder of Leisure World. He purchased property in what is know Rossmoor and started the Rossmoor Corporation. In the early 1960s, as chairman of the Rossmoor Corporation, Cortese developed the Leisure World Corporation, which built the first major planned retirement community of its type in Seal Beach, California. The first residents moved into Leisure World Seal Beach on June 6, 1962. The Rossmoor Corporation broke ground on a second Leisure World in 1963. Thirty-five hundred acres of land located on the former Moulton Ranch in South Orange County was purchased. The first resident moved into this Leisure World on September 10, 1964.

Ross Cortese died in October 1991. He left behind a legacy of seven Leisure World communities, the first two in Orange County, the last in Silver Spring, Maryland. He also developed business parks, retail centers, and non-retirement housing.[42]

❦ His grave is located in the Court of Serenity, East Terrace, 20D. This outdoor mausoleum is located in the northeast section of the cemetery. The Cortese crypt is on the east-facing wall, near the center, three rows from the bottom. His epitaph reads, "Ross W. Cortese, 1916. He made dreams reality and reality a dream 1991."

DONALD DEAN RANDALL

Also interred with the Court of Serenity is Donald Dean Randall (October 30, 1917 to December 23, 2008). In 1946, along with Leo Fender (see lawn J), Francis Hall (see the Court of Prayer), and Charlie Hayes, he established the Fender Musical Instruments Company. At the Fender Company, Randall was known as marketing and sales genius. He is credited with naming two of Fender's greatest guitars, the Stratocaster, and the telecaster. Randall also published Fretts magazine, an early forerunner of today's *Guitar Player* magazine. He was a prominent player in the negotiations, when the Fender Guitar Company was sold to CBS in 1965. He stayed with the company after the merger, serving as President of the Columbia Music Group, a position he held for five years. Donald Randall died on December 23, 2008, at the age of ninety-one.[43]

❦ His cremated remains are found in the Court of Serenity, phase one, east niche room. From the Cortese crypt, proceed north to the inner courtyard. Once inside the courtyard, turn right, and in the corner is a small alcove that has an iron door. Just inside the room on the left, four rows from the bottom, and three rows to the left is the niche containing Randall's remains.

RAYMOND CYRUS "R.C." HOILES

Lawn M holds the mortal remains of Raymond Cyrus "R. C." Hoiles (November 24, 1878 to October 31, 1970), founder of *Freedom Newspapers*, and parent company of the *Orange County Register*. Hoiles was publisher of the *O.C. Register* from 1950 to 1970. He was known for his hard-line approach, conservative ideology, and libertarian viewpoints. In a 1964 *New York Times* interview, he described himself as a "voluntaryist," stating "government should exist only to try to protect the rights of every individual, not to redistribute property, manipulate the economy, or establish a pattern of society."[44]

   Raymond C. Hoiles died on October 31, 1970, at Santa Ana, California, of an undisclosed illness; he was ninety one.[45] His grave is located in lawn M, lot 139, space 1, near the northwest corner of the section on the curb in the first row. His grave marker is adorned with a torch that is the symbol of *Freedom Newspapers*.

DOUGLAS "WRONG WAY" CORRIGAN

Another notable burial in lawn M is Douglas "Wrong Way" Corrigan (January 22, 1907 to December 9, 1995), pioneering aviator and American icon. In July 1938, he infamously attained the nickname "wrong way" after attempting a transcontinental round trip flight from Long Beach, California to New York. Corrigan was supposed to return to Long Beach, but instead landed in Dublin, Ireland on July 18, 1938. Corrigan claimed that this navigational error was due to several factors: heavy cloud cover, the aircrafts fuel tanks obstructed visuals, and an old compass had all contributed to the wrong-way adventure.

Upon exiting the cockpit in Ireland, Corrigan stated to a field officer, "My name is Corrigan, and I am from New York. I started in California, but somehow

Wrong way aviator, Douglas Corrigan's grave site.

I have landed here. My compass fooled me. Am I in Ireland?" Although Corrigan never publicly admitted to planning this wrong-way journey, apparently he had applied multiple times for permission to fly the trans-Atlantic route but was denied.[46] This wrong-way flight caught the imagination of the American people. With the Great Depression at its height, the public was in need of a diversion and thus a reluctant pop culture icon was born.

Primarily known for his wrong-way adventure, Corrigan was also a record-setting pilot in his own right and was also an accomplished aircraft mechanic. While working for the Ryan Aircraft Company in San Diego, he was a member of the team that assembled the wing, gas tank, and instrument panel for Charles Lindbergh's aircraft, *The Spirit of St. Louis*.[47] Douglas Corrigan died on December 9, 1995 in Orange, California.

His grave, located in lawn M, lot 307, space 2, is found on the north side of the section on the curb in the first row. Corrigan's non-descript grave marker bears only his name and dates of birth and death. The marker is unique in its simplicity; it bears a facsimile of his actual signature, a signature that he gratefully obliged to many an autograph seeker.

STANLEY "HERBERT" DUNN

Across the street and to the north of lawn M is the Memorial Garden lawn section; buried here is Stanley "Herbert" Dunn (November 24, 1891 to April 14, 1979), silent film actor and studio prop master. The son of an Irish Sea captain and an Algonquin Indian actress, he began his career in acting at the age of three. In 1913, Dunn got his big break starring in the Éclair films production of The Caballero's Way. Dunn played under the stage name Herbert Stanley, who became Hollywood's first "Cisco Kid," playing in over 100 episodes of the serial from 1913 to 1915. When Éclair Studios shut down in 1915, Dunn shifted career paths from in front of the camera to behind the scenes as a property master for Vitagraph, Biograph, and Columbia Studios. Through the years, he worked with some of Hollywood's biggest stars from silent films to talking pictures. He worked with Howard Hughes on six films including Hell's Angels and The Outlaw. Stanley Herbert Dunn died on April 14, 1979 of a stroke in Costa Mesa, California, at eighty-seven.[48]

His grave is found in the Memorial Garden lawn, lot 462, space 2. Located in the center of the section is the Garden of Remembrance (Angel statue), the grave is on the south side of the statue in the first row. His simple grave marker reads simply; "Love, Stanley H. Dunn, 1891-1979."

ROBERT C. "BOB" NIEMAN

Not far from Herbert Dunn is the final resting place of professional baseball player Robert C. "Bob" Nieman (January 26, 1927 to March 10, 1985). Nieman was an outfielder who played twelve seasons from 1951 to 1962 for the St. Louis Browns, Detroit Tigers, Chicago White Sox, Baltimore Orioles, St. Louis Cardinals, Cleveland Indians, and San Francisco Giants. As a rookie on September 14, 1951, in his major league debut at Fenway Park against the

Boston Red Sox, he was the first player in baseball history to hit two home runs in his first two plate appearances. Both home runs came against Red Sox pitcher Mickey McDermott.[49] Bob's career batting average was .295 with 1,018 hits, 125 home runs, 544 RBIs, in 1,113 games played. His best year statistically came in 1959 with the Baltimore Orioles where he appeared in 118 games, batted .292 with 21 home runs and 60 RBIs. He also played in the 1962 World Series with the San Francisco Giants against the New York Yankees, getting a walk while pinch hitting.[50] On March 10, 1985, while preparing to leave for spring training, he had a fatal heart attack in Corona, California.[51]

❧ His grave is located in the Memorial Gardens, lot 450, space 2 and is on the east side of the section towards the center, roughly five rows diagonally from the southeast curb.

WILLIAM HENRY SPURGEON

A short walk from the Memorial Gardens is lawn L. This is the oldest section of the cemetery and it is here where one of Orange County's founding fathers and early pioneers is buried: William Henry Spurgeon (October 10, 1829 to June 20, 1915). In 1869, Spurgeon purchased sixty-six acres where Santa Ana now stands. He viewed his purchase from a sycamore tree that once stood at the corner of Fifth, Sycamore, and Broadway Streets. Spurgeon was the founder of Santa Ana, represented the district in the 27th State Assembly, and was a Los Angeles County Supervisor, Santa Ana City Trustee, President of the Board of Trustees, and Chairman of the Orange County Board of Supervisors from 1889 to 1891.[52]

William Spurgeon died on the evening of June 20, 1915. He had been ill for sometime and had become feeble. His funeral service was held on June 22, 1915 at the South Methodist Church in Santa Ana, the Reverend Clark presiding. Out of respect for the city founder, the stores in downtown Santa Ana closed for one hour during the service. Pall bearers included some of Orange County's early settlers and leading businessmen, such as, James McFadden, Charles Bowers, John Beatty, and M. M. Crookshank.[53]

❧ Spurgeon's grave is located in lawn L, lot 99, space 1 is under an old oak tree in the center of the Spurgeon family lot on the north side of lawn L.

JAMES MCFADDEN

Lawn R holds the mortal remains of another pioneer of Orange County politics and business: James McFadden (1832 to June 9, 1919). In 1865, James was the first of the McFadden brothers, Robert (see Santa Ana Cemetery), John, and Archie, to arrive in California. James purchased land in and around what was the former Rancho de Santa Ana and what would later become the city of Santa Ana. In 1870, James, along with his brother, Robert, began selling parcels of this land for profit.[54]

The Orange County we see today is very different from the Orange County of the 1870s. The county was basically devoid of any natural building materials and all such materials had to be shipped from other places. The McFadden brothers saw a need for such materials and, in 1874, they established the Newport Wharf and Lumber Company. This company was able to facilitate the raid growth of Orange County through building materials.[55]

Politically, James McFadden was a powerhouse; his restless energy saw no limits. He was a fighter and threw every ounce of himself into battles—an ardent prohibitionist who fought for an alcohol free city and county.[56] James was also an early proponent of Orange County's drive for independence from Los Angeles County.[57]

❧ James McFadden died on June 8, 1919 at the age of seventy-nine of natural causes[58] and his grave is found in lawn R, lot 128, space 1. Locate the Viola Clark grave marker on the curb in the northeast section of the lawn, three rows south is his final resting place.

John McFadden

His brother, John McFadden's (d. June 24, 1915), grave is located just a short distance away in lawn L, lot 32, space 1. John was a successful businessman and politician in his own right, and the third McFadden brother to arrive in Orange County. He was engaged with his brothers, James and Robert, in the family lumber business, but also purchased and ran a hardware store in downtown Santa Ana. He was a highly respected businessman and was a founding member of the Merchants and Manufacturers Association, for which he was the first president. In 1906, he was elected trustee from the first ward in the city of Santa Ana, a position he held for many years.[59]

❧ John McFadden died on the morning of June 24, 1915; he had been suffering from a weakening heart condition and on the morning of the 24th, while reading a newspaper at his hardware store, he suffered a massive heart attack.[60] His grave can be found in the southern area of lawn L; locate the grave stone of Ernest Marks on the curb and nine grave markers north is John's final resting place.

Charles John "C.J." Segerstrom

Charles John "C.J." Segerstrom (1856 to 1928) was the patriarch of the Segerstrom family and a pioneering horticulturalist. Charles was a native of Sweden who left his native country in 1882 for a better life in the United States. His journey to Southern California took several years, with short stays in Chicago, Wisconsin, and Minnesota. In 1898, the Segerstrom family settled in Orange County in what was then known as "Old Newport," and to a life of farming. At first, Charles concentrated on dairy farming, and he had one of the largest operations in the state. In 1918, he realized that the land he owned was much better suited for other things and began to cultivate lima beans. Through the systematic acquisition of local land, he amassed a huge amount of acreage. His determined hard work allowed Charles and the Segerstrom family to become the largest independent producers of lima beans in the United States. The label "grown by Segerstrom," became widely known and famous for its quality.[61]

In 1928, Charles died, but his farm and empire continued to grow. His legacy today is seen in the real estate he acquired. By the mid-1950s, Orange County's population was expanding rapidly and the Segerstrom family land holding were right in the middle of the development. In 1967, a portion of the Segerstrom property was developed into what became Orange County's first enclosed upscale mega-shopping mall. The South Coast Plaza was very successful and has become the centerpiece of the Segerstrom family empire. Charles J. Segerstrom's bequest is felt today in his family's continued philanthropic contributions to Orange County. They have emerged as caretakers of its heritage through creation of the C. J. Segerstrom Company.[62]

❦ Segerstrom's final resting place is found in the southwest section of lawn R, in lot 87, space 1. First locate Dorothy M. Lau's grave marker on the curb, four rows northwest from there is Segerstrom's simple grave.

VICTOR MONTGOMERY

Lawn U holds the mortal remains of Confederate veteran and pioneering Orange County settler Victor Montgomery (April 28, 1846 to October 19, 1911). Montgomery was born in Nashville, Tennessee, and attended the Nashville Military Academy. In 1862, as a young boy of sixteen, Victor enlisted in the Confederate Cavalry. As a cavalry scout he was known for his daring and ability. It was this notoriety and reputation that led Confederate General Nathan Bedford Forest to name him chief of scouts in 1864. Under Forest's command, Montgomery participated in the battles of Tupelo, Franklin, and Nashville.[63]

After the war, Victor studied law, and in 1875, moved to Santa Ana where he established a successful law practice. He was a local leader in the bar association and politics. Victor was the draftee of the original bill of independence for Orange County. He was also a rancher, known to be one of the county's foremost horticulturists.[64]

Victor Montgomery died on the evening of October 18, 1911, of apoplexy (today, known as a stroke) at the Huntington Beach home of his daughter, Gertrude. He had been ill for sometime, suffering from severe exhaustion, and had gone to his daughters home for some relaxation.[65]

❦ His grave is found in lawn U, lot 28, space 6; locate the large upright Montgomery monument, three rows from the curb on the north side of the section. His monument reads: "C.S.A" (Confederate States of America, first line) "Victor Montgomery" (second line), "1846-1911" (third line), "upright, honest, brave, tender, true" (fourth line), and "loyal to every duty, he loved God and his fellow man" (fifth line).

JOHN ALPHEUS WILLSON

John Alpheus Willson (October 22, 1838 to June 15, 1916) was a civil war veteran and local politician. He was not well known, but he did participate in shaping Orange County and the Nation. Willson was born in Rockridge County, Virginia. In 1838, at the outbreak of the Civil War, he enlisted in the 25th Virginia Infantry, Confederate States of America. He rose quickly through the ranks attaining a commission as second lieutenant. John participated in the Battles of Rich Mountain, the Seven Days Battles, Gaines Mill, Malvern Hill, Second Manassas, Antietam (wounded in the hip), and the Shenandoah campaigns. Later in the war, he was assigned to General John McCausland's staff and was present at Appomattox Court House on April 10, 1865, when Robert E. Lee surrendered. Following the war, he moved to Orange County, where he served as Justice of the Peace, Secretary of the Santa Ana Chamber of Commerce, and City Recorder. An interesting side note, on October 12, 1870, Robert E. Lee died and due to Willson's alleged intimate relationship with the Lee family was named as one of the general's pallbearers.[66] John Alpheus Willson died on June 15, 1916, in Santa Ana, California, and is buried in lawn S, lot 137, space 1. At the time of his death, he was known to be the last surviving pallbearer of General Lee.

❧ Willson's grave can be found in the southwest sector, located near the large Rolfe family tombstone, two rows to the west and six graves from Rolfe. His marker reads; "CSA, J. Alph Willson, 1838-1916."

CHARLES W.
ADA E. BOWERS

Also buried in lawn section S are philanthropists Charles W. and Ada E. Bowers (d. 1929) and (d. 1931). Charles came to Orange County in the late 1800s. He was a landowner, developer, and citrus cultivator. His property was located on land that was originally part of the Yorba-Peralta Spanish land grant of 1810. He developed a keen interest in local history and its preservation. In 1924, Charles endowed a trust that created a museum to preserve Orange County's rich history.[67]

Following the deaths of both Charles and his wife, Ada, their former residence on Main Street in Santa Ana was razed and The Charles W. Bowers Memorial Museum was erected. The museum officially opened its doors on February 15, 1936; it houses collections of historical interest from California and Orange County history, as well as Native American artifacts.[68]

❧ The Bowers grave site is found in lawn S, lot 12, space 1 and 2. Locate the large Bowers monument on the southwest corner of the section; their final resting place is just behind the monument.

CORNELIA JOHANNA ARNOLDA "CORRIE" TEN BOOM

Lawn A is the final resting place of Cornelia Johanna Arnolda "Corrie" ten Boom (April 15, 1892 to April 15, 1983) Holocaust survivor, author, and Christian evangelist. She was born in Amsterdam in 1892. Shortly after her birth, the family moved to Holland, where her father owned a watch repair shop. At a young age she followed in her father's footsteps, training as a watchmaker, becoming the first female watchmaker in the Netherlands. When Nazi Germany invaded the Netherlands in 1940, the ten Boom family became active in the Dutch underground helping to hide Jewish refugees from persecution.[69]

Holocaust survivor and author, Corrie ten Boom's burial plot at Fairhaven Memorial Park.

On February 28, 1944, the ten Booms were arrested[70] and sent to the Scheveningen concentration camp where her father died ten days after arrival. In September of 1944, Corrie and her sister Betsie (their mother had died many years earlier) were transferred to the notorious Ravensbruk concentration camp in Germany.[71] Betsie died shortly after arriving, Corrie was miraculously released from the death camp the day after Christmas, December 26, 1944, due to a clerical error.[72] After her release, ten Boom learned that most of the women her age had been killed less than a week after her release.[73]

After the war, Corrie returned to the Netherlands, where she helped to heal the physical and mental wounds of those affected by the Nazi occupation.[74] She told the story of her family's wartime ordeal in the book *The Hiding Places* (1971), which in 1975, was made into a movie of the same title. In 1967, she was honored by the State of Israel as one of the "righteous among the nations," and planted a tree on the avenue of the righteous gentiles in Jerusalem. She was also knighted by the Queen of the Netherlands, recognized for her work towards humanity. Additionally, there is a museum in the Netherlands dedicated to her family.[75]

Corrie ten Boom traveled the world preaching God's love for humanity and emphasized forgiveness. She appeared on many Christian television programs telling her ordeal of the Holocaust and spreading God's love. ten Boom moved to Orange, California in 1977, and on her ninety-first birthday April 15, 1983, she died of a stroke.[76] She was said to have been very happy about dying on her birthday, stating "she could celebrate with the Lord."[77] The epitaph on her grave stone states that "Jesus is Victor" this phrase was a favorite of Corrie's mother and a tile plaque with this phrase hung above the ten Boom fireplace in their home in Haarlem, Holland.[78]

※ Ten Boom's grave is located in lawn A, lot 501, space A. Locate Leonard A. Ross on the curb in the south east corner, fifteen rows from there is Ten Boom's grave.

JOSE E. "PEPITO" PEREZ

Also interred in lawn A, is actor Jose E. "Pepito" Perez (February 16, 1898 to July 13, 1975). Perez known as "Pepito the Spanish Clown" was a screen, stage, vaudeville, and television actor. Pepito was the one time court jester to the Spanish Royal Court of King Alfonso. Also good friends with Desi Arnaz, and Lucille Ball, he devised clown bits for their vaudeville act in early 1950s. Lucy once said that Jose was the driving force in her development as a top comedienne, helping her with pantomime. Perez appeared in the 1952 pilot episode for the *I Love Lucy* show as Pepito the Clown. He was instrumental in development of the plot, prop design, and costumes for this first show.[79] Other film credits include:

- *Army Girl* (1938)
- *Annabella Takes a Tour* (1944)
- *Lady in the Dark* (1945)
- *A Medal for Benny* (1951)
- *The Raging Tide* (1951)[80]

Perez died on July 13, 1975, in Santa Ana from cancer.[81] He is buried in lawn A, lot 196. space 2. Find the grave of Rosa McClintock on the southeast corner of the lawn, and Pepito's final resting place is in the second row.

PAMELA SUSAN COURSON

North of lawn A is the modern outdoor mausoleum of the Court of Prayer, Meditation Garden, and Court of Reflection. Here you will find the mortal remains of three very different but unique individuals. Pamela Susan Courson (December 22, 1946 to April 25, 1974), the long time companion and alleged common-law wife of Jim Morrison, lead singer of the iconic 1960s rock group the Doors. Pamela grew up in Orange, California, and attended Orange High School. Considered a free spirit, she was intelligent but did not apply herself in school. She liked the beach and Newport Beach's Balboa Pier in particular.

Prior to her senior year in high school, Pamela left Orange County for the fast lane of Los Angeles. How Pamela met Jim Morrison is in dispute, some say it was at the Whiskey a Go Go in Hollywood; others say that they met in Venice, California. According to John Densmore, the drummer of the Doors, Pam and Jim met in the Summer of 1966 at the London Fog club in Hollywood.[82] They had a very tumultuous relationship with very little monogamy, but remained companions from 1966 until his death in 1971. Morrison considered Courson to be his "cosmic soul mate." She was the inspiration behind several songs written by Morrison: "Love Street" and "Twentieth Century Fox."[83]

Courson traveled with Morrison to Paris, France, in 1971, for a much-needed break from the recording industry and personal problems. On

Common law wife of legendary rock star Jim Morrison, Pamela "Courson" Morrison's cremation niche.

July 3, 1971, Jim Morrison was found dead of alleged natural causes in the bathtub of their apartment. He was known to be a heavy drinker and drug abuser and this hard living life style may have contributed to his final demise. To this day questions still remain as to how Morrison died. Was it an overdose on heroin? These questions will remain illusive because there was no autopsy performed.

He is buried in Pere-Lachaise Cemetery in Paris.[84] Following Morrison's death Pamela returned to California, becoming a recluse, using heroin, and slowly falling into mental instability. Courson inherited Jim Morrison's entire estate; she fought many lawsuits, which tied up the estate for years.[85]

On April 25, 1974, Pamela Courson died in Los Angeles of a heroin overdose on the couch of a friend. An acquaintance later said that Pamela spoke about seeing Jim again very soon. Whether her death was an accident or a suicide, no one will ever know, but Jim and Pam, "cosmic soul mates," are again united. She was twenty-seven at the time of her death, ironically the same age as Morrison when he died. Her parents had intended for Pamela's cremated remains to be buried with Morrison's in France, but red tape and legal complications made this impossible.[86]

  ❧ Pamela Courson's final resting place is found in the Garden Courts, compartment 164. After entering the Court of Meditation, make a quick left, follow the hall way to a small alcove on the left, and in the center section, bottom left, is Pamela's niche. Her niche is often adorned with fresh flowers, and pictures of Pam and Jim. Her plaque reads Pamela Susan Morrison, and although the pair was never officially married, Pamela saw herself as Jim's common law wife.

WILLIAM BROOKS CHING

Located directly across the hall from Morrison is the final resting place of film and television actor William Brooks Ching (October 2, 1913 to July 1, 1989). Ching was a supporting actor in many film and television programs from the mid 1940s through the late 1950s. His film credits include :

+≋ *D.O.A.* (1950)

+≋ *Pat and Mike* (1952) with Spencer Tracy and Katharine Hepburn

+≋ *Never Wave at a* WAC (1952) with Rosalind Russell

+≋ *Scared Stiff* (1953) with Dean Martin and Jerry Lewis.

Television credits include:

+≋ *77 Sunset Strip*

+≋ *Perry Mason*

+≋ *Science Fiction Theater*

+≋ *Our Miss Brooks*

+≋ *Jane Wyman Presents: The Fireside Theatre*[87]

≋ William Brooks Ching died on July 1, 1989, after a long undisclosed illness.[88] His cremated remains are interred in the Rose Alcove, row two, niche 18G, on the wall seven rows from the right and seven rows from the bottom.

FRANCIS C. HALL

Around the corner and to the right in the Court of Prayer is the crypt of Francis C. Hall (1909 to 1999), pioneering electric guitar manufacturer. Hall was a local Orange County electronic storeowner who in 1953 purchased controlling interest in Rickenbacker Guitars (the company has been credited with making the world's first electric guitar). Rock musicians and groups such as the Beatles (John Lennon), The Byrds (Roger McGuinn), and Tom Petty, have all favored the twelve-string version of the Rickenbacker guitar. Known as a very astute businessman, Hall's successes also helped Leo Fender (also interred at Fairhaven). Francis Hall died on August 25, 1999, of heart failure at the age of ninety.[89]

≋ His crypt is on the west side of the Court of Prayer, tier A, crypt 11-T, towards the middle, five rows from the bottom.

JOHN HOWARD MORROW

From the Court of Prayer a short walk directly to the east is lawn AZ. Here is the grave of John Howard Morrow (1910 to January 11, 2000), an American Diplomat. In 1959, during President Eisenhower's administration, Morrow was appointed Ambassador to Guinea. During the Kennedy administration, Morrow was the first representative from the United States to the United Nations Educational, Scientific, and Cultural Organization. Along with his brother E. Fredric Morrow, they were among only a handful of African-American high-level diplomats who worked for the United States government during the 1950s and 1960s.[90] John Morrow died January 11, 2000, in Fountain Valley, California, from Alzheimer's disease.[91]

❧ His grave is located in lawn AZ, lot 252, space (D) in the middle of the section, nine rows from the curb.

PIERCE LYDEN

Lawn AY holds the mortal remains of one of Hollywood's most prolific B-western villain actors, Pierce Lyden (January 8, 1908 to October 10, 1998). Lyden appeared in over 300 films with another 100 television and serial roles to his credit from the 1930s to the early 1960s. Throughout his long career in show business, Lyden appeared alongside every famous western movie star, including John Wayne, Gene Autry, Roy Rogers, and Hopalong Cassidy. He was awarded the title of "Villain of the Year" in 1944 by the Photo Press Fan Poll. Lyden was also inducted into the Cowboy Hall of Fame in 1979, received a star on the Palm Springs "Walk of Fame" in 1992, and was awarded the Golden Boot award, a kind of "Oscar" for Westerns that same year.

❧ Pierce Lyden died October 10, 1998, at his home in Orange, California, one of the last surviving Hollywood cowboy villains.[92] His grave, AY, lot 6, space 1, and is found on the west side of the lawn, the first row from the curb.

CLARENCE LEONIDAS "LEO" FENDER

One of Rock and Rolls great innovators is buried in lawn J, Clarence Leonidas "Leo" Fender (August 10, 1909 to March 21, 1991). Fender's electric guitars revolutionized modern music, and in 1946, the Fender Electric Instrument Company was established.[93] He was the first to successfully design and market the solid body guitar with his "Broadcaster" in 1948, which was subsequently renamed the "Telecaster." Fenders "Precision bass" liberated the bassist from the cumbersome stand up variety in 1950.

The mainstay, and arguably the best creation of Fenders, was the "Stratocaster" created in 1954. This guitar is and was favored by rock legends such as Eric Clapton, Keith Richards, Jeff Beck, Jimi Hendrix,

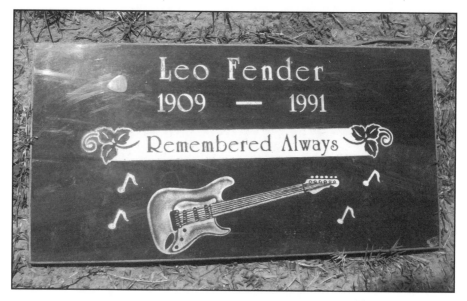

Rock and Roll Hall of Fame guitar maker, Leo Fender's burial plot.

and Stevie Ray Vaughn. This guitar has been in continuous production since its creation.[94]

Along with his contemporary Francis Hall (buried in the Court of Prayer), they revolutionized modern music like no others have since. "He appreciated the artistry of rock and roll, but he didn't like the noise it made," and yet he was the one responsible for the noise." Ironically, Fender favored country and western music over rock and roll. He had a strong work ethic and worked everyday of his adult life, actually working the day before his death. In 1992, one year after his death, he was posthumously inducted into the Rock and Roll Hall of Fame. Leo Fender died March 21, 1991 of complications from Parkinson's disease.[95]

His grave in lawn J, lot 522, space B, can be found in the center of lawn, eleven rows from the eastern side of the section. Fender's simple marker reads; "Leo Fender, 1909-1991, always remembered, with a rendering of his famous Stratocaster."

C.J. "PAPPY" HART

Another "Hall of Famer" that is buried in lawn J is motor sports pioneer C.J. "Pappy" Hart (April 29, 1911 to June 25, 2004). Hart the "Father" of modern drag racing, held races at an unused runway at the Orange County Airport (now called John Wayne Airport) during the 1950s. In the 1960s he moved the races to Riverside Raceway. C. J. "Pappy" Hart was inducted into the International Drag racing Hall of Fame in 1991 and the Motor Sports Hall of Fame in 1999. He is sited with inventing drag racing because he was the first to have a commercial drag strip. Hart died June 25, 2004 in Placentia, California, due to complications from a stroke.[96]

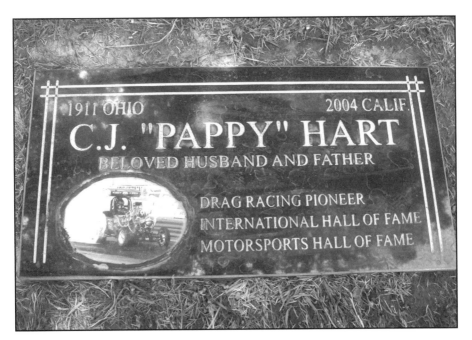

Drag race pioneer Pappy Hart's final resting place.

❧ His grave in lawn J, lot 546, space (E) is located on the east end of the section in the center under an oak tree, three rows from the curb. His marker reads; "C. J. 'Pappy' Hart, beloved husband and father, drag racing pioneer, international hall of fame, motor sports hall of fame." There is also a picture of a drag racer adorning the marker.

ROBERT "BOBBY" NELSON

Also buried in lawn J is child actor Robert "Bobby" Nelson (July 21, 1923 to August 5, 1993). As a child actor, he primarily appeared in westerns from 1926 to 1937. He appeared along side iconic western actors Hoot Gibson, Ken Maynard, Tom Tyler, and Buffalo Bill Jr., in films such as:

- *Custer's Last Stand* (1936)
- *Boot Hill Brigade* (1937)
- *Valley of the Lawless* (1936)
- *The Ghost Rider* (1935)[97]

He left Hollywood in the early 1940s to pursue a career in accounting. Robert Nelson died August 5, 1993 in Orange, California, due to complications from stomach cancer.[98]

❧ His final resting place in lawn J, lot 477, space (E) can be found on the north side of the section four rows from the curb under a tree.

WILLIAM T. GRACE

William T. Grace (1907 to 1989) is the founder of Helen Grace Candy (he named the company after his ex-wife Helen; she is buried at Pacific View Memorial Park). Grace died in 1989 of unknown causes.[99]

His final resting place in lawn H, lot 654, space (E) can be found on the west side of the section, twelve rows from the curb near the center. Grace's ornate marker shows a California mission scene with a sunburst motif. It reads: "W. T. 'Bill' Grace, an inspiration to all who loved him, 1907-1989."

HENRY A. "HANK" EDWARDS

Not too far from Grace is the final resting place of professional baseball player Henry A. "Hank" Edwards (January 29, 1919 to June 22, 1988). Hank Edwards' baseball career lasted eleven years from 1941 to 1953. During this time, he played for six teams, the Cleveland Indians, Chicago Cubs, Brooklyn Dodgers, Cincinnati Reds, Chicago White Sox, and St. Louis Browns. Primarily a reserve outfielder, Hank was often injured throughout his career. His best year statistically was 1946, while with the Cleveland Indians. During the 1946 season, Edwards led the American League in triples (16) with a batting average of .301.[100] Edwards died in Anaheim, California on June 22, 1988.

His grave is located in lawn H, lot 657, space A. On the south west side of the lawn, locate the grave of Herman Garland on the curb; sixteen rows to the north is Edwards simple grave marker and final resting place.

ROBERT SQUIRES
CALVIN E. JACKSON
LEONARD A. WEST

There are several other notable internees at Fairhaven Memorial Park, their stories, and final resting places will be discussed in Chapter Eight, "The Battle of Tomato Springs." They include Robert Squires (the first O.C. Deputy Sheriff killed in the line of duty), Calvin E. Jackson, and Leonard A. West.

4

PACIFIC VIEW MEMORIAL PARK

Tomorrow is the most important thing in life.
Comes into us at midnight very clean.
It's perfect when it arrives and it puts itself in our hands.
It hopes we've learned something from yesterday.

~John Wayne
actor (1907 to 1979)

3500 Pacific View Drive
Corona del Mar, California 92625
Telephone: 949-644-2700

Pacific View Memorial Park is one of the largest and most beautiful cemeteries in Orange County. Founded in the late 1950s, it is situated on over 100 acres of prime coastal property. The cemetery is located two miles inland from the coast, and is perched high above the Pacific Ocean with a sweeping vista of Newport Harbor, and Catalina Island. The grounds are well manicured with sloping lawns, beautiful private gardens, family estates, and a gigantic Spanish-style mausoleum that crowns the peak of the park.

There are two special memorials that grace the grounds, and both are near the entrance to the park: the Armed Forces Memorial (that honors all branches of the U.S. Military), and a Drunk Drivers Victims Memorial (that memorializes those who were killed by drunk drivers). This cemetery is peaceful and calm, and unlike other cemeteries, it is not a place of sadness, but rather a place to celebrate life. There is no better place to contemplate or spend eternity, than overlooking the blue expanses of the Pacific with its cool ocean breezes.

This cemetery has the highest concentration of famous and noteworthy graves in Orange County. The grounds are easy to navigate, and lawn markings are clearly visible on all curbs. If all the noteworthy graves mentioned are to be visited, you will need to set aside at least three hours.

George H. Yardley

The first area of interest in the Vista del Mar lawn section, buried here are numerous famous people. First is professional basketball player and hall of famer George H. Yardley (November 3, 1928 to August 12, 2004). Yardley was a 6-foot 5-inch power forward, who played seven seasons in the National Basketball Association for the Fort Wayne and Detroit Pistons, and Syracuse Nationals from 1953 to 1960. During his playing career, Yardley amassed a career points per game average of 19.2, and scored a total of 9,063. He appeared twice in the NBA Finals with the Fort Wayne Pistons. He was a six time all-star, who led the NBA in scoring (27.8 PPG) in the 1957-58 season. During that same season he broke George Mikan's record by scoring 2,001 points, the first player to break the 2,000 barrier. In 1996, he was elected into the National Basketball Hall of Fame.

On August 12, 2004, he died from Amyotrophic Lateral Sclerosis (Lou Gehrig's disease).[1]

His unmarked grave is found next to his wife, Diana (who died in 1999), in the Vista del Mar lawn section, lot 60. On the southeast side of the lawn, locate the grave of Margaret Kale on the curb; four graves north is their final resting place. The Yardley's grave marker is adorned with a picture of Diana and George but does not reference the basketball hall of famer.

Edmund J. "Eddie" Burns

Also buried in the Vista del Mar section is actor Edmund J. "Eddie" Burns (September 27, 1892 to April 2, 1980). Burns was an actor who appeared in nearly 100 films from 1915 to 1936.[2] Notable film credits include D. W. Griffith's epic, *Birth of a Nation* (1915), and Frank Capra's Academy Award winning film, *It Happened One Night* (1934), starring Clark gable and Claudette Colbert.[3] Burns died on April 2, 1980.

His grave is located in the Vista del Mar section, lot 216, space C. Find marker 195 on the south curb, then locate the grave marker of Leslie Furlong, thirty-three graves north is Burns plot.

Kam Tong

Another actor who is interred in Vista del Mar lawn is Kam Tong (December 18, 1906 to November 8, 1969). Tong was a Chinese-American actor who appeared in numerous films and television shows from the 1930s through the 1960s. He is best known for his role as Kim "hey boy" Chan in the 1960s television series *Have Gun Will Travel*. Other television credits include appearances on:

- *Bonanza*
- *The Man from U.N.C.L.E,*
- *The Big Valley*[4]

He died on November 8, 1969 in Costa Mesa, California. His burial site is located in the Vista del Mar lawn, lot 560, space E. Locate marker 604 on the curb, then find the grave of Fred Hewitt, twenty-three graves north is Kam Tong's grave site.

JEANNE CAROLYN CAGNEY

Jeanne Carolyn Cagney (March 25, 1919 to December 7, 1984) was a screen and television actress in the 1930s through 1960s. She is the sister of James Cagney and appeared with him in:

- *Yankee Doodle Dandy* (1942)
- *The Time of Your Life* (1948)
- *A Lion is in the Streets* (1953)
- *Man of a Thousand Faces* (1957)

Television credits include appearances in:

- *The Adventures of Wild Bill Hickok* (1952)
- *The Red Skelton Show* (1956)[5]

She died on December 7, 1984 in Newport Beach, California. Her final resting place is also in the Vista del Mar lawn, lot 694, space D.

WILLIAM CAGNEY

Just to the left of Jeanne Cagney is her brother, film producer William Cagney (March 26, 1904 to January 3, 1988). William was a producer, actor, and business manager for his brother. He was the producer for many of James Cagney's films during the 1940s and 1950s. The most famous of which being the Academy Award winning film *Yankee Doodle Dandy* (1942). As an actor he appeared along side his brother in *Kiss Tomorrow Goodbye* (1950).[6]

William died on January 3, 1988 in Newport Beach, California, and his grave is located just to the right of his sister Jeanne Cagney, in the Vista del Mar Lawn, lot 694, space E. The Cagney's graves are found on the southeast side of the lawn; locate curb marker 708. Seven and eight graves respectively from the curb are Jeanne and William Cagney.

JAMES ALGER WILSON

Also buried within the Vista del Mar lawn are several professional baseball players, one of which is James Alger Wilson (February 20, 1922 to September 2, 1986). Wilson, a right-handed starting pitcher, played twelve seasons in the major leagues for the Boston Red Sox, St. Louis Browns, Philadelphia Athletics, Boston Braves, Milwaukee Braves, Baltimore Orioles, and Chicago White Sox from 1945 to 1958. An all-star in 1955 through 1956, he also pitched a no-hitter on June 12, 1954 against the Philadelphia Phillies. After his playing career, Wilson worked as a scout for the Houston Astros, and director of player development for the Milwaukee Brewers.[7] Wilson died on September 2, 1986 in Newport Beach, California.

❖ His burial site is locate in the Vista del Mar lawn, lot 816, space A, locate marker 802 on the curb, and from the grave of Mary Keyes walk north, five spaces.

ARTHUR E. STODDARD

Buried nearby is Arthur E. Stoddard (July 28, 1895 to March 24, 1969), the president of the Union Pacific Railroad from 1949 to 1965. Stoddard was an innovative chief executive who oversaw the switch from diesel-electric power locomotives to gas-turbine-electric engines. These so-called "super turbines" were powerful enough to pull a 734 car freight train at a steady pace of twelve miles per hour.[8]

In 1906, and at the age of eleven, Arthur joined his father (a sub-contractor, who was building the Rock Island Line from Oklahoma to Texas) in the railroad industry. In 1916, after attending schools on the East Coast, began work for the Union Pacific as a station helper, worked his way up the ladder to the presidency of the railroad.

Stoddard was a veteran of both World Wars, serving in both the Navy and Army, and rising to the rank of major general in Army. In 1942, as the United States became entangled in World War II, Stoddard was called into active military service. As a colonel in the transportation corps, he was initially stationed in Iran. There he made a study of the railroads of the Middle East, and helped the Russian Army with railway issues. After a year, he was transferred to Allied Supreme Headquarters, in England to over see the rail service. Following the invasion of Europe in June of 1944, he was promoted to manager of the military railway service in France, and for this was awarded the "Croix de Guerre with palms," from France (the country's most cherished military decoration) for exceptional service during the liberation.[9] In 1949, he was promoted to the rank of brigadier general in the officers reserve corps, and assumed the role of commander of the military railway service. Prior to retiring from the reserve corps in 1951, he was promoted to major general. He continued to work his way up the ladder of the Union Pacific, retiring from the company in 1965.

Arthur Stoddard died on March 24, 1969 in Ogden, Utah.[10]

❖ He is burial site is in the Vista del Mar lawn area, lot 166. First find the grave of Jose Lamoso on the curb, near the 802 marker, and then walk fourteen spaces to the north to the Stoddard family plot.

DALE R. COOGAN

Also interred in the Vista del Mar lawn is professional baseball player Dale R. Coogan (August 14, 1930 to March 8, 1989). Coogan played fifty-three games for the Pittsburgh Pirates in 1950. Coogan's career statistics include 129 at bats, 31 hits, with a batting average of .240.[11]

❧ Dale Coogan is buried in Vista del Mar lawn, lot 909, space F, find marker 904 on curb, and his final resting place is twenty-five spaces north from Giovanna Misserville.

CHARLES J. QUILTER

Not far from Coogan is the last famous burial of the Vista del Mar lawn area, interred here is Major General Charles J. Quilter (December 7, 1914 to March 18, 1978). Quilter was a veteran of three wars, World War II, Korea, and Vietnam. He was commissioned a second lieutenant in the Marine Corp in 1937. He completed flight school that same year, and was a classmate of another famous flying ace, Gregory "Pappy" Boyington, who is best known as the commander of the famous Black Sheep Squadron. At the outbreak of World War II, Quilter was assigned to the fighter squadron on Midway Island. He flew twenty-one combat missions in the Pacific theater during the war, and for gallantry, was awarded the Distinguished Flying Cross, Bronze Star, and two air medals. He rose in the ranks rapidly, and by the end of World War II, had been promoted to lieutenant colonel.[12]

After the war, Quilter served as assistant director of the service test division at the Naval Air Test Station, Patuxent River, Maryland. He was also the assistant chief of staff at the Marine Air Reserve Training Command at Glenview, Illinois. At the outbreak of the Korean Conflict, he was assigned to the 1st Marine Aircraft Wing as liaison officer. For his service during the Korean War, he was awarded the Legion of Merit with combat "V," and an Oak Leaf Cluster in lieu of a second Bronze Star.[13]

Between the Korean and Vietnam wars, Quilter served as deputy chief of staff at the Marine Headquarters, and as a staff officer for the Joint Chiefs of Staff, Washington, D.C. In 1963, he was promoted to brigadier general and major general in 1966. He served as the commanding officer at the Marine Corp Air Station, El Toro, California from 1966 to 1968. In 1968, he was transferred to Vietnam and became the commanding general of the 1st Marine Corp Air Wing. He held this position until his retirement from active service in 1969. General Quilter lived peacefully in Laguna Beach until his death from cancer on March 18, 1978.[14]

❧ He is buried in the Vista del Mar lawn, lot 889, space C; find curb marker 904 on the south side of the lawn, then locate the grave of Linda Johnson, seventeen graves north is the generals final resting place.

ALFRED H. SONG

East of the Vista del Mar lawn, and at the top of the hill is the peaceful Reflection Cremation Garden. The garden area has sweeping views of the Pacific Ocean, and is located at the apex of the cemetery. With its small ponds, winding paths, and beautiful waterfalls, it a serene setting.

Interred within the garden area are several notable people, including California State politician Alfred H. Song (February 16, 1919 to October 11, 2004). In 1962, Alfred Song, a Democrat was the first Asian-American elected to the California State Legislature, representing the San Gabriel

Valley. In 1966, he was elected to the State Senate, where he chaired the Senate Democratic Caucus, and Judiciary Committee. Among his many accomplishments, Song was the author of the first California state Consumer Warranty Act.

In 1978, allegations of political wrong doings, and an F.B.I. probe into political corruption brought an end to his political career. The charges against Song were eventually dropped but the damage had already been done; he lost a re-election bid to "good government" candidate Joseph B. Montoya (who would later be convicted of seven felony corruption charges, and was sentenced to six and half years in prison). On October 11, 2004, at the age of eighty-five, Alfred Song died of natural causes at an Irvine assisted living center.[15]

❦ His final resting place can be found in the Reflection Garden, E5, #2, niche 420; take the left path to the first large marble niche holder on the left, on the top row four niches from the right is Senator Song.

DAVID STEWART FREEMAN

Also interred within the Garden of Reflection is the co-author of *100 Things to Do Before You Die*, David Stewart Freeman (February 21, 1961 to August 17, 2008). Stewart along with Neil Teplica wrote the quirky travel book in 1999. It was a spiritual, cultural, and physical adventure book that heralded the 100 must-do things in the world, with a reminder that time is short. Their idea for the book grew out of a website they ran which featured travel events that could not be missed. David died on August 17, 2008 at his home in Venice, California, after hitting his head in a fall. Ironically, at the time of his death, Freeman had only visited half the places in his book.[16]

❦ His cremated remains are interred in the Garden of Reflection, D1, #4, niche 941. From Senator Song's niche, take the path to the interior section of the garden, enter through the green gate, make an immediate right and follow the wall to the end—David's niche is four spaces from the left, and two from the top. His very poignant epitaph reads:

"This life is a short journey.
Make sure you fill it with the most fun
and visit the coolest places on earth
before you pack those bags for the very last time."

MYFORD IRVINE

In the Palm Garden lawn area, located at the top of the hill, and south of the outdoor crypt areas is the burial plot of philanthropist, and land developer Myford Irvine (1898 to January 11, 1959). Myford Irvine was the grandson of Orange County pioneering developer James Irvine Sr., son of James Irvine Jr., and brother of James Irvine III (see Fairhaven Memorial Park). Myford was a land developer in his own right. He financed the building of the Irvine Bowl in

Laguna Beach, where the annual Festival of the Arts is held. He also donated a portion of the Irvine Ranch to the Boy Scouts of America in 1957, for their annual jamboree.

In the late evening of January 11, 1959, Irvine was feeling overworked and despondent, and took his own life. In the basement of their house on the Irvine Ranch, Myford shot himself first with a .22 caliber handgun, failing in his first attempt; he then used a shotgun that was successful. His body was then discovered by his wife, Gloria. After his death, there was some speculation that Irvine did not commit suicide but had been murdered.[17] These rumors were quickly squashed, when no real tangible evidence developed. Myford Irvine was originally interred at Melrose Abbey in Anaheim, but at some unknown point the family chose to rebury Myford at Pacific View Memorial Park.[18]

❀ Today, he rests beside his wife Gloria at the peak of the cemetery in the Palm Garden lawn, lot 23, space B. Locate the large tree on the south curb of the lawn, from there walk seven graves north to Myford and Gloria Irvine's burial plot.

MARGARET EARLY-WALLACE

The Bay View Terrace lawn section has the highest concentration of famous gravesites; first is actress Margaret Early-Wallace (December 25, 1919 to November 29, 2000). Early was a screen actress who appeared in numerous films during the 1930s and 1940s. Eight of the films she appeared in won or were nominated for Academy Awards, they include:

+─❀ *Stage Door* (1937), starring Katharine Hepburn and Ginger Rogers

+─❀ *Jezebel* (1938), starring Bette Davis and Richard Cromwell (see Santa Ana Cemetery)

+─❀ *The Young in Heart* (1938)

+─❀ *Forty Little Mothers* (1940)

+─❀ *Strike Up the Band* (1940) starring Judy garland, and Mickey Rooney

+─❀ *Shores of Tripoli* (1942), starring Randolph Scott, and Maureen O'Hara

+─❀ *Stage Door Canteen* (1943)

+─❀ *Three is a Family* (1944)

She appeared as the character Clarabelle Lee in several of Mickey Rooney's Andy Hardy films, *Judge Hardy and Son* (1939), and *Andy Hardy's Private Secretary* (1941).[19]

❀ Early died on November 29, 2000 in Laguna Beach, California. Her grave is located in the Bay View Terrace lawn, lot 9, space F. Find the 10 marker on the south curb; her grave is in the first row.

ROBERT DeGRASSE

Not far from Margaret Early is award-winning cinematographer Robert DeGrasse (February 9, 1900 to January 28, 1971). DeGrasse was the nephew of director Joseph DeGrasse, and actor Sam DeGrasse. Robert's career in film and television photography spans the 1920s through the 1960s. During the 1930s, he was the director of photography for many of RKO Studios great pictures. His film credits include:

- *Stage Door* (1937)
- *Vivacious Lady* (1938), for which he was nominated for an Academy Award for best cinematography
- *Care Free* (1938), starring Fred Astaire and Ginger Rogers
- *Bachelor Mother* (1939)
- *Kitty Foyle* (1940), starring Ginger Rogers (she won Academy Award for best actress)
- *The Mayor of 44th Street* (1942)
- *The Body Snatchers* (1945), starring Boris Karloff and Bela Lugosi
- *The Bachelor and the Bobby-Soxer* (1947), starring Cary Grant

DeGrasse's television credits include:

- *I Love Lucy*
- *Make Room for Daddy*
- *The Jack Benny Show*
- *The Dick Van Dyke Show*[20]

Robert DeGrasse died on January 28, 1971 in Newport Beach, California. His grave is located in Bay View Terrace lawn, lot 107, space E, from Margaret Early's grave walk fourteen markers north, and one row west.

FRANK GIFFORD TALLMAN

Frank Gifford Tallman (April 17, 1919 to April 15, 1978) was a Hollywood stunt pilot, and business partner of aviator Paul Mantz (interred in the Alcove of Devotion). Tallman like Mantz was a stunt pilot, who appeared in numerous motion pictures and television shows from the 1950s to the 1970s. Major film credits include:

- *Layfette Escadrille* (1957)
- *How the West was Won* (1962)

- *It's a Mad, Mad, Mad, Mad World* (1963)
- *Catch-22* (1970)
- *The Hindenburg* (1975)
- *Funny Lady* (1975)
- *The Great Waldo Pepper* (1975)
- *MacArthur* (1977)
- *Capricorn One* (1978)
- *1941* (1979)

His television credits include:

- *The Twilight Zone* (1960)
- *Hogan's Hero's* (1965)
- *The Six Million Dollar Man* (1974-77)
- *The Bionic Woman* (1976)
- *Baa Baa Black Sheep* (1976-78)
- *Starsky and Hutch* (1977)

During this time Tallman became friends and eventually partnered with fellow Hollywood aviator Paul Mantz. Together they formed Tallmantz Aviation. This company quickly moved to the forefront of the movie aviation business. They developed experimental aircraft and restored old antique planes for the movie business.

When Paul Mantz was killed on the set of *The Flight of the Phoenix* in 1965, Tallman had a difficult time keeping the company afloat. After settling his financial difficulties, the company again began to shoot films and television shows.

Tragedy struck again on the afternoon of April 15, 1978. Tallman, flying a Piper Aztec aircraft out of Orange County Airport, was killed when the plane he was piloting slammed into a cloud-shrouded mountainside, fifteen miles from the airport.[21]

At his funeral, nearly 300 friends, co-workers, and fellow pilots gathered to pay their final respects to the famed stuntman. Six police helicopters from local police departments flew overhead and performed the missing man formation. A half dozen of his movie co-workers flew over the rites in their World War II-era aircraft, two Corsairs, P-51 Mustang fighters, and Japanese Zeros to honor their fallen comrade.

Ironically, Frank Tallman, and Paul Mantz are both buried at Pacific View, with Tallman's grave located in Bay View Terrace, lot 146, space, A, not far from Director Robert DeGrasse.

Albert Charles "Bert" Delmas

A short distance from Tallman is professional baseball player Albert Charles "Bert" Delmas (May 20, 1911 to December 4, 1979). Delmas, a second baseman who threw right but batted left, played twelve games for the Brooklyn Dodgers in 1933. He played alongside future Hall of Famer Hack Wilson, who was near the end of his legendary playing career, and four years removed from his record setting 191 runs batted in season (1930) with the Chicago Cubs. Bert Delmas' career statistics include twenty-eight at bats, seven hits, with a batting average of .250. He died in Huntington Beach, California, on December 4, 1979 at the age of seventy-eight.[22]

His grave is located in Bay View Terrace, lot 172, space C; it is located nine graves north of Robert DeGrasse, and one row west.

Daniel Mandell

Also at rest in Bay View terrace is three-time Academy Award winning film editor Daniel Mandell (July 13, 1895 to June 8, 1987). Mandell's film career spanned the silent era to the mid-1960s. He edited some of Hollywood's biggest productions, working with such famed directors as Billy Wilder, and Frank Capra. Mandell's career highlights include:

- *Wuthering Heights* (1939)
- *Meet John Doe* (1941)
- *The Little Foxes* (1941), which was his first Oscar nomination
- *The Pride of the Yankees* (1942), his Oscar win
- *Arsenic and Old Lace* (1944)
- *The Best Years of Our Lives* (1946), he won his second Academy Award
- *Guys and Dolls* (1955)
- *Witness for the Prosecution* (1957), he was Oscar nominated
- *Porgy and Bess* (1959)
- *The Apartment* (1960), for which he won his third and final Academy Award

Daniel Mandell died at the age of ninety-two in Huntington Beach, California.[23] His final resting place is Bay View Terrace, lot 333, space A; find curb marker 353 on the west side of the lawn, ten rows east, under a large eucalyptus tree, and in front of a marble memorial bench is the acclaimed film editor's grave.

JACK FAULKNER

Just east of Daniel Mandell's grave is the final resting place of NFL coach Jack Faulkner (April 4, 1926 to September 28, 2008). Faulkner began his coaching career in 1955 with the Los Angeles Rams. His tenure with the team lasted five years, when in 1960, he shifted to the fledgling American Football League's Los Angeles Chargers franchise, where he coached the defense for two seasons. In 1961, he was hired to be the head football coach for the Denver Broncos. His career record of ten wins, twenty-one loses, and one tie were less than spectacular, but he did attain the honor of being named the AFL Coach of the Year in 1962. In 1965, after being fired as the head coach of the Broncos, Faulkner was hired by the Minnesota Vikings as the defensive backs' coach. After one year in Minnesota, he moved to the New Orleans Saints, becoming the defensive coordinator, a position he held until 1971. In that year, he again joined the Los Angeles Rams as a scout, moving on to coach the defensive line in 1973, a position he held for seven years. In 1980, the Los Angeles Rams won the NFC Championship but lost to the Pittsburgh Steelers in Super Bowl XIV. After the 1980 season, Faulkner left the sidelines for the front office, first as Assistant General Manager of the Rams, and finally being named Director of Football Operations. In 1994, when the Rams franchise moved to St. Louis, Faulkner was one of only a handful of front office personnel that did not relocate with the team. Jack Faulkner died on September 28, 2008, in Newport Beach, California; he was eighty-two.[24]

❧ His grave is located in Bay View Terrace, lot 309, space E, six rows east of Daniel Mandell. Locate the silver in-ground marker 309, to the right is Faulkner's presently unmarked grave.

ROBERT C. "BOB" WIAN

After leaving Jack Faulkner's grave, get in your car, and head to the north side of Bay View Terrace lawn, find curb marker 974; near here is the final resting place of restaurant entrepreneur Robert C. "Bob" Wian (June 15, 1914 to March 31, 1992). Bob Wian was the founder of the Bob's Big Boy restaurant chain. In 1936, he opened his first "hamburger joint" restaurant, Bob's Pantry in Glendale, California. Bob's Big Boy was known for inexpensive drive-in style food, such as its classic double-decker hamburgers and thick milkshakes. By the late 1960s, the restaurant chain had grown to over 1,000 outlets worldwide. In 1967, Bob sold his interest in the restaurants to the Marriott Corporation. Bob was also mayor of the city of Glendale for two years, 1948-49. His son Casey Wian is a journalist, and correspondent for the Cable News Network (CNN). Bob Wian died on March 31, 1992 of a cerebral hemorrhage at Hoag Hospital in Newport Beach, California.[25]

❧ His grave is found in Bay View Terrace, lot 959, space W; find curb marker 974, then locate the large bronze "N" in ground lawn marker. Six graves south is Wian's final resting place.

Mary Antonia "Toni" Wayne-La Cava
Josephine Alicia Saenz-Wayne

After viewing Robert Wian's grave, drive or walk to the east side of the lawn to stand in front of the outdoor mausoleum and crypts. Locate marker number 557 on the curb. Near here, in the first row, are the graves of actress Mary Antonia "Toni" Wayne-La Cava (February 25, 1936 to December 6, 2000), daughter of John Wayne, and Josephine Alicia Saenz-Wayne (1909 to June 24, 2003), the first wife of John Wayne. Toni Wayne whose birth name was Mary Antonia Morrison is the sister of actor Michael, and Patrick Wayne. She is also the mother of actor Brendan Wayne. Toni appeared in several of her father's films, including The Quiet Man (1952), and The Alamo (1960), in which she plays the wife of the one of the Alamo defenders. In a poignant scene at the end of the film, Toni Wayne, her on-screen daughter, and a small black child are the only survivors of the battle. In moment of grandiose compassion, Mexican General Santana spares their lives, allows them to leave the Alamo unharmed, and has the Mexican Army salute her to honor the fallen heroes of the Alamo. Toni Wayne's acting career was limited to only a few roles. Instead, she chose to raise a family outside of the limelight of Hollywood's glare. She died on December 6, 2000 in Los Angeles, California from cancer.[26]

Toni's mother Josephine Saenz-Wayne was the daughter of Jose Saenz, the Consul General to Panama from the United States, and was the first wife of actor John Wayne. The Waynes were married in 1933, and after twelve tumultuous years, divorced in 1945. Josephine was a devout Catholic, and morally objected to the divorce, but publicly allowed the proceeding to progress. She never acknowledged the disunion, and always considered herself John Wayne's first, and only, legitimate wife. Their marriage produced four children, actors Michael, Patrick, Antonia, and Melinda Wayne. Josephine died on June 24, 2003 from cancer.[27]

❧ Toni's and her mother's graves are located next to one another on the east curb of Bay View Terrace lawn, in the first row, near curb marker 557.

John Wayne

Ironically, just west of Toni, and Josephine, a few yards down the slope, is the most famous grave in this cemetery, and in all of Orange County. Here is the final resting place of legendary screen actor John Wayne (May 26, 1907 to June 11, 1979). He was born Robert Michael Morrison in Winterset, Iowa in 1907, to Mary and Clyde Morrison. Mary soon had a change of heart, and re-named him Marion Michael in honor of a wealthy relative. The young Morrison grew to despise the name, and his early childhood was not happy. He felt unloved by his mother, who favored his younger brother Robert. Because of his name, Marion was teased, and bullied at school. He found himself in many fights, his father, Clyde, advised him not to go looking for a fight, but if he found it unavoidable, make sure he won at all costs. The tough image that would be a hallmark of later film characters was being developed at an early age.[28]

In 1915, the Morrisons moved to the Los Angeles area. Clyde had been diagnosed with tuberculosis, and a hot dry climate was suggested. At the age of eleven, a big event in Marion's life took place; he was befriended by a local fireman, a man that Marion looked up too. This man gave young Morrison his nickname: "big Duke."[29] The nickname stuck, and with the new name came a fresh bravado, the young "Duke" Morrison began to prosper emotionally and academically. He began to excel in school, and by his senior year, was a member of the National Honor Society, and at graduation was named the class salutatorian.

Morrison grew to be a tall and very handsome young man. Because of his size he excelled in athletics. He was named captain of the high school football team, and this team was very successful. These triumphs gave Morrison his first glimpse of fame. As for college, his greatest desire was to attend the U.S. Naval Academy, at Annapolis, but instead was offered a full scholarship to play football at the University of Southern California. Morrison's college years were filled with great joy, and he prospered. He gained tremendous fame on and off the football field. These accolades led to a part-time summer job on the back lot of the Fox Studios. Morrison's first taste of the movies came as an assistant to cowboy actor Tom Mix. This small job was the catalyst that propelled Morrison into his legendary film career. During that summer at the Fox Studios, Morrison would meet a person that would forever alter his life.[30]

In 1930, John Ford was one of Hollywood's most successful directors. He was directing a film called *Mother MacCree*, when fate sent the young Morrison to the set of the film. The director took an immediate liking to Duke, and a life-long friendship ensued. John Ford saw something special in Morrison. He was young, raw, and he saw a potential for stardom. Over the next few years, Ford cast Morrison in several of his films, and he was a natural in front of the camera. Fate again entered Morrison's life when he was introduced to another director, Raoul Walsh. Walsh also saw potential in Morrison, but thought his name was not marketable. A more "American" sounding name was needed, and Walsh came up with John Wayne. The name stuck, and John "Duke" Wayne the movie star was born. It was with Raoul Walsh that John Wayne got his first big break as a leading man in *The Big Trail* (1930).[31]

For the next few years, Wayne starred in numerous serials and

View of the Pacific Ocean from John Wayne's grave.

B-westerns, his six-foot-three-inch frame and silent good looks made him very marketable. Wayne felt he was being type cast and yearned to break free to super stardom. The year 1939 was to be very significant for John Wayne. Director John Ford had not forgotten his friend and protégé; he was casting for a new film, *Stagecoach*. Ford thought that Wayne would be perfect for the lead role in the film. This was the break that Wayne needed. *Stagecoach* was critically acclaimed, a box-office success, and it propelled Wayne to new level of recognition.[32]

It was the beginning of many successes for Wayne, and provided the impetus for the development of the hero image that would prove to be Wayne's lasting legacy in film. The dynamic duo of Ford and Wayne would become box-office gold, and over the years, their film partnership would produce some of Hollywood's greatest and most successful motion pictures.

John Wayne's award-winning acting, producing, and directing career spanned five decades, beginning in the late 1920s through the late 1970s—a prolific film career that saw him star in over 250 motion pictures. During this time, he starred alongside many of Hollywood's greatest actors and actresses. The characters he portrayed in many of his films personified the image of the true patriotic American. Some of Wayne's many legendary films credits include:

- *Dark Command* (1940
- *Reap the Wild Wind* (1942)
- *Flying Tigers* (1942)
- *The Fighting Seabees* (1944)
- *Fort Apache* (1948)
- *Red River* (1948)
- *Wake of the Red Witch* (1948)
- *The Sands of Iwo Jima* (1949)
- *Rio Grande* (1950)
- *The Quiet Man* (1952)
- *Hondo* (1953)
- *The High and the Mighty* (1954)
- *The Searchers* (1956)
- *The Alamo* (1960)
- *The Longest Day* (1962)
- *In Harms Way* (1965)
- *The Green Berets* (1968)

He was nominated for a best acting Academy Award for his portrayal of Marine Sergeant John Stryker in *The Sands of Iwo Jima* (1949). In 1969, he won

Legendary film actor John Wayne's grave marker.

the best actor Academy Award and Golden Globe for his portrayal of Marshall Rooster Cogburn in *True Grit*. Wayne's last film was *The Shootist* (1976). In the film, he played an over-the-hill gunfighter who was dying of cancer. Ironically, in real life, Wayne was also battling cancer. He was a life-long smoker, and had been waging a fight with lung cancer for several years. Illness was nothing new to Wayne, he had a cancerous lung removed in 1963, had open-heart surgery in 1978, and had his stomach removed in 1979. He died on the evening of June 11, 1979, at the U.C.L.A. Medical Center in Los Angeles, California, from lung and stomach cancer.[33]

According to his widow Pilar, John Wayne final wish was to be cremated, and his ashes scattered at sea, near Catalina Island. He also wanted all of his friends to gather at his home for a party, not wanting a sorrowful occasion; but instead, wanted a joyful celebration of his life—an Irish type wake.[34] These arrangements were never carried out; Michael Wayne the executor of his father's estate, chose to have a "more dignified" arrangement.

Wayne was to be buried at Pacific View Memorial Park, which over looked his beloved Newport Harbor. At 6 a.m. on June 15, 1979, Wayne's bronze flower draped casket was brought into Our Lady Queen of Angels Catholic Church in Corona del Mar for funeral mass. In attendance were only immediate family, his seven children, twenty-seven grand children, Pilar Wayne, and a few close friends. After the conclusion of the mass, the funeral procession of only twenty cars made its way to Pacific View Memorial Park. After the procession had entered the cemetery, the gates were closed, and no one else was allowed admittance. As the sun arose in the east, on that June morning, a brief graveside ceremony was conducted by the archbishop Marcos G. McGrath, and John Wayne was laid to rest.[35] This was not the end the legendary actor had envisioned. It is interesting to note that the plot in which Wayne is buried was given to the Wayne family by his close friend, Chick Iverson.

John Wayne's final resting place lay unmarked for over twenty years, his son, Michael, was very protective of his father's image and was adamant about keeping fans away. He feared fans would desecrate the grave and wanted the location of his father's burial kept as secret as possible. It was only after Michael's death in 2003 that the surviving Wayne siblings decided it was time to pay tribute to their father's legacy, and at long last had a flat bronze marker (which plays homage to his image of the ultimate cowboy) erected at his gravesite.

Today, John Wayne's legacy is found in his films, and the characters he portrayed will be remembered forever. He was a true American icon, an original, a legend bigger than life.

✿ John Wayne's grave is located in Bay View Terrace lawn, lot 573. It is a few yards from his daughter, Toni, and first wife Josephine's graves. Walk west down the slope and six rows to the legendary actors final repose.

MARION MACK

After viewing Wayne's gravesite, return to the summit of the lawn, and locate curb marker 229. Interred a short distance from here is silent screen actress Marion Mack (April 8, 1902 to May 1, 1989). Her given name was Joey Marion McCreedy, and in her early films, she went by the name Joey McCreedy, and eventually Marion Mack. She had a short (nine film) screen career that started in 1921, when she was hired by legendary comic film producer Mack Sennett as one of his "bathing beauties," in On a Summer Day. Mack's first starring role was in Mary of the Movies (1923), which was written by her future husband, Lewis Lewyn. Her most famous role was that of heroine, Annabelle Lee, in Buster Keaton's classic comedy, *The General* (1927). Other film credits include:

⇢ *One of the Bravest* (1925)

⇢ *Alice in Movieland* (1928)

Alice in Movieland was her last on the screen film. She then retired from acting and began to write movie scripts with her husband. In the 1970s, there was a renewed interest in the silent-film era, and Marion traveled around the country, appearing at screenings of her films. Marion Mack died on May 1, 1989, in Costa Mesa from heart failure at eighty-seven.[36]

✿ She is buried next to her husband, film producer Lewis Lewyn, in Bayview Terrace, lot 222, space F. Find curb marker 229, walk west down the slope, seven rows to their plots. Marion's grave marker reads Joey Marion Lewyn.

JAMES EDWARDS II

Return to the crest of the lawn, and across the street in front of the mausoleum area is the Catalina Estates. Interred here is movie theater mogul

James Edwards II (November 23, 1906 to April 26, 1997). In 1930, Edwards bought his first movie theater, a run-down establishment in Monterey Park, California. He was one of the first theater owners to install sound systems, and also the first to have a multi-screen theater (1939). In 1961, Edwards brought the movies to Orange County. His first theater was located in Costa Mesa, and the opening night movie was Doctor Zhivago.

By 1997, the Edwards theater empire had 90 theater locations, with 560 screens in California. On April 26, 1997, Edward—a spry ninety year old—was preparing for a day of sun and fun at his home in Newport Bay. After apparently lowering a wave runner into the water behind his home, he suffered a fatal heart attack. A short time later, he was found floating in the water near their boat dock by his wife, Bernice. All attempts to revive the theater mogul failed.[37]

❧ Edward's final resting place is located in the Catalina Estates, lot 166. The plot is found on the curb, in front of the Lagunita Court entrance.

The sweeping views of the Pacific Ocean and Newport Beach from the crest of Bay View terrace are breath taking; lingering here with the cool ocean breezes, brings peace to the soul, and one can understand why so many have chosen to spend eternity in this place.

PAUL MANTZ

After taking in the beauty of the scenery, move on to the massive outdoor mausoleum, and crypt area. Start at the Palm Court entrance on the south side of the complex. After entering the Palm Court hallway, walk east to the end of the hall, turn right, and again walk to the end; located here is the Alcove of Devotion. In niche 43, are the cremated remains of pioneering Hollywood stuntman and aviator Paul Mantz (August 2, 1903 to July 8, 1965). Mantz was one of the most talented and daring movie stunt pilots during the 1930s through the mid-1960s. During these three and one-half decades he appeared in nearly fifty films. His first movie was on Howard Hughes' Academy Award nominated film Hell's Angels (1930). Other motion picture credits include:

+→❀ *Airmail* (1930)

+→❀ *Men with Wings* (1938)

+→❀ *Only Angels have Wings* (1938)

+→❀ *Flying Tigers* (1942)

+→❀ *Twelve O'Clock High* (1949)

+→❀ *Around the World in Eighty Days* (1956), *The Flying Leathernecks* (1957)

+→❀ *The Spirit of St. Louis* (1963)

+→❀ *It's a Mad, Mad, Mad, Mad World* (1963)[38]

On July 8, 1965, Mantz was killed while attempting a stunt during the filming of Robert Aldrich's *The Flight of the Phoenix*, near Yuma, Arizona. As cameras were rolling, he attempted to maneuver his experimental Tallmantz Phoenix P-1 aircraft near the desert floor; the aircraft clipped a small hill, and broke into two pieces, killing Mantz instantly.[39]

His cremated remains are interred within the Alcove of Devotion in niche 43, which is on the left side of the alcove, four niches from the bottom.

JOHN COLLIN "JACK" FULTON, JR.

After leaving the Alcove of Devotion, retrace your footsteps until you find the Alcove of Time hallway on the right. On both sides of this hallway are cremation niches, and the first famous internee within the alcove is noted big-band era musician, singer, and songwriter John Collin "Jack" Fulton, Jr. (June 13, 1903 to November 12, 1993). Fulton, a singer and trombone player, began his music career in New York City during the Roaring Twenties with the Mason-Dixon, George Olsen, and Paul Whitman Orchestras. Fulton was also a staff musician at radio station WBBM in Chicago from 1935 to 1955.

As a lyricist, he wrote and co-wrote over 100 songs. He teamed with Lois Steele to write Perry Como's 1954, number one hit single, "Wanted."[40] The duo had another hit in 1956, with Ivory Tower, sung by Cathy Carr and Gale Storm. This record hit number two and six on the Billboard music chart, respectively.[41] Ivory Tower was also re-recorded by singer Martina Blanque, for the sound track to the motion picture *Carried Away* (1996), starring Dennis Hopper, Amy Irving, and Gary Busey.[42]

Fulton's greatest achievement as a lyricist came when he teamed with renowned composer Moe Jaffe to write "If You Are But A Dream" (1941). In 1944, this song was recorded by Frank Sinatra as a "B" side to his single "White Christmas," and it became one of Sinatra's all time greatest hits. The following year, the song was included in the Academy Award Winning short film, *The House I Live In*, also featuring Sinatra on vocals. In 1987, Sinatra again reprised his hit song for the motion picture sound track to Woody Allen's film, *Radio Days*.[43] Fulton's other notable music credits include "Mrs. Santa Claus," recorded by Nat King Cole, "My Greatest Mistake," and "Until."

Jack Fulton died on November 12, 1993, in Rancho Bernardo, California.[44]

His cremated remains are found in the Alcove of Time, niche 61G. Locate the first glass case on the right wall, one row above this case, and four niches from the right is his place of rest.

JOSEPH H. "COUNTRY" WASHBURNE

Interred near Fulton is Joseph H. "Country" Washburne (December 28, 1904 to January 21, 1974). Washburne was a composer and bandleader during the 1930s and 1940s. Born and raised on the Gulf Coast of Texas, he began his career as the bass player in the Ted Weens and Spike Jones bands, before forming his own group. Country Joe Washburne appeared regularly on the Fiber McGee and Molly and Great Gildersleeve radio programs during the 1930s. As a composer, he is best known for writing the hit *One Dozen Roses*, which topped the Hit Parade for eighteen weeks in the 1940s. His other noteworthy musical compositions are:

+=$ "Oh Mona, You Don't Know What Lonesome Is"

+=$ "I Saw Esau, and That's the Reason"

&% Washburne retired to Newport Beach, and died on January 21, 1974 of a heart attack.[45] His cremated remains are interred in the Alcove of Time, niche 55K. Again, find the first glass case on the right wall, ten niches from the right, and four above the first glass case is Washburne's cremation niche.

RUBEN SALAZAR

The final noteworthy internee of the Alcove of Time is award-winning *Los Angeles Times* columnist, and television news director Ruben Salazar (March 3, 1928 to August 29, 1970). Salazar was an award-winning columnist for the *Los Angeles Times* from 1959 to 1970, and was an outspoken proponent for Chicano rights. He spotlighted injustices against Mexican-Americans and other minorities. A controversial reporter, he prided himself on telling the truth. Once he enraged the Mexican-American community by covering a story on the original founders of the city of Los Angeles. In that story, he showed that many of the founders of the city were not Spanish Dons, but rather low-income Indians, Negros, and poor Mexicans. In addition to the *Times*, he was also the news director for local Los Angeles Spanish news station KMEX channel 34.[46]

In the late afternoon of August 29, 1970, Salazar was killed, while reporting on the National Chicano Moratorium March against the Vietnam War in East Los Angeles. The peaceful march attracted over 200,000 people but erupted into a riot. Violence swept the East LA neighborhood along twelve blocks of Whittier Boulevard. During the chaos, there were tremendous amounts of looting, and vandalism. Nearly 500 police were called to disperse the crowd, and quell the rioting.[47]

At around 5 p.m., Sheriff's Deputies were alerted to a possible gunman near the Silver Dollar Café on Whittier Boulevard. Salazar and KMEX cameraman Guillermo Restrepo were observing the riot from inside the café, when an unprovoked tear gas canister was fired into the restaurant. Restrepo and other patrons were able to escape through a back door, but Salazar was not as lucky. Hours later it was discovered that Salazar had been struck in the head, and killed by one of the tear-gas canisters. In the aftermath of the rioting, Salazar was the only reported fatality, while there were forty others injured.[48] A coroner's inquest ruled Salazar's death was a homicide but Tom Wilson, the Los Angeles Sheriff's Deputy who fired the tear gas canister, was never prosecuted.

Tributes to Salazar poured in from around the country. President Nixon, vacationing at western White House in San Clemente, issued a statement expressing his sorrow at learning of the newsman's death. California Senator Alan Cranston issued a statement from the floor of the U.S. Senate, "Salazar was a peaceful and compassionate man who dedicated his life to the eradication of poverty, injustice, prejudice, and ignorance."[49] After his death he received many awards, and honors. One such was the Robert F. Kennedy Award for excellence in journalism; another honor was the re-naming of Laguna Park in east LA, the site of the riots, to Salazar Park, and in October 2007, the U.S. Postal Service announced that a commemorative stamp would be issued to honor Salazar, and well as other noteworthy journalists.

✤ Ruben Salazar's cremated remains are interred in niche 36A in the Alcove of Time; they are on the right side of the hallway, bottom row, and four niches from the left.

HARRY F. PERRY

On the right side of the hallway after leaving the Alcove of Time is an enclosed crypt area. At the end of this hallway is the Alcove of Faith; interred here are two Hollywood personalities, first Harry F. Perry (May 2, 1888 to February 9, 1985). Perry was an Academy Award nominated cinematographer from 1920 to 1943. He has nearly thirty films to his credit, mainly from the silent era. Major film credits include:

- ✤ *Wings* (1927), which won the Academy Award for Best Picture
- ✤ *Hell's Angels* (1930), for which Perry was nominated for an Academy Award for Best Cinematography
- ✤ *Corvette K-225* (1943), for which he was again nominated for best cinematography

After filming *Corvette K-225*, other than a few film credits for special effects in the late 1940s, for unknown reasons, he vanished from Hollywood. Harry Perry died on February 9, 1985 in Woodland Hills, California at the age of ninety-eight.[50]

✤ His cremated remains are found in the Alcove of Faith, niche 25, two rows from the bottom, and eight niches from the right.

WILLIAM COSBY PIERCY AUSTIN

Also interred within the Alcove of Faith is actor William Cosby Piercy Austin (June 12, 1884 to June 15, 1975). Austin, a British citizen, was born in Georgetown, British Guyana. A prolific character actor, he appeared in eighty-nine films from 1920 to 1947. Major film credits include:

- ✤ *Duck Soup* (1927)
- ✤ *The Mysterious Dr. Fu Manchu* (1929)
- ✤ *High Society* (1932)
- ✤ *The Private Life of Henry VIII* (1933)
- ✤ *National Velvet* (1944)

William is the younger brother Albert Austin, who was also a prolific actor appearing in many silent era films, mostly with Charlie Chaplin. William Austin died on June 15, 1975 in Newport Beach, California.[51]

❧ His cremated remains are located in the Alcove of Faith, niche 251, in the top row, six niches from the right.

RALPH C. SMEDLEY

After leaving the Alcove of Faith, walk west past the Alcove of Time hallway to the Lagunita Court area. On the left are a row of crypts; here is the final resting place of Toastmaster's International founder Ralph C. Smedley (February 22, 1878 to September 11, 1965). Smedley, an Illinois native, came to Santa Ana, California, in 1922. There he worked as the educational director of the YMCA. Smedley noticed that many of the young men at the "Y" needed help with confidence and speech training. On October 22, 1924, he founded Toastmasters. The organization would help members improve their communication, public speaking, and leadership skills, with careful, constructive evaluation. Today, Toastmasters has 230,000 members, 11,500 clubs, can be found in 92 countries.

Smedley also penned several books on public speaking:

- *The Amateur Chairman*
- *The Voice of the Speaker*
- *Speech Evaluation*
- *The Story of Toastmasters*

❧ Ralph Smedley died on September 11, 1965, at age eighty-seven.[52] He is entombed within the Lagunita Court, crypt 601, level one. It is on the left side, and four crypts west on the bottom row.

HAROLD MINJIR

After viewing Smedley's crypt, retrace your footsteps back to the hallway near the Alcove of Time, turn left, and then, directly on the right, is the Lagunita Alcove wall (south). Interred here on the top row, four niches from the left is actor Harold Minjir (October 5, 1895 to April 16, 1976). Minjir was a prolific character actor who starred in sixty plus films, from 1930 to 1945. His major film credits include:

- *Wife vs. Secretary* (1936)
- *Blondie* (1938)
- *Edison the Man* (1940)
- *The Feminine Touch* (1941)
- *Mr. and Mrs. North* (1942)
- *Jack London* (1943)[53]

❧ Minjir's cremated remains are interred in the Lagunita Alcove wall (south) in niche 327.

ALBERT C. CLARK

Also interred within the Lagunita Alcove is award-winning film and television editor Albert C. Clark (September 15, 1902 to July 13, 1971). Clark's film editing career spanned four decades, beginning in 1933 and ending in 1969. He was nominated for five Academy Awards, and one Emmy Award. His Academy Award nominated films were:

↦ *The Awful Truth* (1937)

↦ *Mr. Smith Goes to Washington* (1939)

↦ *All The Kings Men* (1949)

↦ *Cowboy* (1958)

↦ *Pepe* (1960)

He also was the film editor for five of the *Blondie* series movies that starred Arthur Lake and Penny Singleton during the 1940s. In television, Clark was nominated for an Emmy Award for his editing on *Ben Casey* (1961). Other television credits include:

↦ *The Twilight Zone*

↦ *Perry Mason*

↦ *Gilligan's Island*

↦ *Gidget*

↦ *I Dream of Jeannie*[54]

❧ Clark died on July 13, 1971 and is interred in Lagunita Alcove wall (south), niche 237, four niches from the bottom, and nine from the left.

THEODORE J. KENT

A third and final internee of Lagunita Alcove is another award-winning film editor Theodore J. Kent (October 6, 1901 to June 17, 1986). Kent was a prolific film editor who worked exclusively for Universal Pictures for forty years, from 1927 to 1967. He was nominated for a best editing Academy Award for 1964's *Father Goose*. He also worked as a film editor on many of Universal's classic monster movies of the 1930s through the 1950s, such as:

↦ *The Invisible Man* (1933)

↦ *Bride of Frankenstein* (1935)

↦ *Son of Frankenstein* (1939)

+—⚶ *The Black Cat* (1941)

+—⚶ *The Wolf Man* (1941)

+—⚶ *The Ghost of Frankenstein* (1942)

+—⚶ *The Creature from the Black Lagoon* (1954)

Other notable film credits include:

+—⚶ *My Man Godfrey* (1936)

+—⚶ *Bedtime for Bonzo* (1951)

+—⚶ *The Private War of Major Benson* (1955)

+—⚶ *The Man of a Thousand* Faces (1957), and *Operation Petticoat* (1959)[55]

⚶ Ted Kent's cremated remains are located in niche 177 on the bottom row, six niches from the left.

LOH SEN TSAI

From the Lagunita Alcove (south), proceed to the back wall (east) of the Lagunita crypts courtyard area. Interred in the crypts along the east wall is Noble Peace Prize Nominee Loh Sen Tsai (February 6, 1901 to December 31, 1992). Tsai was born in China and received his PhD in psychology in 1928 from the University of Chicago. He served on the faculty of four universities: Brown, University of California, Los Angeles, Tulane, and Cal State Fullerton.

During the 1940s, he returned to China, and became Dean at the University of Nanking. Tsai also served as an advisor to the Chinese Ministry of Education. Professor Tsai returned to the United States in the late 1940s, joining the faculty at Tulane University in New Orleans. In 1951, while at Tulane, he conducted studies on peace and cooperation that led to his nomination for the Nobel Peace Prize. He researched animal behavior and found that natural enemies (such as cats and rats) could live together in harmony under the right circumstances.

Tsai was the author of more than 150 research papers, focusing on brain damage, vitamin B-deficiency, and electro convulsive shock. These studies led the professor to be the focus of three feature articles in *Life* magazine. Towards the end of his career, Tsai came to Cal State University, Fullerton. There he was named outstanding professor in 1971, and he retired in 1973.

Loh Sen Tsia suffered a fatal heart attack on December 31, 1992, in Newport Beach; California.[56]

⚶ He is buried in the Lagunita Court Crypts, #306. The distinguished professor's final resting place is found on the east wall in the back of the courtyard, bottom row, and seven crypts from the left corner.

OTTO W. TIMM

From the Lagunita courtyard area, walk to the main hallway, go north a short distance; on the right hand side of the hallway is the Lagunita Alcove (north). Interred here are the cremated remains of two noteworthy people, first of which is pioneer aviator Otto W. Timm (October 28, 1893 to June 29, 1978). His career in aviation began in 1910, and these early days were filled with many failures and dangers. Timm attempted to build several planes, but none were successful. He barnstormed and held exhibitions of flight around the country prior to the outbreak of World War I. In 1916, he became the senior flight instructor at Rockwell Field in San Diego. It was during this time that he built the successful "Model T-18," trainer bi-plane.

After the war, he moved to Venice, California, and opened the Pacific Aeroplane and Supply Company. Here he helped design and construct the six-passenger bi-plane known as the "Pacific Hawk," and "C-1" racing monoplane.

In 1922, while working as chief engineer at the Nebraska Aircraft Company, he met a young Charles Lindbergh. Lindbergh had come to the airfield to learn how to fly. On July 16, 1921, Timm gave Lindbergh his first flight lesson. Five years later, Lindbergh would make his historic transatlantic flight. Timm and Lindbergh remained close friends the remainder of their lives. In 1928, Timm returned to California, where he opened another aircraft company at the Grand Central Airport in Glendale. The O.W. Timm Aircraft Company produced the "840 bi-motor" passenger era bi-plane, and "T-S140," high wing twin-engine monoplane. During World War II, the company designed and manufactured the "N2T1 Navy Trainer," and "CG4R troop transport aircraft.

In 1965, towards the end of his career in aviation, Timm was contacted by the TallMantz Company to design a plane for the movie, *Flight of the Phoenix*. The "Phoenix P-1" had a short and tragic lifespan. Famed stunt pilot Paul Mantz was killed in this plane while performing a stunt for the movie. Otto W. Timm died on June 29, 1978 at eighty-five in a nursing home in Torrance, California.[57]

His cremated remains are interred within the Lagunita Alcove (north), niche 151. This niche is found in the upper right hand corner of the wall, two niches from the right, and two from the top.

JOHN BEURY GALLAUDET

The second famous internee of the alcove is character actor John Beury Gallaudet (August 23, 1903 to November 5, 1983). Gallaudet was a very productive character actor who appeared in nearly 175 films, and television shows from the 1930s to early 1970s. Film credits include:

    Pennies from Heaven (1936)

    Manhattan Shakedown (1937)

- *Knute Rockne All American* (1940)
- *The Strange Case of Doctor RX* (1942)
- *The Farmers Daughter* (1947)
- *The Babe Ruth Story* (1948)
- *The Kid from Left Field* (1953
- *In Cold Blood* (1967) Truman Capote's Oscar nominated film

His television credits include appearances on:

- *I Love Lucy*
- *The Beverly Hillbillies*
- *Perry Mason*
- *Batman*
- *My Three Sons*
- *Bewitched*
- *Adam-12*[57]

Gallaudet died on November 5, 1983, in Los Angeles and his cremated remains are interred in the Lagunita Alcove wall (north), niche 75, second row from the right, and four from the bottom. He does not have a name plaque on the niche. He shares the space with his wife, Helen Constance Gallaudet, who does have name plaque.

ROY ROWLAND

Continue to walk to the Alcove of Horizon, which is located north of the Valencia Court area in a passageway between the Valencia Courts, and Magnolia Court (south) area. Here, on the right, are the niches that hold the mortal remains of noted film director Roy Rowland (December 31, 1910 to June 29, 1995). Rowland directed fifty-eight full-length and short-subject films from 1934 to 1966. He is best known for his short-subject film series of the 1930s:

- *Robert Benchley's: How to*
- *Pete Smith Specialties*
- *Crime Doesn't Pay* series

His feature film credits include:

- *A Night at the Movies* (1937)
- *A Stranger on a Train* 1943)

- *The Outriders* (1950)
- *Witness to Murder* (1954)
- *Meet Me in Las Vegas* (1956) for which he was nominated for a Directors Guild of America Award

He is also the father of western actor Steve Rowland.[58]

Roy died in Orange, California, on June 29, 1995. His ashes are interred in niche 22 of the Alcove of Horizon, four niches from the right, and three from the bottom.

CLARENCE UPSON YOUNG

Also interred here is screenwriter Clarence Upson Young (October 14, 1895 to January 22, 1969). Young was a Hollywood writer with twenty-four screenplays to his credit from the 1930s to the 1960s. He was primarily a writer of westerns, which included:

- *The Law West of Tombstone* (1938)
- *Badlands* (1939)
- *North to the Klondike* (1942)
- *Albuquerque* (1948)
- *Showdown at Abilene* (1956)
- *Gunfight at Abilene* (1967).

Other notable film credits are:

- *Hot Steel* (1940),
- *Night Monster* (1942), horror classic, starring Bela Lugosi[59]

Young's ashes are interred within the Alcove of Horizon, niche 322.

ROBERT D. WEBB
BARBARA MCLEAN-WEBB

After leaving the Alcove of Horizon, walk north through to the Magnolia Court (south) area, and to the fountain; directly north of here is a wall of crypts, and in the top right corner are the Academy Award-winning husband and wife team of Robert D. Webb (January 8, 1903 to April 18, 1990, and Barbara McLean-Webb (November 16, 1903 to March 28, 1996).

Robert Webb was an award winning director and producer during the 1950s and 1960s. Noted are:

- *In Old Chicago* (1937) best assistant director Academy Award
- *Beneath the 12-Mile Reef* (1953) a Cannes Film Festival nominee

Other notable film credits include:

- *The Agony and the Ecstasy* (1965)
- *The Seven Cities of Gold* (1955)
- *Love Me Tender* (1956), starring Elvis Presley in his first motion picture,
- *The Cape Town Affair* (1967)

He also worked with his wife, film editor Barbara McLean on nine films. Robert died on April 18, 1990 in Newport Beach, California.[60]

※※※※※※※※※※

Barbara McLean was a film editor for 20th Century Fox Studios. When she began her film editing career in the early 1930s, she was one of only a handful of woman working in Hollywood. In 1949, she was named Fox's editing director. She was well liked and was a favorite editor of director Darryl F. Zanuck.[61] She and her husband Robert Webb teamed together on numerous films from the 1930s through the 1950s. During her career, she was nominated for six Academy Awards, winning one for best editing for the motion picture *Wilson* (1944). Her Academy Award nominated films were:

- *Les Miserables* (1935)
- *Lloyd's of London* (1936)
- *Alexander's Ragtime Band* (1938)
- *The Rain Came* (1939)
- *The Song of Bernadette* (1943)
- *All About Eve* (1950)

Other film credits include:

- *Captain from Castille* (1947)
- *Twelve O'Clock High* (1949)
- *David and Bathseba* (1951)
- *The Snow's of Kilmanjaro* (1952)
- *Niagra* (1953), *The Robe* (1953)
- *King of the Kyber Rifles* (1953)
- *Untamed* (1955)[62]

She retired from 20th Century Fox in 1969. Barbara McLean-Webb survived her husband Robert Webb by six years. The two are entombed side by side in the top row of the Magnolia Court (south), crypt 691.

FRIEDA PUSHNIK

From the Webb's crypt area, proceed east along the sidewalk to the back area of the section. Along the back wall of crypts in the bottom row, in the breeze way between the Magnolia Court (north and south) sections, is interred Frieda Pushnik (February 10, 1923 to December 24, 2000). Pushnik is known as the armless, legless girl wonder, who toured with *Ripley's Believe It or Not*, and Ringling Brothers Circus from 1933 to 1956. Her deformities were the result of complications her pregnant mother encountered during an emergency appendectomy surgery. Nonetheless, Frieda enjoyed a happy childhood, attending school regularly, and learned to do everything that a normal person could do.

In 1933, she was discovered by a scout for Ripley's, and was put on display in the "odditorium" exhibit at the 1933 World's Fair. After the fair closed, she and the other Ripley oddities toured the country for six years. In 1943, she was hired by Ringling Brother Circus for their sideshow attraction, which included the bearded lady, the giant eight-foot tall man, and the doll family of little people. Pushnik stated that she did not regret her time in the circus, never felt exploited, and actually enjoyed traveling.

In 1956, sideshows like the one Ringling Brothers exhibited were outlawed, and Frieda returned home, settling in Orange County, California. She appeared in several movies such as the campy horror classic *The House of the Damned* (1963), and *Side Show* (1981).

Freida Pushnik died on December 24, 2000 from bladder cancer. She is buried in the Magnolia Court crypts 313.[63]

FREDRICK ALFRED "FREDDY" MARTIN

Just around the corner from Pushnik's crypt, on the left wall, is the final resting place of big band leader Fredrick Alfred "Freddy" Martin (December 9, 1906 to September 30, 1983). Martin nicknamed "Mr. Silvertone," was born in Ohio. An orphan at an early age, he was raised in various orphanages. At the age of sixteen, Martin took up the saxophone and auditioned for local big band leader Guy Lombardo (who would go on to great national success). He impressed Lombardo who encouraged the young man to form his own band.

Martin's band was invited to stand in for Lombardo regularly. This big break launched Freddy's career in the music industry. In the early 1930s, he and his band toured the country. His first big recording hit was with Brunswick Records in 1934 with *Louisiana Hayride*. Two members of Martin's band were trombone players, Tommy Dorsey and Jerry Colonna. They would go on to have great success with their own bands. Other notable members of Martin's band were Russ Morgan, Terry Shand, and Buddy Clark. Merv Griffin played piano in the band in the late 1940s. Griffin was the singer on the band's hit record, *I've Got a Lovely Bunch of Coconuts*.

In 1938, Martin and his band came to the west coast and played a performance at the Ambassador Hotel in Los Angeles. This led to a twenty-five-year engagement at the hotel as the house band in the famed Coconut Grove Ballroom. His band was one of the most popular big bands of the era and was best known for adapting classical music into contemporary recordings. Hit records such as:

- "Cumana"
- "The Hut-Sut Song"
- "Bumble Bee Boogie"

All were adaptations from classical music. All big bands of the era had theme songs, and Martin's was *Tonight We Love*, which was a contemporary version of Tchailovsky's First Piano Concerto. The band peaked during World War Two, and was featured in numerous films such as:

- *The Mayor of 44th Street* (1942)
- *Seven Days Leave* (1942)
- *Stage Door Canteen* (1943)[64]

He and his band recorded the theme song for *The Wonderful World of Disney* television program in 1958.[65]

Freddy Martin continued to perform up until the late 1970s, when he suffered a series of strokes that led to his retirement. On September 30, 1983, Martin died at Hoag Hospital in Newport Beach, California, from complications of earlier strokes.[66]

He was interred in the Magnolia Court (north), crypt 884, located around the corner from Frieda Pushnik in the middle of the wall, bottom row, and seven crypts from the left.

LINDA MARIE BROWN

Proceed to the fountain on the western side of the courtyard. Interred in the right hand corner of the fountain is murder victim Linda Marie Brown (1961 to March 19, 1985). In the early morning hours of March 19, 1985, Linda Brown was shot to death as she slept in her Garden Grove home. She was the twenty-four years old, and the fifth wife of David Arnold Brown, the owner of a successful Irvine computer business.

Earlier in the day, Linda and her fourteen-year-old stepdaughter, Cinnamon, had an argument, and because of the turmoil, David left the house. He returned to the family home around 3:30 a.m., and found his wife unconscious lying in a pool of blood in the couple's bedroom. She had been shot several times in the stomach. She was rushed to a nearby hospital, but died shortly after arriving. Cinnamon was found several hours later hiding in the doghouse in the back yard of the family home. She was unconscious, and near death herself having taken an overdose of prescription medication. A note was found in her hand that read:

"Dear God, Please forgive me, I didn't mean to hurt her."[67]

At the outset of the investigation police detectives were leery that a young girl could have masterminded, and carried out such a cold-blooded killing on her own, but with all the evidence, including a confession pointing directly at Cinnamon, the case seemed cut and dry. She was found guilty of Linda's murder, and sentenced to twenty-seven years to life in prison. Due to her age, she would be housed in the California Youth Authority, and released at the age of twenty-five.[68]

During the trial, her father had kept close tabs on his daughter, visiting her often, giving her money, and buying her gifts. He lived the life not of a grieving widower but of a bachelor on the loose. He cashed in several life insurance policies totaling nearly $900,000, bought a new home in Anaheim Hills, and had Linda's seventeen year old sister, Patty Bailey, move in with him. Police were suspicious of David's activities, but had no hard evidence that would incriminate him in the slaying.

Several years passed by and Cinnamon had a change of heart. She was jealous of the attention Patty was receiving from her father, and she was upset with the prospects of being in jail until she was twenty-five. Cinnamon contacted police investigators, and recanted her original confession. She told investigators that her father, David Brown, had recruited her to assist him in killing her stepmother. She stated that her father had told her that Linda was a member of the Mafia, and that she was plotting to kill him in order to take over the family computer business. He wanted Cinnamon to take the blame for the killing, and that because of her age, she would not spend a lot of time in jail. The impressionable young girl believed the story her father had told. In the weeks leading up to the murder, he instructed Cinnamon on how to act, and how to write a suicide note. Cinnamon told the detectives that the night before the killing, Patty Bailey, instructed her on how to use a hand gun, and on the day of the slaying, her father, David Brown, had mixed a concoction of drugs for her to take that would make the suicide attempt seem real.

This evidence, as well as Cinnamon's recanted confession, and tape-recorded conversations between Cinnamon and David, led to his, and Patty's arrest. Under intense pressure, Patty Bailey turned against her former lover, and confessed that David had manipulated her and Cinnamon into helping him carry out the murder. She also said that David had promised to marry her if she helped with the killing. With all this evidence, David Brown was compelled to agree to a plea bargain to escape the death penalty. He pleaded guilty to masterminding the murder of his wife, Linda Brown. In exchange, six other charges were dropped, and the death penalty was not sought.

In August 1992, he was sentenced to life in prison without the possibility of parole.[69] Patricia Bailey was also found guilty of lesser crimes, and was remanded to the California Youth Authority. She was released on her twenty-fifth birthday in 1993. Cinnamon was paroled from the California Youth Authority in 1992; she was twenty-one. In custody, she was able to complete her high school education.[70] Prior to her release from CYA, she made a national television appearance on the Oprah Winfrey Show, via satellite, stating that she was anxious to return home, and never wants to see her father again.[71]

As a side note, after his arrest, and during his confinement, prior to trial for Linda's murder, David Brown was charged with, and eventually confessed to, an elaborate murder for hire scheme, in which he attempted to hire his cellmate Richard Steinhart to kill the prosecutor, Patty Bailey, and several police investigators. For this crime he was sentenced to additional time in prison. Today, David Brown sits in Folsom prison. At his sentencing in 1991, the judge was stunned at his evil describing him as a killer whose cold-blooded cunning made Charles Manson "look like a piker."[72]

The sensational murder case became the subject of two books, and in February 1991, a four-hour made-for-television movie, *Love, Lies, and Murder,* detailing the case was shown on NBC. The two-night miniseries was the third highest rated miniseries of the 1990-91 television season.[73]

❀ Linda Marie Brown's cremated remains are found in the Magnolia Court (north), niche 35, in the southeast corner of the fountain. Her simple plaque is adorned with a Jesus peace fish insignia, and reads in part "your love, kindness, caring and beauty will shine forever, love: Krystal and David.

E. NILES WELCH

After leaving the fountain area, proceed west to the portico crypts; interred within this section of the Magnolia Courts is silent film actor E. Niles Welch (July 29, 1888 to November 21, 1976). Welch was a screen actor during the silent era. His prolific career included over 121 films from 1913 to 1940). He was a versatile character actor who appeared in a variety of movie genres, which included historical drama, murder mystery, comedy, war, and westerns. With the dawn of talking pictures, Welch's career waned but he still found bit-part roles, mostly in westerns, and historic dramas. His major film credits include:

- *Miss George Washington* (1916)
- *One of Many* (1917)
- *The Secret of Storm Country* (1917), starring Norma Talmadge
- *The Count of Monte Cristo* (1934)
- *The Story of Louis Pasteur* (1935)
- *Wife vs. Secretary* (1936)
- *Mary of Scotland* (1936), directed by John Ford, and starred Katharine Hepburn[74]

❀ Welch is interred in the Magnolia Courts (west) portico, crypt 651, three vaults from the left, and three rows from the bottom.

PETER PLOTKIN

Also interred in this section is artist Peter Plotkin (April 1, 1879 to January 1, 1960). He was born in Mogilev, Belarus Russia in 1879 to impoverished parents of Jewish descent. On March 13, 1881, Czar Alexander II was assassinated. His death was blamed on Jewish anarchists, and his successor Czar Alexander III ordered mass retribution against the Jewish people. The Russian "progroms" of 1881 to 1884 that were ordered by the Czar killed thousands of innocent Russian Jews, including Peter's parents and immediate family. He was later adopted by a Russian aristocrat named Count Gunzberg, and was afforded all the luxuries that life could afford, including the best education.

Peter received an education in fine arts, literature, and dramatics from the Russian Royal University in St. Petersburg. It was during this time that Peter was befriended by literary giant, Leo Tolstoy. After graduation, Peter continued his education traveling to Paris, Rome, and London. He immigrated to the United States in 1910, residing in New York City for a period, until he was invited to Dallas, Texas in 1915. There, he was commissioned to paint a mural on the walls of the Burton-Merritt house. He taught art and literature at Simmons University 1929-1931, after which he moved to Los Angeles, California. There he worked as a commercial artist and private art teacher. He opened his own art school in the late 1940s. His primary form of painting was with oil, and portraiture was a specialty. He was very religious and he painted numerous biblical scenes. In addition, he painted many historical landscapes. In the late 1920s he was commissioned by the Hilton Hotel chain to paint several historical scenes for lobbies of their hotels,

The Cossacks (1929)

The Colonial Blacksmith (1929)

King Solomon (1929)

The Landing of Henry Hudson (1929)

He also painted full-size portraits of the early presidents of McMurray College in Texas, as well as the following art work:

Lottie Moon (1927), a portrait of the first female Baptist missionary to China (it is on display at the Southwest Baptist Seminary in Louisville, Kentucky)

Chaim Weitzmann (1948), the first president of Israel

George Washington as a Mason (1950)

Robert E. Lee (1950)

The Good Samaritan (1950)

Today, many of his more famous pieces of art are on display at a family-owned gallery in Lake Forest, California.[75]

Peter Plotkin died on January 1, 1960. He is interred in the Magnolia Court crypts, four rows from the left, and two spaces from the bottom. Directly opposite from Plotkin crypt, in the corner of the portico is a touching family memorial that pays tribute to the artist and his wife. It always adorned with flowers and other decorations.

JEANNE LAVERNE CARMEN

After leaving the Magnolia Court (west) portico area, retrace your footsteps north to the modern Sunset Court area. Walk north along the sidewalk past the center lawn area to the north side of the court, turn right, and along the back wall is interred actress Jeanne Laverne Carmen (August 4, 1930 to December 20, 2007). Carmen was a blonde bombshell actress, and pin up model during the 1950s. She was known as the "Queen of the B-Movies." Platinum blond, with a curvaceous hourglass figure (with measurements of 36-26-36), she first found employment in 1948 as a dancer in the chorus line of Bert Lahr's Burlesque. (Lahr is best known for playing the Cowardly Lion in the Wizard of Oz.) During this same period, she posed as a pin-up model for numerous risqué gentlemen's magazines, which led to her appearing in numerous bawdy, low-budget films. Her major screen credits include:

- *The Three Outlaws* (1956)
- *War Drums* (1957)
- *Untamed Youth* (1957)
- *Born Reckless* (1958)
- *The Monster of Playa Blancas* (1959)

These films were low on plot and high on sexual content.[76]

Alleged confidant and friend of Marilyn Monroe, actress Jeanne Carmen's burial crypt at Pacific View Memorial Park.

Jeanne was also known as a trick-shot golf hustler. She discovered that she had this talent while modeling clothes for a golf manufacture. She took her trick shot skills on the road touring with golf professional Jack Redmond. She was able to make a good living at hustling on the golf courses of America.[77]

In the early 1960s, Jeanne found herself in Las Vegas, and was often seen in the company of famous actors, politicians, and mobsters. She claimed to be best friends with Marilyn Monroe, but no actual photographic evidence has ever surfaced to substantiate her claims. By 1967, Carmen had virtually vanished from the limelight, and for almost twenty years, nothing was heard from her. Then in 1987, she re-surfaced appearing on numerous television shows claiming wild and outlandish associations with the likes of the Kennedys, Marilyn Monroe, Frank Sinatra, Elvis, prominent members of the Mafia, and others.[78]

The flamboyant blond bombshell died on December 20, 2007 at her home in Irvine from lymphoma.[79] Her final resting place is found in the Sunset Court, crypt 153-CC, along the back wall, seven crypts from the left corner, and three rows from the bottom. Her crypt is adorned with a beautiful picture of Jeanne taken in her prime as "Queen of the B-Movies," and her epitaph reads, "She Came, She Saw, She Conquered."

LES BAXTER

The final famous internee of the out door mausoleum area is only a temporary visitor, composer and music arranger Les Baxter (March 14, 1922 to January 15, 1996). Early in his career Baxter sang with Mel Torme and the Mel-Tones (1945), and he conducted the orchestra for the Abbott and Costello radio show, as well as Bob Hope's radio program. He was a versatile and prolific composer who penned over 250 songs during his long music career. His hit songs included (just to name a few):

- *Ruby* (1953)
- *Unchained Melody* (1955), made famous by the Righteous Brothers (Bobby Hatfield is interred at Pacific View)
- *The Poor People of Paris* (1956)[80]

Baxter also arranged musical scores for over 100 motion pictures that included:

- *War Drums* (1957)
- *The Lone Ranger and the Lost City of Gold* (1958)
- *The House of Usher* (1960)
- *The Pit and the Pendulum* (1961)
- *The Man with the X-Ray Eyes* (1963)

✦ *The Raven* (1963

✦ All nine campy back to the beach movies starring Frankie Avalon and Annette Funicello such as *Beach Party* (1963), *Beach Blanket Bingo* (1965), and *How to Stuff a Wild Bikini* (1965).

Baxter also wrote the theme song for the television series *Lassie* (1958). As an actor, he appeared in several films, *Hot Blood* (1956), and *Untamed Youth* (1957), that starred Jeanne Carmen, and he also wrote several songs for the movie. Les Baxter died on January 15, 1996 in Newport Beach from heart and kidney failure.

✿ His cremated remains were unclaimed by family members, and are being held in an unused crypt 162, in the Sunset Courts area. This blank and unassuming crypt is on the same wall as Jeanne Carmen, eight vaults to the north, and on the bottom row. If this crypt were to be purchased, the remains stored within would be moved to a new location within the cemetery. Perhaps one day the famous composer will find peace, and his final resting place.

HELEN GRACE

After leaving this area, return to your car and drive to the Newport Vista lawn area. Locate marker 1113 on the east curb. Buried down the slope from here is Helen Grace (January 10, 1914 to December 21, 2002). Helen Grace along with her husband, William Grace (see Fairhaven Memorial Park) founded a chocolate candy store empire. In 1944, William secretly purchased a small store front in San Pedro, California. On his wife's thirtieth birthday, he gave her the candy shop, and named it in her honor, Helen Grace Chocolates.

The duo worked long hours to make their business a success. Helen worked the counter, while William made the candy in the back. The family business grew rapidly, and by the 1970s they had over twenty-five retail locations.

In 1963, Helen and Bill retired, moving to Northern California, and entrusting the company to their eldest son, James Grace (he is buried next to his mother). He managed the

Famed candy entrepreneur, Helen Grace's final resting place.

company until his untimely death in 1989. In the mid-1980s, Helen and Bill divorced, and she returned to southern California, settling in Huntington Beach. In 2001, the Grace family sold their remaining interests in the candy company to Robert and David Worth. Helen never lost her love for the business, and would occasionally stop into one the stores to see how things were going.

❁ She died on December 21, 2002, in Huntington Beach of natural causes at eighty-eight.[82] She is buried in the Newport Vista lawn, lot 1104, space G. After locating marker 1113 on the east curb, walk nine rows west to the Grace family plot. Helen's grave is topped by a large bronze marker, and the family plot has a lovely marble memorial bench.

ROBERT L. "BOBBY" HATFIELD

Proceed to the Lido Terrace, interred here is rock and roll legend Robert L. "Bobby" Hatfield (August 10, 1940 to November 5, 2003). Hatfield was born in Wisconsin but at a young age the family moved to Anaheim. Bobby met his future musical partner Bill Medley while the two were attending Cal State Long Beach. In 1963, while performing with the Paramours, Hatfield and Medley were discovered by legendary record producer Phil Spector. He persuaded them to leave the Paramours and form their own band. Legend has as it that they got the name "The Righteous Brothers" after a black fan referred to them as being "righteous." The name stuck, and the duo was signed to a record contact with Philles Records. The Righteous Brothers, with their style dubbed "blue-eyed soul," had a string of hit records from 1964 to 1965, hits that include:

- "You've Lost that Lovin' Feeling" (1965), that was number one on the Billboard Music hits
- "Unchained Melody" (1965), which reached number four, Bobby was actually the solo singer on this recording
- "Ebb Tide" (1965),
- "Just Once in My Life" (1965)

In 1965, Phil Spector lost interest in the pair, and they moved onto Verve Records, where they recorded another number one hit, "You're My Soul and Inspiration" (1966). In 1968, the Righteous Brother broke up; Hatfield kept the Righteous Brothers name, and continued to perform. Medley and Hatfield reunited briefly in 1974 to record a tribute album to fellow rock and roll artists who had died, hits included:

- "Rock and Roll Heaven"
- "Give It to the People"
- "Dream On"

In 1990, the pair enjoyed a renaissance, and returned to the charts when their hit song, "Unchained Melody," was included in the soundtrack for the

Righteous Brother and Rock and Roll Hall of Famer, Bobby Hatfield's grave.

movie *Ghost*.[83] In March 2003, the Righteous Brothers were inducted into the Rock and Roll Hall of Fame.[84] That November, they were on a national tour, and had made a stop in Kalamazoo, Michigan. Bobby died of a heart attack while napping, and an autopsy reveled that the heart failure was precipitated by a cocaine overdose.[85]

❧ Bobby Hatfield's final resting place is in the Lido Terrace, second garden enclosure. Find the Lido Terrace area; walk north along the sidewalk to the second enclosed plot. Here you will find the final resting place of rock and roll icon Bobby Hatfield. His large ornate flat to the ground grave marker is adorned with a picture of the singer, his epitaph reads,

> *Bobby was an amazing talent,*
> *Through his beautiful voice and*
> *Wonderful sense of humor*
>
> *Our memories and your*
> *"Unchained Melody"*
> *will live on through eternity,*
> *We love you, and we miss you,*
>
> *If you believe in forever*
> *then life is just a one night stand.*

KEVIN DUBROW

From Hatfield's grave site proceed to the Garden of David lawn; interred here is another rock and roll legend, Kevin Dubrow (October 29, 1955 to November 25, 2007). In 1975, Dubrow, a southern California native, formed the heavy metal rock band Quiet Riot, with guitarist Randy Rhodes, bassist Kelly Garni, and drummer Drew Forsyth. The band was a major draw on the Los Angeles club circuit during the late 1970s but never scored a major record contract. In 1983, they were signed by Pasha Records, and released the album *Metal Health*, the record was a number one hit with such iconic rock anthems as "Cum on Feel the Noise," and "Bang Your Head."[86] The band is widely recognized as being responsible for igniting the 1980s hair band pop metal movement. They paved the way for other metal bands such as Motley Crue and Rat. Quiet Riot's second album release *Condition Critical* in 1984 was not as well received, and topped out at number fifteen on the Billboard charts.

Kevin Dubrow was known for his rabble rousing vocal delivery, and in-your-face stage presence. He did not get along with his fellow band mates, and this led to constant personnel changes.[87] In 1987, he was fired from the band, which claimed that he was an out-of-control egomaniac. Dubrow with guitarist Carlos Cavaso reformed in 1990 as Heat, but toured the club scene under the name Quiet Riot.[88]

❧ On November 25, 2007, while staying at his home in Las Vegas, Nevada, Kevin was found dead of an over dose of cocaine; he was fifty-two.[89] Dubrow is buried in the Garden of David lawn, lot 60, space D. Walk west down the path until you locate a bronze "G" marker in the grass on the right; six graves north

Kevin Dubrow was the lead singer of the heavy metal band Quiet Riot.

is the singer's final resting place. The epitaph on his grave marker reads, "The music and memories live on."

MITCHELL HALPERN

Also interred in the Garden of David is famed boxing referee Mitchell Halpern (July 14, 1967 to August 20, 2000). Halpern was a well-respected professional boxing referee who oversaw eighty-seven championship fights in a career that started in 1991. Some of his biggest fights were:

- Mike Tyson vs. Evander Holyfield (1996
- Oscar De La Hoya vs. Felix Trinidad (1999)
- Lennox Lewis vs. Evander Holyfield (1999)
- Oscar De La Hoya vs. Ike Quartey (1999)
- Erik Morales vs. Marco Antonio Barrera (2000)

In 1997, Mitch was supposed to referee the infamous "bite" re-match fight between Evander Holyfield and Mike Tyson, but Tyson's camp vocally opposed this and Mills Lane filled in.

On the evening of August 20, 2000, after a domestic dispute in his Las Vegas home, Mitch shot himself.[90] He is buried in the Garden of David, lot 63, three rows west from Kevin Dubrow's grave. The epitaph on his grave reads in part:

"In loving memory of Mitch whose genuine compassion for others brought joy and happiness to those he touched; A renowned and respected world class boxing referee who felt his greatest accomplishments were being a father and making children's wishes come true; His love and laughter will be missed by all."

PAUL DONALDSON KING

From the Garden of David, drive to the Seaview lawn; buried here are two noteworthy people. First is versatile Hollywood screenwriter and executive Paul Donaldson King (July 14, 1926 to July 10, 1996). King was a screenwriter in both film and television from 1958 to 1988. Major film and television credits include:

> *Operation Petticoat* (1959), for which he was nominated for an Academy Award for best screen play

> *Bonanza* (1960)

> *Rawhide* (1963)

> *Daniel Boone* (1964)

King was also a television executive at Warner Brothers, Quinn Martin Productions, and NBC. He died on July 10, 1996 at his home in Newport Beach.[91]

His grave is located in Seaview lawn, lot 1452, space F. Find marker number 1448 on west curb; three rows east is his unassuming final resting place.

ARTHUR K. "SPUD" MELIN

Also buried in the Seaview lawn is the co-founder of Wham-O toys, Arthur K. "Spud" Melin (1924 to June 28, 2002). In 1948, Melin with his boyhood friend, Richard Kerr, co-founded Wham-O toys. They were known as the gurus of fads.

The first product they developed was the Wham-O Slingshot; this was the product that gave the company its name. When the slingshot hits its target, the sound it made sounded like wham-o. In 1958, they developed the biggest fad of them all—the hula-hoop. It was a thin plastic ring that you swung around your hips. The simple toy took off and became a national phenomenon. The first few years of production saw the company churn out over 25,000 hula-hoops a day, and over the years has made over twenty-five million.

Other sensational fad products included:

> The Frisbee (1958)

> Slip and Slide (1961)

> The Limbo Party Kit (1962)

> The Super ball (1965)

> The Air Blaster (1965)

In 1982, Melin sold his interest in Wham-O to the Kansco Group and retired. Spud Melin died on June 28, 2002 in Newport Beach, from Alzheimer's disease.[92] He is buried in the Seaview lawn, lot 1475, space D. Locate marker 1472 on the east curb, and four rows west is the guru of fads final resting place.

Raymond J. "Ray" Malavasi

Proceed to the Ocean View lawn area; interred here are numerous noteworthy people, including NFL head football coach Raymond J. "Ray" Malavasi (November 8, 1930 to December 15, 1987).

Malavasi was the head football coach for the Los Angeles Rams from 1977 to 1982. In 1980, he coached the team to their first Super Bowl appearance, losing 31-19 to the Pittsburgh Steelers. After a dismal 1982 season in which the team went 2-7, he was fired, and replaced by former USC coach John Robinson. Malavasi's statistics with the Rams were 40 wins against 33 defeats, NFC West division champions 1978, and 1979, and NFC champions 1979. Following his firing from the Rams, he never again coached in the NFL. He was also a very close friend of fellow coach Jack Faulkner (see Bay view Terrace). Ray Malavasi died of a heart attack on Tuesday, December 15, 1987, in Santa Ana, California.[93]

His grave is located in Ocean View, lot 824, space A. From marker 790 on the west curb of the lawn, walk five rows east to Malavasi's grave. His simple marker is adorned with a small football icon in the upper left corner.

Nan Leslie

Not far from Malavasi is actress Nan Leslie (June 4, 1926 to July 30, 2000). Leslie was an actress in the late 1940s to late 1960s. She starred in over thirty films, and also appeared on numerous television programs. Primarily a B-western actress in her early films, she co-starred with cowboy actors Gene Autry and Tom Holt. Major film credits include:

- *Under the Tonto Rim* (1947)
- *Western Heritage* (1948)
- *Indian Agent* (1948)
- *Rim of the Canyon* (1949)
- *Pioneer Marshal* (1949)

Her noteworthy television credits include:

- *The Cisco Kid*
- *The Lone Ranger*
- *The Adventures of Rin Tin Tin*
- *Perry Mason*
- *Lassie*

In 1968, she married Jason Coppage and retired from acting. Nan Leslie died on July 30, 2000 in San Juan Capistrano, California, from pneumonia.[94]

🍀 Her grave is located in Ocean View lawn, lot 951, space C; find marker 913 on the west curb. Eight markers east, under a large tree, is the unmarked grave of the actress.

BRYAN MARIS STEPHENS

Buried a short distance from Leslie is professional baseball player Bryan Maris Stephens (July 14, 1920 to November 21, 1991). Stephens was a right-handed relief pitcher who played two seasons for the Cleveland Indians, 1947-48. He appeared in 74 games, winning 8 and losing 16, with an earned run average of 5.16.[95] An interesting note, in 1940, while Stephens was a member of the Detroit Tigers minor league system, he and several other players were declared free agents by baseball Commissioner Landis, who was clamping down on team rule violations.

While Stephens was serving in the military during World War Two, he suffered an injury to his non-pitching hand in which the pinky finger was amputated.[96]

🍀 Stephens burial plot is located in Ocean View lawn, lot 1045, space A. Locate marker 1070 on the north curb and then walk three rows south to the grave.

JAMES ROOSEVELT

After viewing Stephens' grave, get back in your car and drive to the west side of Ocean View lawn. Locate curb marker 817. Near here is the grave of James Roosevelt (December 23, 1907 to August 13, 1991). James was the second child, and oldest son of President Franklin D. Roosevelt. He was born in New York City into a life of wealth and prestige. A graduate of Harvard University (1933), while in his junior year (1932), he was manager of his father's presidential campaign staff in Massachusetts. Following his graduation, he briefly served as FDR's White House Press Secretary.[97]

In 1941, James left politics for a brief time to explore opportunities in Hollywood, where he was employed by Samuel Goldwyn as a movie producer. His film credits include:

↤🍀 *Yes, Indeed*

↤🍀 *Lazybones*

↤🍀 *Easy Street*

↤🍀 *Alabamy Bound*

↤🍀 *Pot O' Gold*

All these films were made in 1941.[98] At the outbreak of World War II, he enlisted in the Marine Corp and rose to the rank of Brigadier General. While attached to the 2nd Marine Raider division, he was awarded the Navy Cross and Silver Star for gallantry during the raid on Makin Atoll in the South Pacific.[99]

Following the war, James entered politics and was appointed chairman of the California Democratic Party in 1946. He was dismissed as chairman in 1948, after opposing President Truman's re-election efforts. In 1950, undaunted by his dismissal from the Democratic Party, he ran for Governor of California. But with limited support from the Democratic Party, he lost the election to Earl Warren. Undaunted, by these failures, Roosevelt ran for a seat in the U.S. House of Representatives in 1954, and finally won an election. He went on to much success representing California for ten years, 1955 to 1965. During his tenure in Congress, one of his greatest achievements was his work on the 1964 Civil Rights Act.[100]

In 1965, he left Congress and ran an unsuccessful campaign for Mayor of the City of Los Angeles. Shortly after which, he was appointed ambassador to the United Nations Economic and Social Council by President Johnson. His days of controversy were not over. He bucked the Democratic political establishment, and endorsed Republican Richard Nixon for President in 1968. Then in 1976, he again reversed course, endorsing Democratic presidential candidate Jimmy Carter. James Roosevelt's days of flip-flopping political allegiance were not over. In 1984, he endorsed Republican President Ronald Reagan's re-election. After all this political flip-flopping, neither political party wanted his association, and he was banished to political oblivion.

After the election of 1984, Roosevelt switched his attention to preserving his family's historical legacy, and social responsibility issues. In 1983, he founded the National Committee to Preserve Social Security and Medicare, a non-profit organization that lobbied Congress for the preservation of the programs started by his father. He was a proponent of these issues the rest of his life.

❧ On August 13, 1991 in Newport Beach, California, James Roosevelt, the last surviving child of Franklin and Eleanor Roosevelt, died from complications of Parkinson's disease and stroke.[101] He was buried with full military honors in the Ocean View lawn, lot 815, space B; locate marker 817 on the east curb, and three rows west is his final resting place.

GEORGE G. SIPOSS

After leaving the grave site of James Roosevelt, head south. Located between curb markers 454 and 527 is the grave of inventor and author George G. Siposs (April 18, 1931 to November 21, 1995). George Siposs was a renaissance man who had many interests; he was an inventor, musical composer, and author. Born in Hungry in 1931, his family immigrated to Austria in 1949 to escape the communists. Soon after, they all moved to Canada where George finished school, graduating from the University of Toronto with a degree in engineering. As a bio-engineer, he was instrumental in helped start Orange County's first medical manufacturing company, Edwards Laboratories, in Irvine. He founded his own medical manufacturing company's, Delta Medical (1972), and American Omni Medical (1985). He was a pioneering inventor who helped develop many medical devices such as the implanted insulin pump, blood oxygenator, and arterial bubble traps. In 1983, he invented the pocket-sized insulin pump, for which he won the California Governors Award.

Siposs was not just an inventor, but was also an acclaimed author who wrote seven fiction novels, and eleven non-fiction books, which included:

+─❦ *The Green Team* (A Techno Medical Thriller)

+─❦ *Out of the Red*

+─❦ *How to Cash in on your Bright Idea*

George Siposs developed leukemia in 1991, and battled the disease for four years. He was a positive thinker and even as the end loomed near, he remained optimistic. Siposs succumbed to the ravages of the illness on November 21, 1995.[102]

❦ His grave is located in Ocean View lawn, lot 492, space E, located between curb markers 454 and 527. Find the grave of Esther Walters on the curb and then go ten rows west down the slope to Siposs' plot. The epitaph on his grave marker reads:

"Life is what happens while you're busy making other plans."

JUNE STOREY-CLARK

Continue south along the eastern ridge of Ocean View lawn to curb markers 383 and 454. Interred near here is actress June Storey-Clark (April 20, 1918 to December 18, 1991). Storey was a screen actress in the 1930s and 1940s and she starred in forty-five motion pictures. She was primarily, a lead actress in B-westerns for Republic Pictures, and was Gene Autry's leading lady in ten of his films. Her major screen credits include:

+─❦ *In Old Chicago* (1937)

+─❦ *Home on the Prairie* (1939)

+─❦ *Colorado Sunset* (1939)

+─❦ *In Old Monterrey* (1939)

+─❦ *South of the Border* (1939)

+─❦ *Carolina Moon* (1940)

+─❦ *Ride Tenderfoot Ride* (1940)

+─❦ *Lone Wolf Takes a Chance* (1941)

June retired from acting in the late 1940s, and married an Oregon rancher. She died on December 18, 1991, in Vista, California, from cancer.[103]

❦ Her grave is found in Ocean View lawn, lot 423, space B. It is located between east curb marker 383 and 454, seven rows west down the slope, and reads June S. Clark.

WILFRED M. CLINE

Interred nearby is Academy Award nominated cinematographer Wilfred M. Cline (September 3, 1903 to April 9, 1976). Cline was the director of cinematography on nearly ninety films, in a career that spanned forty years (1928 to 1969). In 1941, he was nominated for a best cinematography Academy Award for his film *Aloma of the South Seas*. He worked with actress Doris Day on many of her films such as:

- *Tea for Two* (1950)
- *Lullaby of Broadway* (1951)
- *April in Paris* (1952)
- *Lucky Me* (1954)

Other noteworthy film credits include:

- *Ain't Misbehavin'* (1955)
- *April Love* (1957)

Cline also dabbled in television photography with credits that include:

- *The Detectives* (1959)
- *Tate* (1960)
- *The Big Valley* (1965-1969)[104]

Wilfred Cline's final resting place is in Ocean View lawn, lot 282, space A. On the east curb, find marker 289; seven rows west is his grave site.

DOROTHY DARE

From the east rim of Ocean View lawn, drive to the south side area. Interred near the curb is actress Dorothy Dare (August 6, 1911 to October 4, 1981). The actress was born Dorothy Herskind, but after arriving in Hollywood in the early 1930s, she changed her name to be more recognizable. The vivacious red head was a versatile actress who had a wonderful singing voice, and her screen presence made her roles always memorable. In a relatively short Hollywood film career (1934-1942), she appeared in seventeen films. Dare's movie credits are wide-ranging, and include musicals, comedies, and dramas such as:

- *Private Lessons* (1934)
- *Happiness Ahead* (1934)
- *Sweet Adeline* (1934)
- *Gold Diggers of 1935* (1935)

- *Romance of the West* (1935)
- *High Hat* (1937)
- *Cut Out for Love* (1937)
- *The Yanks are Coming* (1942)[105]

The final resting place for this actress is in Ocean View lawn, lot 104, space E. Locate south curb marker 78, then find the grave of Katherine Herskind (Dorothy's mother); Dorothy's rests beside her mother, one row from the curb.

JOHN D. ELDRIDGE

From the Ocean View lawn area, proceed to the Lakeside lawn. Interred here are two noteworthy people; first prolific character actor John D. Eldridge (August 30, 1904 to September 23, 1961). Eldridge was a character actor who appeared in nearly 200 motion pictures and television programs from 1934 to 1961. His screen credits include:

- *Mysterious Crossing* (1936)
- *The Black Cat* (1941)
- *Life Begins for Andy Hardy* (1941)
- *Saboteur (1942)*
- *An American in Paris* (1951)

Television roles include appearances on:

- *Death Valley Days*
- *My Little Margie*
- *I Love Lucy*
- *The Adventures of Superman*
- *Perry Mason*
- *Leave it to Beaver*
- *Bonanza*
- *Mr. Ed*
- *Peter Gunn*

He is the younger brother of actor George Eldridge (a prolific actor in his own right with nearly 250 screen credits).[106]

John Eldridge died on September 23, 1961. His burial plot is in Lakeside lawn, lot 7, space B. Locate curb marker 12 on the east side of the lawn; twenty graves west is the actor's final resting place.

Rudolph Ishing

Also buried in Lakeside lawn is award-winning cartoonist Rudolph Ishing (August 7, 1903 to July 18, 1992). Ishing was a cartoonist, director, and producer, who got his start under Walt Disney in the early 1920s. Disney hired Ishing to work in his Kansas City studio drawing for Newton's Laugh-O-Grams, and later Alice in Cartoonland, and Oswald the Rabbit.[107]

Ishing and fellow cartoonist Hugh Harman left Disney's employment in the late 1920s to form their own company. Their first cartoon was Bosko the Talk-Ink Kid (1929). The character Bosko had a catch phrase, "That's all folks," that would be used later in Ishing's Porky Pig cartoons. The cartoon "Bosko" was the first animated film to coordinate movement to speech. In 1930, the success of this film caught the eye of studio executives at Warner Brothers, and the duo of Ishing and Harman were hired to develop the "Looney Tunes" cartoon franchise starring Bugs Bunny, Daffy Duck, and Porky Pig.

In 1931, they added "Merrie Melodies" to the cartoon family. Ishing was nominated for his first short-subject Academy Award in 1935 for The Calico Dragon, and was nominated the following year for The Old Mill Pond. He left Warner Brothers for Metro-Goldwyn-Mayer in 1934, and successes continued to come his way, winning his first Oscar as producer for the short-subject film *The Milky Way*. This film was the first non-Disney-related animated short to win the Academy Award.

Ishing's legendary career in animation spanned six decades, 1928 to 1988, and in that time, he had a hand in developing some of the greatest animated characters of all time. He produced or directed over 200 animated short-subject films.

❧ He died on July 18, 1992 in Newport Beach, California, from cancer.[108] Ishing is buried in Lakeside lawn, lot 156, space A. On the east curb, locate marker 123 and 157, two rows west is the grave site of the innovative cartoon mogul.

John Gordy

The final two famous internees at Pacific View Memorial Park are located in the Garden of Valor, near the entrance to the cemetery. First is professional football player John Gordy (July 17, 1935 to January 30, 2009). Gordy was a 6-foot, 240-pound star offensive lineman for the University of Tennessee in the late 1950s. In 1957, he was drafted by the Detroit Lions in the second round. In his ten-year professional career (1957-1967), he teamed with left guard Harley Sewell as one the best tandem guards of their time. Gordy also appeared in three pro-bowls, 1964-66, and was voted second team all-NFL in 1964, 1966, and 1967. In 1968, he was elected to lead the NFL players union, and was successful in negotiating the league's first collective bargaining agreement, and other important issues, such as increases in pension fund contributions. In 1968, Gordy starred along side Alan Alda in the motion picture, *Paper Lion*. It was a film about sports writer George

Plimpton's experiences as a rookie quarterback for the Lions. John Gordy died on January 30, 2009, in Orange, California, from pancreatic cancer.[109] The year 2009 marked the 75th anniversary of the founding of the Detroit Lions football franchise, and John Gordy was posthumously voted a member of their all-time team.

His grave is located in the Garden of Valor, lot 144, space D. It can be found in front of the Armed Forces, near the parking lot.

JAY MIGLIORI

The final famous burial at Pacific View belongs to musician Jay Migliori (November 14, 1930 to September 2, 2001). Migliori, a jazz saxophonist, made his recording debut in 1955 with the Woody Herman Band. He worked for many years as a session player for artists such as Frank Sinatra, Frank Zappa, and Maynard Ferguson. In 1972, he helped form the band Supersax, a Charlie Parker tribute band. In 1974, Supersax won a best jazz performance Grammy Award for their album, *Supersax Plays Bird*. Jay Magliori died on September 2, 2001 in Mission Viejo, California, from colon cancer.[110]

He is buried in the Garden of Valor, lot 79, space B. From Armed Forces Memorial, his plot is eighteen graves north.

KEITH HARRINGTON
PATRICIA HARRINGTON
JANNELLE CRUZ

Also buried at Pacific View are three victims of the original night stalker unsolved murder case from the early 1980's, Keith and Patricia Harrington and Jannelle Cruz. Their stories will told in Chapter Eight, "Murder and Mayhem."

5

Forest Lawn Memorial Park:

Cypress

*"A sign of a celebrity is that his or her name
is often worth more than his services."*

~*Daniel J. Boorstin,
historian (1914 to 2004)*

4471 Lincoln Avenue
Cypress, California 90630
Telephone 800- 204-3131

Park hours are 8 a.m. to 5 p.m. seven days a week.

Forest Lawn Memorial Park in Cypress is just one of ten corporate-run private non-denominational cemeteries that are owned and operated by the Forest Lawn Memorial Park Association. These ten cemeteries are situated throughout the greater Los Angeles area, and the most famous of which are located in the Hollywood Hills and Glendale, California. Forest Lawn Cypress has its own unique flare with its peaceful natural setting, green lawns, tree-lined vistas, and numerous works of art. There are many historic reproductions of art and architecture within the grounds. They includes the only exact bronze replica of Michelangelo's "David," a wonderful rendition of John La Farge's "The Ascension," and a faithful re-creation of the old St. John's Church in Richmond, Virginia. This is the same church in which Patrick Henry gave his famous speech, "Give me liberty or give me death."

The large ascension mausoleum complex on the grounds houses both interior and exterior crypt areas. The John La Farge's "Ascension" mosaic replica is awe inspiring and graces the entrance to the mausoleum complex. The grounds of the cemetery are fairly expansive and navigating the park is easy with a map (which can be obtained at the information booth at the entrance). The curbs and lawns are not well marked, but there are plenty of landmarks that allow for easy directions to the gravesites of the famous that are interred within the grounds.

Buried within the grounds of Forest Lawn Cypress are a variety of noteworthy people that include numerous Hollywood celebrities, sports stars, rock and roll icons, history makers, as well as infamous victims of heinous crimes.

DANIEL "DANNY" FLORES

The best place to start a tour of Forest Lawn Cypress is in the far northeast side of the grounds in the Everlasting Hope lawn section. Interred here are two famous people, first of which is Daniel "Danny" Flores (July 11, 1929 to September 29, 2006). Flores, known professionally as Chuck Rio, was a composer, performer, and Grammy Award winner of the hit song, "Tequila." Flores' musical career took off in the late 1950s playing with rockabilly singer Dave Burgess and the Champs. In 1957, the group recorded their most famous hit "Tequila," which was actually a b-side to a single called "Train to No Where."

"Tequila" reached number one on the Billboard music chart in March of 1958. Flores played sax on the recording, and his voice is the one heard yelling "Tequila!" during the song. Not only did it win a Grammy Award for best R & B recording in 1958, it has since sold over six million records world wide.[1] [Two members of the Champs who went on to fame of their own are Jimmy Seals and Dash Crofts, they formed Seals and Crofts. They had several pop hits in the early 1970s with such songs as "Summer Breeze," and "Diamond Girl.[2]] The Champs, as an original group, had a short career, and this was their only chart-topping hit record.

Danny Flores signed away the U.S. rights to the song in the late 1960s, but retained world wide rights. Since then, the song has become a pop culture icon; in 1980, it was used in the movie *Pee Wee's Big Adventure*, and because of this new found fame, Flores was able to regroup, and toured (with much success) under the name Chuck Rio and the Champs. He died on September 29, 2006, from pneumonia in Huntington Beach, California.[3]

❦ Flores' grave is found in Everlasting Hope lawn, lot 1007, space 2A. Follow Guardian Drive north, just before going over the bridge; then locate a small staircase on the west side of the lawn. Follow the tree line along the flood control channel, near the middle of the section. Along the fence is a large double-trunked tree; from here, walk south four rows to Flores's standard-sized bronze grave marker.

ANGEL FLOREZ

Retrace your footsteps back to the staircase, along the short brick wall south is the final resting place of Angel Florez (August 13, 1963 to April 25, 1995). He was an original "mousekeeter" on the *New Mickey Mouse Club* television show. The show ran for two seasons, 1977-1978. It was an updated version of the successful 1950s Disney television show. Cast members often refer to themselves as the "forgotten" mice because later versions of the show were more popular and had more famous stars.[4]

This version had several noted performers such as Lisa Whelchel, who had some success in the hit television show, *The Facts of Life* (1979-1988), playing the role of Blair.[5] Another cast member, Kelly Parsons, became Miss California, and was fourth runner up for Miss U.S.A. in 1986.[6]

Angelo Florez did not have much success in the entertainment industry after the show's conclusion, and faded into obscurity. He died from complications of A.I.D.S. on April 25, 1995, at age thirty-three.[7] His death went unreported in all the local area newspapers.

❧ Angel's grave is located in the Everlasting Hope lawn, lot 329. From the staircase on the northwest side of the lawn, follow the top of the small brick wall south six markers, and in the first row closest to the wall, you will find his final resting place.

George Grandee

Moving on to the Sheltering Trees lawn section are the final resting place of two noteworthy people. First drive south along Guardian Drive, turn left onto Cypress Drive, then right onto Evergreen Drive, and take this to the southeast side of the lawn. Buried near here is actor George Grandee (May 20, 1900 to August 1, 1985). Grandee was a character actor who appeared in fourteen motion pictures from the mid-1920s to the late 1930s. His major film credits include:

- *The Meddler* (1925)
- *The Man From the West* (1926)
- *The Great Garbo* (1929)
- *Rainbow Over Broadway* (1933)
- *Marry Widows* (1934)
- *Swing It Professor* (1937)[8]

❧ George Grandee is buried in the Sheltering Trees lawn, lot 5730, space 4; first find the grave of Mary A. Kinninger near the southeast curb, and thirteen markers west is the actors burial plot.

Richard Carter "Dick" Wantz

The second famous burial in this lawn section is professional baseball player Richard Carter "Dick" Wantz (April 11, 1940 to May 13, 1965). Wantz was a promising young pitcher for the Los Angeles Angels, whose career was tragically cut short after the diagnosis of a brain tumor. In April of 1965, he made the opening day roster of the major league club; his major league debut came on April 13th, appearing in one inning of relief, striking out two batters, while allowing three earned runs. After the game, he complained of a severe headache and was examined by team doctors. The doctors found a rapidly growing malignant brain tumor that was deemed inoperable; the highly touted rookie pitcher never played again.

He died exactly one month later, on May 13, 1965, following emergency surgery at Daniel Freeman Hospital in Los Angeles. His funeral was held on Tuesday, May 18th at the Church of Our Fathers at Forest Lawn Cypress, and it was attended by the entire Los Angeles Angels organization, as well as numerous friends and family.[9]

🐝 Dick Wantz is buried in the Sheltering Trees lawn, lot 493, space 3. Drive to the west side of the lawn; on the curb, locate the grave of John E. Thomas. Four markers east is the pitcher's final resting place.

PHILIP FORD

Just across the street from Wantz's grave site is the Garden of Protection lawn. Interred near the east side of this section are two famous people. First, is noted film and television director Philip Ford (October 16, 1900 to January 12, 1976). Ford was a director of numerous television and motion pictures from the mid-1940s until the mid-1960s. His father was noted actor Francis Ford, and his uncle was Academy Award winning director John Ford. Philip's major screen credits include mostly westerns, and B-level films. Among the most famous are:

- *Crime of the Century* (1946)
- *The Mysterious Mr. Valentine* (1946)
- *The Timber Trail* (1948)
- *Train to Alcatraz* (1948)
- *Angel in Exile* (1948)
- *The Wyoming Bandit* (1949)
- *Prisoners in Petticoats* (1950)
- *The Dakota Kid* (1951)
- *Utah Wagon Train* (1951)

His television film credits include:

- *Lassie* (1955-1958)
- *The Adventures of Superman* (1956-1958)
- *Beware of the Dog* (1964)

The director died on January 21, 1976, in Woodland Hills, California.[10]

🐝 His final resting place is located in the Garden of Protection, lot 5190. Locate the stairs on the east side of the lawn; proceed west along the center isle. A short distance on the left is the grave of Karl Howland; sixteen grave markers south is Ford's burial plot.

Buried not far away is pioneering rock and roll drummer Sandy West (July 10, 1959 to October 21, 2006). West was a co-founder and drummer of the 1970s all-girl, punk rock group, The Runaways, that had several hit songs such as, "Cherry Bomb," and "Born to be Bad." West along with Joan Jett, Lita Ford, Cherie Currie, Micki Steele, and Kim Fowley founded the group in Los Angeles in 1975. They signed with Mercury Records, and released their first album *The Runaways* (1976), the album was critically panned, and did not sell well. Their second release *Queens of Noise* (1977), faired no better in the United States, but in Japan it was a smash hit.

The group was viewed by critics as a novelty, and was not taken seriously; they were seen as being over hyped by their record label. Their subsequent albums *Waintin' on the Night* (1978), and *Little Lost Girls* (1981) did no better than their previous releases.

In 1978, the group was the opening band for the Ramones concert tour, and garnered a large cult following. This alone was not enough to keep the group together; they played their last concert on New Year's Eve 1979, in San Francisco. Soon after, the group disbanded and never again played together. Band mates Joan Jett, and Lita Ford went on to successful solo music careers, and Micki Steele joined another all-girl group, The Bangles.[11] Sandy West continued to perform in her own group, The Sandy West Band, releasing one album *The Beat is Back*. She did not have much success; she struggled financially and emotionally for years after the break up of the group.

On October 21, 2006, West died of lung cancer at a hospice in San Dimas, California. She was forty-seven.[12] When informed of Sandy West's death, former band mate Joan Jett was quoted as saying:

Sandy West, drummer in the all-girl rock band, the Runaways.

"We shared the dream of girls playing rock and roll. Sandy was an exuberant and powerful drummer; I am overcome from the loss of my friend. I always told her we changed the world."[13]

Today, the legacy of the Runaways is seen in their influence on all-girl bands such as, the X-Ray Spex, the Bangles, and the Go-Go's. They paved the way and helped revolutionize the world of rock and roll.

🍀 Sandy West's grave is found in the Garden of Protection, block 20, lot 4324, space 3. Walk west from the staircase a short distance, four rows on the right locate the grave of Norman Shepard, and eleven markers directly north is the punk drummer's final resting place.

HAROLD EUGENE WERTZ

Drive to the southwest corner of Memory Lane and Cypress Drive; this will also be the southwest corner of the Garden of Protection. Park along the west curb (note the section with the small statues), and take the staircase up into the brick wall enclosed lawn area. Interred here are two famous people, first is Harold Eugene Wertz, Jr. (August 3, 1927 to November 21, 1999). Wertz was best known as "Bouncy" the little chubby kid in the early Hal Roach *Our Gang* comedies. When Wertz outgrew the part, he was replaced by George McFarland (better known as Spanky). After leaving the *Our Gang* comedies, Wertz did not continue in Hollywood, and settled into a life of obscurity. When these comedies again became popular in the 1970s, Wertz, along with other fellow alumni, made public appearances to sign autographs and to talk about the series. Harold Wertz died on November 21, 1999 in San Diego, California.[14]

He is buried in the Garden of Protection, block 2, lot 7295, space 1. His large bronze grave marker is located inside the brick wall enclosed area near the southwest corner of the lawn. Follow the sidewalk up the stairs into the enclosure; walk east. On the right, count seven rows. Harold Wertz's grave site is just to the right of this walkway.

ABE KASHEY

Buried not far from Wertz in the southwest corner of the enclosure is famed wrestler Abe Kashey (November 28, 1903 to September 24, 1965). Known as "King Kong," Kashey in his professional wrestling days, was a born in Syria. He made his professional wrestling debut in 1930. He was best known as a villain in the wrestling ring with his best feud being with fellow wrestler Dirty Dick Raines. In 1949, Kashey lost a highly publicized match with Verne Gagne (his debut), that was referred by boxing champion Jack Dempsey.[15] Kashey had a very long and lucrative career as a professional wrestler, but he also made cameo appearances in several motion pictures. His film credits include:

📽 *King of the Mounties* (1942)

📽 *Nazty Nuisance* (1943)

+—❧ *The Crime Doctor's Courage* (1945)

+—❧ *Tarzan and the Leopard Woman* (1946)

❧ Kashey died on September 24, 1965 of congestive heart failure in Lynwood, California.[16] His grave is located in the Garden of Protection, block 1, lot 8274, space 2, which is found in the southwest corner of the enclosure, and is one row from the wall.

GLENN MARTIN QUINN

One final famous internee of the Garden of Protection lawn area is Irish born actor Glenn Martin Quinn (May 28, 1970 to December 3, 2002). Glenn is best known for his role as the boyfriend/ husband of Becky Connor on the hit sitcom *Roseanne*. He joined the cast of the sitcom in its third season of production (1990), and stayed with the show seven seasons until it was cancelled it 1997. A native of Dublin, Ireland, Quinn often had to play roles that hid his accent.[17] His television credits include:

+—❧ *Beverly Hills* 90210 (1990)

+—❧ *Call Me Anna* (1990)

+—❧ *Silhouette* (1990)

+—❧ *Covington Cross* (1992)

+—❧ *Jesse* (1999)

+—❧ *At Any Cost* (2000)

From 1999 to 2002, he co-starred as the half-demon Allen Doyle in the *Buffy the Vampire Slayer* hit television series spin off, *Angel*.[18] Quinn must have been battling his own inner demons when on December 3, 2002, he was found dead of a heroin overdose at a friend's home in North Hollywood, California.[19]

❧ His grave is located in the Garden of Protection, block 4, lot 7324, space 2. Find block 4 on the cemetery map. It is best to access the area from the south side of the lawn along Cypress Drive; locate a small staircase near the south curb. Once up the stairs, follow the small brick wall west to the grave of Mae Alice Prescott; nineteen markers north is Quinn's final resting place. His simple bronze grave marker is adorned with a symbol of Jesus with his arms outstretched and a Celtic Cross. Hs epitaph (an old Irish poem) reads:

"May the road rise to meet you,
may the wind be always at your back,
may the sun shine warm upon your face,
and rain fall soft upon your fields,
and until we meet again,
may God hold you in the hollow of his hand."

This is a fitting farewell for the soul of a lost Irish lad.

H.B. "Toby" Halicki

Moving on to the large lawn area known as Eternal Peace, buried on the east side of this area is H. B. "Toby" Halicki (October 18, 1940 to August 20, 1989). Halicki was a versatile Hollywood director, producer, actor, writer, and stuntman. He is best known for starring and producing action car chase movies in the 1970s and 1980s. The most famous of these was *Gone in 60 Seconds* (1974). Other notable films, in which he acted, directed, produced, and performed stunts in are:

- *The Junkman* (1982)
- *Deadline Auto Theft* (1983)
- *Deadly Addiction* (1988)

In August of 1989, while filming *Gone in 60 Seconds II*, a remake of his original film, Halicki was tragically killed on the movie set in Buffalo, New York. He died when a cable that was attached to a water tower broke, and severed a telephone pole that fell on top of him. The stunt in question called for a truck to crash through a series of cars ramming the support for a water tower. Prior to shooting the scene, the stunt crew had already weakened the supports for the water tower. Immediately things began to go wrong, and the tower began to come down. Most of the crew was able to escape the falling tower unharmed, but Halicki was not so lucky. Ironically, just hours before his death, he told an Associated Press reporter, that close calls while performing stunts on movies had made him more cautious, and that "you can always have a chase sequence where things go wrong."[20]

His grave is located in the Eternal Peace lawn, block 3, lot 4046, space 1. On the east curb of the lawn near the intersection of Cypress Drive and Memory Lane, locate the grave marker of Thomas L. Schwarz; ten rows west is Halicki's burial plot. The epitaph on his grave marker reads:

"My darling husband,
the love we shared will always be...
Toby-The Dream Maker,
your life has touched us all,
I'll love you always,
Denise."

Edward Raymond "Eddie" Cochran

Buried in the Tender Promises lawn area is rock and roll legend Edward Raymond "Eddie" Cochran (October 2, 1938 to April 17, 1960). Cochran was born in Oklahoma and moved to Southern California at the age of eleven. He had a very brief career in rock and roll, but in that short time, he was able to make an important impact. Cochran was a flashy performer, and exceptional guitarist. His stage presence was very energetic; he was considered a rebel rocker, and one of the first real rock guitar heroes. His music would influence generations of future rock and roll legends such as Pete Townsend and Jimmy Page. Cochran had a string of hit singles in the late 1950s, with songs such as:

- "Sittin' in the Balcony," that reached number eighteen on the billboard hits list in 1957
- "Summertime Blues" (1958), was a top ten single
- "C'mon Everybody," was a top forty hit in 1958
- "Somethin' Else" (1959), reached number fifty-eight on the charts
- "Three Steps to Heaven," was number one in the United Kingdom in 1960[21]

He was very popular in England, and in the spring of 1960, embarked on a concert tour of the British Isles. On April 17, 1960, he played the last concert of the successful tour at the Hippodrome Theater in Bristol. After the show, Cochran, with fellow rocker Gene Vincent, and Sharon Sheeley (Eddie's fiancée), left the Hippodrome Theater for London's Heathrow Airport. Around midnight, the taxi in which the group was traveling blew a tire, swerved out of control, and slammed into a telephone pole. Wreckage from the crash was strewn over 200 yards up the road. Both Cochran and Vincent were thrown from the car, sustaining serious injuries. Cochran was rushed to a local hospital, and died later that morning on the operating table of massive head and internal injuries. Sharon Sheeley suffered a broken pelvis and back injuries, and the driver of the taxi, George Martin, walked away with only minor scratches.[22] Cochran's body was flown back to the United States; over 200 mourners attended his funeral services at the Maywood Methodist Church. Among the mourners were Conception Valenzuela, the widowed mother of rock idol Richie Valens (who

had been killed a year earlier in a plane crash with Buddy Holly). He was reported to have been buried in a white satin shroud.[23] In 1987, Cochran was posthumously inducted into the Rock and Roll Hall of Fame.

His final resting place is located in the Tender Promises lawn, lot 2996, space 4. In the center of the lawn, find the small statue; left of the statue area and five rows from the south wall is the rockers burial plot. A large bronze marker graces the grave of the legendary rocker.

Rock and Roll legend Eddie Cochran's grave site.

SHARON SHEELEY

One row directly south from Cochran's grave is the burial plot of his fiancée, Sharon Sheeley (April 4, 1940 to May 17, 2002). Sheeley was with the rocker when he died in England and was the youngest woman to ever write a number one hit song in America. Her song credits include:

- *Poor Little Fool*, was recorded by Ricky Nelson in 1958 and reached number one on Billboards Hot One Hundred list
- *Dum Dum*, recorded by Brenda Lee, and was number four on the charts
- *Breakaway*, recorded by Irma Thomas
- *Hurry Up*, recorded by Richie Valens

Eddie Cochran recorded several of her songs:

- "Cherished Memories"
- "Love Again"
- "Somethin' Else"

She also co-developed the hit 1960s television show *Shindig* with her then-husband and host of the show, Jimmy O'Neil. Sheeley died on May 17, 2002, of a cerebral hemorrhage in Los Angeles.[24]

There is some controversy as to whether she is actually interred in this grave. Sharon's marker states that it is a cenotaph, but the death certificate and interviews of cemetery personnel state that her ashes are indeed buried in the grave. The bronze marker is adorned with musical notes, and reads:

> *Together forever*
> *In loving memory of*
> *Sharon K. Sheeley,*
> *She was*
> *"somethin' else,"*
> *We will miss you."*

Sharon Sheeley's cenotaph with Cochran grave marker in background.

KEN MAYNARD

Interred in the Churchyard lawn area, in front of the Church of Our Fathers, are three noteworthy people. First, is famed cowboy actor Ken Maynard (July 21, 1895 to March 23, 19730). Maynard was a cowboy actor with over ninety motion picture film credits, whose career spanned the 1920s and 1930s. He was one of Hollywood's most popular western stars during this period. His contemporaries included William S. Hart, Tom Mix, Hoot Gibson, and Buck Jones. Maynard is credited with being the first singing cowboy, and as being the first actor to make a star out of his horse (named Tarzan). Major film credits include:

- *The Man Who Won* (1923)
- *North Star* (1925)
- *Haunted Range* (1926)
- *The Overland Stage* (1927)
- *The Canyon Adventure* (1928)
- *Cheyenne* (1929)
- *Fighting Thru* (1930)
- *Come, On Tarzan* (1932)
- *The Lone Avenger* (1933)
- *In Old Santa Fe* (1934)
- *Boots of Destiny* (1937)
- *Death Rides the Range* (1939)

Early Western actor Ken Maynard, who died penniless and nearly forgotten is buried at Forest Lawn.

By the late 1930s, Maynard's popularity waned, and he soon was out of films and back on the rodeo circuit. He made only a handful of films after the 1930s, mostly small cameo performances.[25] Maynard spent the last years of his life living alone in a trailer, poor and forgotten. He died on March 23, 1973, at the Motion Picture Country Home in Woodland Hills, California. He was seventy-seven. His funeral was attended by seventy-five mourners, mostly strangers, many of whom were dressed in full western gear. No Hollywood stars came to the services. It had been rumored that Gene Autry would make an appearance, but he did not.[26] Maynard's grave is found in the Churchyard lawn, block 3, lot 2840, space 1. From the east curb of the lawn, find the grave marker of Maxine Pyle; five rows west is the famed cowboy actor's final resting place.

My-ca Dinh Le

The final person of note that is interred within the Churchyard lawn area is child actor My-ca Dinh Le (January 7, 1975 to July 23, 1982). Le, along with Renee Chenn, and veteran actor Vic Morrow, was killed on the set of the movie *Twilight Zone*. During filming of a scene in which a helicopter attacks and destroys a village, Morrow was supposed to lead the two children across a shallow river to safety. Instead, several explosive fireballs got too close to the helicopter, damaging the tail rotor. This sent the helicopter spinning out of control, and it landed on top of the three actors, decapitating Morrow and crushing the two children.[27]

In the aftermath of the tragedy, it was found that the two children had been working in violation of state law that prohibited children under the age of eight from working late hours. Director John Landis and the film production company were put on trial for negligence. The resulting trial ended in a not guilty verdict, but subsequent civil lawsuits commenced with undisclosed settlements being reached. As a result of the accident, tougher rules and regulations were enacted on film companies, pertaining to the use of children and dangerous conditions.

My-ca Le is buried in the Churchyard lawn, block 5, lot 1839, space 1. From the front entrance of the church, locate a small brick wall. Find the left corner of that wall and two rows south is the young actors burial plot.

Walter Lloyd "Kit" Carson

A short walk west from the Churchyard lawn is the lawn of Fond Remembrance. Buried here are three interesting people. First, is professional baseball player Walter Lloyd "Kit" Carson (November 15, 1912 to June 21, 1983). Carson played two seasons for the Cleveland Indians, 1934 and 1935. A light hitting right fielder, he appeared in twenty-one games, had ten hits with a batting average of .250.[28]

His grave is located in the Fond Remembrance lawn area, block 13, lot 5178, space 4. From the east curb of the lawn, locate the grave of John Carlisle; seven rows west is Carson's final resting place.

Also interred here is famed aviator Joan Merriam Smith (1936 to February 17, 1965). Smith learned to fly at the early age of sixteen. On March 17, 1964, she began her historic flight around the world. Smith would use the exact route that Amelia Earhart used in 1937. Earhart failed in this attempt and was never seen or heard from again. Smith's flight soon became a race when another female pilot, Jerry Mock, also took off in an attempt to break the record. Mock ended up beating Smith by twenty-five days and became the first female to fly solo around the world entirely by air. Smith completed her flight on May 12, 1964.

Although, Smith was not the first at this accomplishment, she did make a few firsts of her own:

- She was the first to fly solo along the equator.

- She was the first woman to fly around the world in a twine engine plane.

- She was the first woman to fly solo from Africa to Australia.

- She was the first woman to fly from Wake Island to Midway Island.

On February 17, 1965, Smith, along with biographer Trixie-Ann Schubert, was killed in a plane crash. The two were in route to an important meeting in the Lucerne Valley when the plane Smith was piloting mysteriously crashed near the Big Pines Recreation area, north of Los Angeles. Witnesses to the crash stated that they saw a portion of the right wing come off, and the plane was sent into a vertical dive. Both women were killed instantly, and their bodies

Famous Aviator Joan Smith's final resting place.

were burned beyond recognition. The exact cause of the crash was never determined. Smith was awarded the Harmon Trophy Award posthumously in 1965. This award is given for the most outstanding international achievements in the science of aeronautics.[29]

❦ Joan Merriam Smith is buried in the Fond Remembrance lawn, block 13, lot 5027, space 1. From the east curb of the lawn, locate the grave marker of Larry Dean Taggart; twenty-five rows west along the break between block eleven and thirteen is Smith's grave. Her bronze marker extols her many aviation accomplishments.

JACK R. COLER

The final noteworthy person buried in the Fond Remembrance lawn is Jack R. Coler (1947 to June 26, 1975). Coler was an F.B.I. agent who was killed in a gun battle with Sioux Indians who had occupied a portion of Wounded Knee Village on the Pine Ridge Indian Reservation in South Dakota. Colers, along with fellow agent Ronald Williams, were on the reservation to serve warrants. They were ambushed as they approached a house in the tiny village of Ogala. The agents were shot multiple times. The home in question was owned by John Little. At the time of the attack, it was occupied by nearly thirty people. These people had gathered at the home to protect Dennis Banks, who was staying nearby, and was due to stand trial for the Wounded Knee affair of 1973.[32] Two American Indian Movement members, Robert Robideau and Darelle Butler, were arrested and tried for the agent's murder. Both men were eventually acquitted by a Federal court of the killings. The defense headed by famed attorney William Kunstler had proven that an atmosphere of tension existed between the F.B.I. and Indian Movement, and the Indians believed that they were under attack and that they'd responded in self defense in the shooting of Coler and Williams.[31]

❦ Jack Coler is buried in the Fond Remembrance lawn, block 14, lot 5468, space 1. From the Fond Remembrance wall crypts on the north side of the lawn, locate the grave of Vicki Ruth Blake. Eleven markers south is Coler's unassuming grave.

SIDNEY H. "BUSTER" KELLEY

From the Fond Remembrance lawn area, drive to the Ascension Mausoleum complex. Interred in and around the mausoleum are several noteworthy people.

In the Garden of Memory, located in front of the mausoleum and to the left, is buried Sidney H. "Buster" Kelley (December 16, 1908 to December 5, 2001). Kelley, along with his brother Leslie Kelley, built the largest used car business in the United States and developed the Kelley Blue Book used car price guide. The "Blue Book" was first published in 1926. It contained price values for thousands of used cars. In 1962, the Kelley brothers sold the guide book but maintained a management role in the business. Today, the "Blue Book" is still the leader and largest automobile valuation price guide. Buster Kelley died on December 5, 2001, from complications of cancer.[32]

❧ His grave is located in the Garden of Memory, upper level, lot 1090, space A. After entering the upper garden area, proceed around the sidewalk to the left; follow the sidewalk to the furthest left corner of the interior lawn. Three graves from this corner, near the sidewalk, is Kelley's final resting place. The epitaph of his marker reads:

"only as much as we dream we can be."

KAREN ANNE CARPENTER

Exit the Memory Garden area and proceed to the interior mausoleum to the left of the giant Ascension Mosaic. In the Sanctuary of Compassion, in the left hallway, is the former burial site of pop singer Karen Anne Carpenter (March 2, 1950 to February 4, 1983).

Karen was interred in the Sanctuary of Compassion after her death from heart failure, due to complications of anorexia nervosa. In 2003, Richard Carpenter had her remains moved to Pierce Brothers Valley Oaks Memorial Park in Westlake Village, California. The former epitaph of her Forest Lawn crypt read:

"a star on earth, a star in heaven."

❧ Karen's large crypt at the end of the sanctuary now sits empty.

BRUCE A. JACOBSON
DEBORAH PAULSON

The hallway right of the Sanctuary of Compassion is the Sanctuary of Family Love. Interred here are two victims of the 1976 mass shooting at the library of Cal State Fullerton, Bruce A. Jacobson and Deborah Paulson. Their story will be told in the Chapter Eight, "Murder and Mayhem."

JUANITA MILLENDER-MCDONALD

Exiting the indoor mausoleum, turn left and proceed to the Ascension Gardens, number two area. Interred here is Congresswoman Juanita Millender-McDonald (September 7, 1938 to April 21, 2007). A liberal Democrat, she was elected to the U.S. House of Representatives in 1996. The 37th district of California for which she was the representative included most of South Central Los Angeles, as well as the city of Long Beach. Prior to entering Congress, Millender-McDonald worked as school teacher and as a textbook editor. In 1990, she ran for the Carson City Council, winning the election and became that city's first African-

American elected councilwoman. She then ran and was elected to the California State Assembly in 1992. In 1995, Congressman Walter Tucker was embroiled in an extortion scandal and resigned his seat in the U.S. House of Representatives. Millender-McDonald ran for the seat and won the special election. In Congress she was known for her commitment to protecting human rights. In 2006, she was named the Chairwoman of the House Committee on House Administration. She was the first African-American woman to chair this committee.

❧ In April of 2007, she died from colon cancer. Millender-McDonald, a tireless worker, had only requested a leave of absence from Congress one week prior to death.[33] Her crypt is found in the outdoor Ascension Gardens, section two. Upon entering the garden area, turn right; along the immediate wall on the right are a row of crypts. Three rows from the bottom and five rows from the right is the Congresswoman's final resting place. Her ornate bronze tablature reads:

> *"Congresswoman, Juanita Millender-McDonald, give her the reward she has earned, and let her works bring her praise at the city gate.*
>
> *Proverbs 31:31."*

JOCELYN REINA
LILIBETH MACALOLOOY

The final noteworthy burials at Forest Lawn, Cypress are two victims of the crash of Pan Am flight 103. The aircraft was blown up by a terrorist bomb that exploded over Lockerbie, Scotland, in 1988. The stories of these two flight attendants, Jocelyn Reina, and Lilibeth Macalolooy, as well as other victims of the tragedy, will be discussed in the Chapter Eight, "Murder, and Mayhem."

6

OTHER PRIVATE CEMETERIES

Not life, but good life, is to be chiefly valued.

~Socrates
philosopher (469 BC to 399 BC)

MELROSE ABBEY MEMORIAL PARK

2303 South Manchester Avenue
Anaheim, California 92802
Telephone: 714-634-1981

Hours of operation are from dawn to dusk, seven days a week.

Established in 1929, Melrose Abbey Memorial Park is located just a stone's throw across the 5 freeway from Angels Stadium of Anaheim. Unbeknownst to most baseball fans is the fact that several of baseball's early record setters, infamous scoundrels, and iconic personalities are buried within its grounds. Other famous internees include a wide variety of interesting athletes, politicians, Hollywood actors, and vaudeville performers. The cemetery is boarded by Manchester Avenue to the northeast and Lewis Street to the southwest. The grounds are divided into three distinct sections, the main cemetery, the Vietnamese, and Islamic burial areas.

The cemetery's abbey chapel features Orange County's largest full-size pipe organ and has a magnificent stained glass window depicting Jesus' Sermon on the Mount. The dark gothic interior of the abbey chapel has three floors of crypts. It is a small part of a much larger mausoleum complex. A tiny cemetery by modern standards, Melrose Abbey is situated on ten acres of picturesque manicured lawns. Each section has a unique name which is clearly marked on each curb. Interior roads are not named but are easily maneuvered. There are very few landmarks to guide the visitor and all grave markers are flush to the ground.

A central starting point is the historical abbey chapel area. Located within the chapel are the final resting places of four noteworthy individuals, a U.S.

Congressman, two professional baseball players, and the horticulturalist who created the boysenberry.

JAMES PHILIP "JIMMY" AUSTIN

Entombed in the basement area of the chapel is James Philip "Jimmy" Austin (December 8, 1879 to March 6, 1965), professional baseball player, coach, and manager. Austin played for the New York Highlanders (Yankees) and St. Louis Browns from 1909 to 1929. He was considered to be one of the finest defensive third basemen of his era. He is most famous for a Charles M. Conlon photograph in which Ty Cobb is seen sliding into him at third base.[1] Austin was a player-manager for the St. Louis Browns in 1913, 1918, and 1923. The first of Branch Rickey's first "Sunday manager," Rickey would play or manage on the Sabbath. As a part-time manager, Austin amassed a record of thirty-one wins against forty-four loses. After retiring as a player he also coached for the St. Louis Browns and Chicago White Sox.[2] His career playing statistics were 1580 games played, 5388 at bats, 1328 hits, 661 runs, 390 runs batted in, 244, stolen bases, and a .246 career batting average.[3] Jimmy Austin died March 6, 1965, in Laguna Beach, California, from an undisclosed illness.[4]

❦ His crypt can be found in the basement area under the abbey chapel. The basement crypt can be accessed from the north stairwell of the chapel. Once in the basement, turn left into the first alcove. Through the wrought iron gates on the right side, six rows in and two rows up (companion 13CC) is Austin's final resting place.

EARL ANDREW HAMILTON

Exiting the basement, walk into the main chapel near the front doors. To the right is a staircase that leads to the upper mezzanine level. Here is the final resting place of Earl Andrew Hamilton (July 19, 1891 to November 17, 1968), professional baseball player. He was a teammate of Jimmy Austin who played for the St. Louis Browns, Detroit Tigers, Pittsburgh Pirates, and Philadelphia Phillies from 1911 to 1924. Hamilton a left-handed pitcher who appeared in 410 games, compiled a record of 116 wins, 147 loses with an earned run average of 3.16.[5] On August 30, 1912, Hamilton pitched the American Leagues 18th no-hitter, against the Detroit Tigers. In 1920, he and New York Giants pitcher Rube Benton, pitched an epic sixteen innings of shut-out baseball, with the Giants finally prevailing, for the win in the seventeenth inning.[6] Earl Hamilton died on November 17, 1968, at the age of seventy-seven in Anaheim, California.[7]

❦ His crypt (mezzanine memorial 8-C) is found on the upper floor of the chapel mausoleum, south side, six rows from the stained-glass window, and four rows from the bottom.

JOHN MILLS HOUSTON

Not far from Hamilton is Congressman John Mills Houston (September 15, 1890 to April 29, 1975). Houston served as mayor of Newton, Kansas, from 1927 to 1931 and was Secretary of the Kansas State Democratic Central Committee 1934 and 1935. He also served in the United States House of Representatives from Kansas 1935 to 1943. Houston was defeated for re-election in 1943, but was appointed to the National Labor Relations Board by President Franklin Roosevelt, where he served from 1943 to 1953.[8] John Mills Houston died on April 29, 1975 in Laguna Beach, California.

❧ He is buried near Earl Hamilton on the upper level mausoleum of the abbey chapel in mezzanine memorial crypt, 20-F. It is near the stained-glass window on the bottom row.

RUDOLPH BOYSEN

On the ground floor of the chapel abbey is the Sanctuary of Peace cremation niche room. Interred here is Rudolph Boysen (July 14, 1895 to November 25, 1950). Boysen was a pioneering horticulturalist who owned a small farm in Merced County in Northern California. In the 1930s, Boysen created a new berry, a hybrid of several kinds of blackberries, raspberries, and loganberries. Unable to make the berry or farm commercially viable, he sold the farm and moved to southern California.[9] Walter Knott (see Loma Vista Memorial Park), an expert in berry farming, heard of the new berry and sought out the abandoned farm of Boysen. Knott was able to save several withered vines of the hybrid berry, and brought them back to his farm in southern California. With great care, Knott was able to bring the vines back to life. Knott named the new berry after its creator and it has hence been known as the boysenberry. The boysenberry became the backbone of Walter Knott's successes and is still wildly popular today.[10] Rudolph Boysen went on to work for twenty-five years as superintendent of city parks for Anaheim. He died on November 25, 1950, at the age of fifty-five.[11]

❧ His cremated remains can be found in the abbey chapel, Sanctuary of Peace, niche 65C. This is left of the main doors to the chapel. Once inside the niche area, Boysen's final resting spot is on the front wall, eight niches from the bottom and two from the right.

DALLAS DENVER BIXLER

From the chapel abbey proceed to the main mausoleum and here is the cremated remains of Olympic gold medalist Dallas Denver Bixler (February 17, 1910 to August 13, 1990). Bixler won the gold medal on the horizontal bars at the 1932 Olympics in Los Angeles. He beat out the two favored athletes from Finland by using a new dismount style called the reverse giant. It was Bixler who held the distinction as the only U.S. men's gymnastic gold medalist until Peter Vidmar won gold in 1984.

Dallas was an international gymnastic judge and coach for forty-four years and was instrumental in the career of future Olympian Cathy Rigby. Bixler was an Olympic torch bearer for the opening ceremonies at the Los Angels Olympics in 1984. Dallas Bixler died on August 13, 1990 of natural causes at age eighty. At the time of his death, Bixler was one of the oldest living Olympic athletes.[12]

His cremated remains are found in the Hall of the Cross, which is located in the main hallway of the mausoleum next to the chapel. Look for the wall of black marble on the right. In the middle, top row, is Bixler's unique memorial that shows him on the high bar.

EDWARD MARSHALL STEDMAN

Edward Marshall Stedman (August 16, 1875 to December 16, 1943) was a silent film actor, writer, and director. Stedman appeared in numerous silent films from 1910 to 1919, primarily westerns. He starred along side Tom Mix in:

- *His Father's Deputy*
- *The Law and the Outlaw,*
- *Cupid in the Cow Camp* (1913)
- *The Country Mouse* (1914)

Numerous directing credits include:

- *The Cattle Rustlers* (1912)
- *The Suffragette* (1913)
- *A Prince for a Day* (1917)[13]

He was married to prolific screen actress Myrtle Stedman and is the father of actor Lincoln Stedman. Marshall died on December 16, 1943 of a heart attack at his home in San Clemente, California.[14]

His final resting place (magnolia 43F) is located in the second hallway of the main mausoleum, twenty two crypts on the right, and two rows from the bottom.

BARBARA READ-TALMAN

After exiting the old mausoleum, take the hallway outdoors to the north patio area. To the right is a hallway that leads into the newer wing of the mausoleum. Interred here are the cremated remain of actress Barbara Read-Talman (December 29, 1917 to December 12, 1963). Read appeared in twenty-one motion pictures during the 1930s and 1940s. A versatile actress, Read's career highlights include roles in:

- *The Road Back* (1937)
- *Midnight Intruder* (1938)
- *Curtin Call* (1940)
- *The Shadow Returns* (1946)
- *Death Valley* (1946)
- *Key Witness* (1947)
- *Corner Creek* (1948)[15]

After completing *Corner Creek*, she left Hollywood to raise a family. Married and divorced twice, her second husband was actor William Talman, known for playing the role of Hamilton Burger, the district attorney on the hit television series *Perry Mason*. This marriage was very volatile and also ended in divorce.[16]

On the morning of December 12, 1963, at her Laguna Beach home, despondent over ill health and failed marriages, Read committed suicide by draping a blanket over her kitchen oven, turned on the gas, and stuck her head under blanket. Her body was found later that same day by her uncle, Charles McCollough. She left a long, rambling suicide note that explained her despondency and subsequent actions.[17]

❧ Barbara Read's cremated remains are interred in the Sanctuary of Devotion, niche 120. Enter the indoor mausoleum area from the north patio; the Sanctuary of Devotion is the third alcove on the left. Read's niche is in the right center section, seven from the bottom, and two from the glass case.

CAROLYN JONES

When leaving the mausoleum, take the hallway outdoors to the north patio to see where actress Carolyn Jones (April 28, 1930 to August 3, 1983) is buried. Born in Amarillo, Texas, she is best known for her quirky role as Morticia Addams in the mid-1960s television series, *The Addams Family*. She was a versatile actress who appeared in numerous stage and screen productions. Jones had a unique look and off beat style of acting.[18] Her major film credits include:

- *House of Wax* (1953)
- *Desireee* (1954)
- *The Seven Year Itch* (1955)
- *Invasion of the Body Snatchers* (1956)
- *King Creole* (1958)
- *How the West of Won* (1962)

In 1957, Jones was nominated for an Academy Award for her supporting role as the existentialist in *Bachelor Party*. Numerous television credits include roles on:

- *Batman*
- *Dragnet*
- *Ironside*
- *Wonder Woman*
- *Fantasy Island*

At the time of her death she was filming the television show Capitol.[19]

Actress Carolyn Jones' crypt, she is best known for portraying, Morticia Adams on the campy 1960's television show The Adams Family.

In 1953, she married an unknown director/ producer, Aaron Spelling, who went on to great success. This marriage did not last long.[20] Carolyn Jones died on August 3, 1983 after a long battle with cancer.[21]

❧ Her crypt is found in the North patio, niche 46GG, located on the west end of the hallway on the bottom row, eight niches from the end.

CLIFFORD CARLTON "GAVVY" CRAVATH

Interred in Carnation Lawn number 1B is professional baseball player Clifford Carlton "Gavvy" Cravath (March 23, 1881 to May 23, 1963). He was one of major league baseball's premier power hitting outfielders during the "dead ball" era. Carvath got his nickname "Gavvy" during his minor league playing days with the Pacific Coast Leagues Los Angeles Angels; allegedly he hit a ball that struck and killed a seagull while the bird was in mid-flight. The Spanish word for seagull is "gaviota" and "Gavvy" is a derivative of this term.[22] Gavvy played twelve years in the major leagues, primarily for the Philadelphia Phillies from 1908 to 1920. He is credited with holding two of baseball's pre-Babe Ruth home run records. Cravath hit a career 119 home runs and this mark was eclipsed by Ruth in 1921. During the 1915 season, Gavvy hit a record twenty-four home runs. This mark was eclipsed by Babe Ruth, who slugged twenty-nine in 1919, as a member of the Boston Red Sox.[23] Cravath lead the National League in home runs six times and runs batted in twice. His career statistics of 1220 games played, 3951 at bats, 1134 hits, 119 home runs, 719 RBIs, with a batting average of .287 made him one the "dead ball" era's best players. Gavvy appeared in the 1915 World Series versus the Boston Red Sox.[24]

He also managed 229 games for the Phillies in 1919 and 1920, winning 91 and losing 137.[25]

After retiring from baseball in 1923, he moved to Laguna Beach. He was elected Justice of the Peace and served in this capacity for thirty-seven years. As a judge, he was known for his good sportsmanship and crusty sense of humor. Judge Gavvy Cravath died on May 23, 1963 he was eighty-three.[26]

❧ His grave is located in Carnation Lawn 1B, lot 299, space one. On the north curb, find the grave of Howard and Ida McGaha; eighteen markers south is Cravath's burial plot.

ROBERT M. FELLOWS

A short walk from Carnation Lawn one is the Carnation Urn Garden. Here is found the cremated remains of acclaimed movie producer Robert M. Fellows (August 23, 1903 to May 11, 1969). Fellows was the producer of numerous films from the 1940s and 1950s, movies that starred some of Hollywood's biggest names, such as John Wayne, Errol Flynn, Glen Ford, Bing Crosby, and Ronald Reagan. Acclaimed film credits include:

- *Virginia City* (1940)
- *Knute Rockne*
- *All American* (1940)
- *Santa Fe Trail* (1940)
- *They Died with Their Boots On* (1941)
- *A Connecticut Yankee in King Arthur's Court* (1949)
- *Big Jim McLain* (1952)[27]

In 1953, he produced *Hondo* which starred John Wayne. This film was nominated for two Academy Awards, best actress (Geraldine Page) and for writing.[28] The following year, 1954, brought Fellows more accolades, when he produced *The High and the Mighty*, again starring John Wayne. This film garnered six Academy Award nominations, winning one for Best Musical Score.[29] Robert Fellows died of a heart attack on May 11, 1969 in Hollywood, California.[30]

❧ His final resting place is located within the Carnation Urn Garden, lot 160. In this small unassuming section of cremated remains, first locate the Dexter and Frances Jones marker. This unique grave marker has a depiction of "death" represented by the Grim Reaper and a sundial which represents time. Just to left is the modest grave marker of Robert M. Fellows.

JACK NORWORTH

In the center of Carnation Lawn there is the Psalm 23 memorial wall; interred nearby is singer and songwriter Jack Norworth (January 5, 1879 to

Jack Norworth, penned the lyrics to baseball's iconic anthem, "Take Me Out to the Ball Game" is interred at Melrose Abbey.

September 1, 1959). Norworth was a vaudeville performer, song writer, and film actor. He is best known as the lyricist for the unofficial anthem of professional baseball and 7th inning stretch tradition, "Take Me Out to the Ballgame" (the words were set to music by Albert Von Tilzer).[31] Norworth allegedly penned the lyrics to this song in 1908, while riding a subway train in New York City. He noticed a sign: "baseball today – Polo Grounds." The song is written from a female point of view. In it, the character Katie Casey urges her boyfriend to take her to a baseball game, instead of a show.[32] It is used traditionally during the 7th inning stretch with only the chorus being sung. Norworth ironically had never attended a baseball game before writing the lyrics. It took him thirty-two years to see his first ballgame in 1940. This song has become a part of American popular culture second only to "Happy Birthday" in recognition.[33] Sadly, Norworth never received royalties from this song; it was published prior to the copyright laws.[34]

A native of Philadelphia, he started in vaudeville at an early age, landing a job with the Ziegfeld Follies, where he met his first wife, Nora Bays.[35] Norworth and Bays worked as a team for many years on the vaudeville circuit. A prolific song writing duo their "Shine on Harvest Moon" (1908) was debuted with the Ziegfeld Follies and became a pop culture standard.[36]

Jack Norworth, a longtime resident of Laguna Beach, was a founder of the local little league of which he held the title of honorary president. Each year, he would lead the little league parade and, in the spirit of his iconic song, throw cracker jacks to the youngsters.[37] In 1970, he was elected to the Songwriters Hall of Fame.[38]

Norworth was also an actor, who appeared along side his second wife, Dorothy Norworth, in the *Nagger* film series (1931-1932). He also appeared in other short films such as:

- *Queen of the Night Clubs* (1929)
- *Song and Things; Odds and Ends* (1930)
- *Shine on Harvest Moon* (1942)
- *The Southerner* (1943)[39]

At the age of seventy-nine, Norworth suffered a stroke in a Los Angeles area hospital while under going treatment for a liver ailment. On September 1, 1959, only hours after returning home from Los Angeles, he suffered a fatal heart attack.[40]

He is buried under a very faded marker next to his third wife, Amy, in Carnation Lawn 3E. Locate the Palm 23 wall in the center of the lawn; four grave markers to the south is Norworth's plot.

ROBERT Y. DUDLEY

Towards the back the cemetery is the Paradise Garden Lawns. Here is the burial plot of actor Robert Y. Dudley (September 13, 1869 to November 12, 1955). A character actor, Dudley appeared in numerous films from the silent era to the 1950s. Primarily, appearing in "B" movies, notable film credits include:

- *Seven Keys of Baldpate* (1917)
- *The Traveling Salesman* (1921)
- *Chicago* (1927)
- *Reunion* (1932)
- *The Toast of New York* (1937)
- *The House of the Seven Gables* (1940)
- *The Son of Dracula* (1943)
- *Lady on a Train* (1945)
- *As Young as You Feel* (1951)

In Orson Wells' Academy Award winning film, *Citizen Kane* (1941), Dudley played an uncredited role as a photographer. He was the founder of the "Troupers Club of Hollywood," an organization founded by actors for actors. Robert Dudley died November 12, 1955 in San Clemente, California.[41]

He is buried in the Paradise Garden, section 9, lot 409, space 1. His grave is found near the Armed Forces Memorial, next to a tree, four rows north (towards the abbey), and seven grave markers south of the memorial.

CLAUDE PRESTON "LEFTY" WILLIAMS

Interred in an unmarked grave is Claude Preston "Lefty" Williams (March 9, 1893 to November 4, 1959) a professional baseball player. Williams is best known for his involvement in the World Series fix of 1919, known infamously as the "Black Sox" scandal. A left-handed pitcher, "Lefty" played seven years, breaking into professional baseball with the Detroit Tigers in 1913, and playing for the Chicago White Sox 1916 – 1920. He pitched in 189 games, compiling a record of 82 wins and 48 loses, with an earned run average of 3.13.[42] A roommate of the legendary hitting star "Shoeless" Joe Jackson, Williams was just coming into his own as a pitcher with two consecutive 20 plus win seasons in 1919 and 1920. Williams, along with seven other White Sox players, were implicated and later banned for life for fixing the 1919 World Series.[43]

To his dying day Williams denied involvement in the scandal, but evidence and logic point in another direction. His uncharacteristically poor performance during the World Series helped sink the Sox, allowing the Cincinnati Reds to take the championship. His incongruous series record of zero wins against three defeats with an earned run average of 6.61 was suspiciously weak having been a steady force going 23 – 11 with forty starts (leading the American league) during the regular season.[44] He was promised $10,000 to help throw the series but only received $5,000, which was twice his annual salary.[45] Allegedly, he planned to turn against the fix in his last start due to a double cross by the gamblers. The night before game eight, William's wife's life was threatened and he had no choice but to go through with the fix. In game eight of the 1919 World Series, Lefty Williams lasted less than one inning, throwing fifteen pitches, with five hits, three earned runs, while recording only one out. The White Sox were finished, and the Reds were crowned World Champions.[46]

In 1921, a Grand Jury was convened to investigate whether the "1919 Series" had been fixed. Eight White Sox players—Joe Jackson, Buck Weaver, Eddie Cicotte, Chick Gandil, Happy Felsh, Swede Risberg, Fred McMullin, and Lefty Williams were indicted on five counts of fraud and conspiracy. During the Grand Jury investigation, several players including Williams, testified and later confessed to the fix. At the trial, the transcripts of these confessions mysteriously disappeared and the players recanted their story. This lost evidence, along with shoddy prosecution, brought a verdict of not guilty on all charges. Even though the eight had been found not guilty in a court of law, Major League baseball's newly appointed commissioner, Judge Kenesaw Mountain Landis, permanently disqualified all the players from baseball.[47]

Lefty's life after baseball was filled with many unknowns. What is clear is that he and his wife, Lyria, lived a quiet unassuming life. They lived in Chicago for an indeterminate number of years after the scandal.[48] Later, the Williams moved to Northridge, California, and again, in 1954, to South Laguna Beach. In Laguna, he managed a local garden nursery.[49]

Williams died on November 4, 1959 from pneumonia complicated by Hodgkin's Disease.[50] To his dying day, he denied involvement in the conspiracy and scandal that almost destroyed baseball.

❧ His family wished privacy; his remains were cremated and buried according to Christian Science tradition in an unmarked grave. A search of cemetery records showed that Williams' burial location has been permanently expunged.

SAMUEL JERNIGAN

Also interred at Melrose Abbey is Samuel Jernigan (November 3, 1876 to October 25, 1966). He was Sheriff of Orange County and a prominent participant in the "Battle of Tomato Springs." His story will be told later in the Chapter Eight, "Murder and Mayhem."

WESTMINSTER MEMORIAL PARK

14801 Beach Boulevard
Westminster, California 92683
Telephone: 714-893-2421

Hours of operations are 7 a.m. to 7 p.m. Spring and Summer;
7 a.m. to 5 p.m. Fall and Winter months.

This cemetery, originally named the Central Cemetery of Westminster, was established in 1924. It is set on 150 acres of sprawling grass lawns, with waterfalls, and a small lake. With a map of the grounds, traversing the cemetery is easy, but be aware that the streets and lawns are not well marked. Many of the curb markings are in need of repainting. The main boulevard into the cemetery is named Westminster Avenue of Flags or just Westminster Drive. Every lawn has a unique name and block number; individual graves have a lot and a grave number. These lawns all have lot locator plugs. All the famous graves within the cemetery are located within the grass lawns, none are found in the mausoleums.

As a point of reference, the cemetery is bordered by Beach Boulevard on the west, Bolsa Avenue on the south, and Miller Avenue on the north.

HARRY BUFFUM

The first famous interment of the Oaks lawn area is department store magnate, Harry Buffum (April 11, 1895 to April 6, 1968). Buffum was the president and chairman of the board of the Buffum's department store chain. He was the son and nephew of Charles A. and Edwin E. Buffum, co-founders of the stores.

Founded in 1904, in Long Beach California, Buffum's grew into a sixteen store operation by the early 1990s. Harry began his association with the store at the age of nine as a sweep-out boy in the Long Beach store. He quickly rose through the ranks of the company, and was named president in 1934, and chairman in 1961. He was the brother of Dorothy Buffum Chandler, wife of Norman Chandler, publisher of the *Los Angeles Times*. The Dorothy Chandler Pavilion in Los Angeles is named in her honor.

Harry Buffum died on April 6, 1968 after a long illness. He was originally to have been buried at Sunnyside Memorial Park in Long Beach but was instead interred at Westminster.

His grave is located in the Oaks lawn, block 34, lot 251B, space 4. The grave is found just inside the park after passing the information booth. From the south curb, locate the grave of Robert and Irma McNatt; twenty-eight graves north is Buffum's final resting place.

᪥᪥᪥᪥᪥᪥᪥᪥᪥

As a post script to the Buffum story, shortly after Harry's death, the department store chain was sold to an Australian company, the Adelaide Steamship Company. The new owners struggled for twenty years to keep the stores open. In 1991, unable to find a buyer, the Buffum's department store chain, a southern California tradition, closed its doors and was liquidated.[51]

GEORGE W. PAYNE

Interred nearby is professional baseball player George W. Payne (May 23, 1889 to January 24, 1959). In 1920, at the age of thirty, Payne, a relief pitcher, made his major league debut with the Chicago White Sox. He appeared in twelve games, with a record of one win and one loss, with an earned run average of 5.46. After the conclusion of the 1920 season, Payne was released by the White Sox and never again played professional baseball. He died in Bellflower, California on January 24, 1959.

He is interred in the Oaks lawn, block 34, lot 192, space 1. Find the grave of Henry J. Harris (five rows east of Robert and Irma McNatt) on the south curb; thirty-four grave markers north is Payne's burial location.[52]

REX R. CECIL

Moving on the Gospels lawn area, turn left onto Schiller Drive, and then right onto Riley drive; buried here is another professional baseball player, Rex R. Cecil (October 8, 1916 to October 30, 1966). Cecil was a right-handed starting pitcher for the Boston Red Sox in 1944 and 1945. He appeared in 18 games, had a record of 6 wins and 10 losses, with 5 career complete games in 106 innings of work, with an earned run average of 5.18.[53]

Cecil's grave is located in the Gospel's lawn, block 36, lot 423, space 1. Find the grave marker of Clarence M. Clark on the south curb; seventeen grave markers north is Cecil's burial plot.

PHILIP RYAN SLATTERY

Another professional baseball player is buried nearby in the Garden of Heavenly Peace: Philip Ryan Slattery (February 25, 1893 to March 2, 1968). Slattery, a left-handed relief pitcher, played one season for the Pittsburgh Pirates in 1915. He joined the Pirates late in the season, and appeared in three games.[54]

He is buried in the Garden of Heavenly Peace, block 22B, lot 63, space 1. This area is found along the south wall of the cemetery. The divide between the Trees lawn and the Garden of Heavenly Peace lawn areas were at one point divided by a road, but this is no longer the case. The line between the two lawn areas is continuous, and blends together. Slattery's grave is found along the fence line of in section "B" and is unmarked.

LILY GRAY

A short walk due north is the Trees lawn area, buried within section "A" is Lily Gray (January 11, 1920 to May 31, 1972). Gray was one of the victims in the landmark Ford Pinto rear-end gas tank explosion case. On May 31, 1972, Lily Gray of Orange was driving her Ford Pinto to Barstow. On interstate 15 just outside of the city of San Bernardino, Gray's car stalled in the middle lane of the highway. Her car was rear-ended and burst into flames. Gray and her passenger, thirteen-year-old Richard Grimshaw, were burned over ninety percent of their bodies. Both victims were transported to Loma Linda University Hospital. Gray died later that day from complications of the burns and heart failure. Grimshaw survived the accident but was badly hurt.

The families of Lily Gray and Richard Grimshaw both filed suit against the Ford Motor Company for wrongful death and personal injury. In the subsequent trial, the plaintiffs argued that Ford knew the gas tanks on the Pinto were defective, and that the victims of the accident would have walked away from the crash without serious injury, if only the gas tank had not exploded. In February of 1978, the jury in the case found that Ford was liable, and had intentionally fitted the Pinto with defective gas tanks to save expenses. The family of Lily Gray was awarded $659,680 in compensatory damages, and $6,600 in medical costs. Richard Grimshaw was awarded $2,841,680 in compensatory damages and $125 million in punitive damages. At the time of this judgment, this case was the largest ever returned in such a lawsuit.

Ford produced the Pinto from 1971 to 1980. Early models of the car were prone to leaking fuel after low speed rear-impact collisions. After many lawsuits and public outcry, Ford implemented new improved safety measures on the Pinto but the public's perception of the car never improved, and in 1981, Ford stopped production. In spite of this bad press, there were over three million Pintos sold during its nine year run of production.[55]

🐾 Lily Gray is buried in the Trees lawn section, block 46A, lot 487, space 1. From the north curb, locate the grave of Eva Estella Carver. This is near the divide between section "A" and "B." Gray's final resting place is eleven rows south.

STAFFORD REPP

Next, we move on to the lawn of Remembrance, and the graves of two noteworthy people. First is veteran character actor, Stafford Repp (April 26, 1918 to November 5, 1974). Repp was a prolific character actor who primarily appeared in television from the mid-1950s until the mid-1970s. He best known for playing the role of Chief O'Hara on the 1960's hit television show *Batman*.

Repp began his show business career in radio, and appeared in several movies, but he made his biggest impact in television. He appeared in over 600 television episodes in various programs. His major television credits include:

- *Perry Mason*
- *The New Phil Silvers Show*
- *Dennis the Menace*
- *The Twilight Zone*
- *The Lucy Show*
- *My favorite Martian*
- *Gunsmoke*
- *M.A.S.H.*

Repp died on November 11, 1974 in Inglewood, California at fifty-six.[56] He is buried in the Remembrance lawn, block 56C, lot 279, space 1. Locate the grave marker of June L. Ellis on the east curb; ten rows west is the veteran actor's burial plot.

ROBERT H. "BOBBY" STURGEON

Another noteworthy person interred within the lawn of Remembrance is professional baseball player Robert H. "Bobby" Sturgeon (August 6, 1919 to March 10, 2007). Sturgeon, a utility infielder, played six seasons in the major leagues from 1940 until 1948 for the Chicago Cubs and Boston Braves. In 1941, he won the starting short stop position with the Cubs, but had a severe leg injury in 1942, and a three-year military stint during World War II, which both shortened his promising playing career.

Upon his return from the war, he found himself as primarily a back-up player with limited playing opportunities. He was traded to the Boston Braves from the Cubs on March 1, 1948, for light hitting infielder Dick Culler. Sturgeon played thirty-four games for the National League pennant winning Boston Braves; he filled in on occasion at second base for Hall of Famer Eddie Stanky but was not part of the post season roster. His career statistics are 420 games played, 1,220 at bats, 313 hits, 80 runs batted in, with an batting average of .257.[57] Sturgeon died on March 10, 2007, in San Dimas, California.

He is buried in the lawn of Remembrance, block 56C, lot 144, space 4. Find the grave marker of Kathryn Claar on the east curb; fifteen rows west is the final resting place of Sturgeon. The Meditation lawn area is the largest section of the cemetery. It is broken up into six areas with a small lake area in the middle. This section of the cemetery holds the highest concentration of noteworthy burials. The famous burial is within walking distance of the Sturgeon's grave in section "A" of the Meditation lawn.

LOYAL GRIGGS

Interred in the south west section is Academy Award winning cinematographer Loyal Griggs (August 15, 1906 to May 6, 1978). Griggs began his career in show business in the silent film era as a cameraman and moved steadily up the ranks to director of photography. He was nominated for three Academy Awards:

- ⊷ *The Ten Commandments* (1956)
- ⊷ *The Greatest Story Ever Told* (1965)
- ⊷ *In Harm's Way* (1965)

He won the Academy Award for best cinematography in 1954 for *Shane*. Other major film credits include:

- ⊷ *White Christmas* (1954)
- ⊷ *The Bridges at Toko-Ri* (1954)
- ⊷ *We're No Angels* (1955)
- ⊷ *The Buccaneer* (1958)
- ⊷ *G.I. Blues* (1960)
- ⊷ *Man-Trap* (1961)
- ⊷ *Girls! Girls! Girls!* (1962)
- ⊷ *The Night of the Grizzly* (1966)

❀ Griggs died on May 6, 1978 in Laguna Beach, California at seventy-two.[58] He is buried in the Meditation lawn, block 19A, section 49, space 4. Locate the grave of Avis Kritzer near the south west curb; four rows east is the burial spot of the award winning cinematographer.

JERRY AVRITT

Follow Lakeside Drive around to section "F" of the Mediation lawn on the east side of the cemetery. Interred here is Jerry Avritt (July 30, 1942 to December 21, 1988). Avritt was the flight engineer on Pan Am flight 103, which exploded and crashed in Lockerbie, Scotland, on December 21, 1988. His story, along with other Orange County victims of the crash will be told in Chapter Eight, "Murder and Mayhem."

❀ His grave is located in Meditation lawn, block 19F, lot 424, space 4.

MASS GRAVESITE

Ironically, buried a short distance away from Jerry Avritt is the mass gravesite of over 100 victims of the twentieth century's worst airline crash. On March 27, 1977, on the tiny island of Tenerife (one of the Canary Islands), 583 people were killed in the collision of two Boeing 747 Jumbo Jets.

Due to a tragic chain of events on the day of the crash, KLM Royal Dutch Airlines flight 4805 and Pan Am flight 1736 found themselves at Los Rodeos Airport in Tenerife. Early in the afternoon of the day of the crash, a terrorist

Canary Islands crash victims memorial at Westminster Memorial Park.

bomb exploded in the terminal of Las Palmas International Airport. Both KLM 4805 and Pan Am 1736, along with other planes, were diverted to the smaller Los Rodeos Airport. This airport was not familiar with large amounts of traffic and confusion developed. The runways and taxiways of the airport were jammed with aircraft, the control tower was overwhelmed, and aircraft crews became anxious. After hours of delay, both KLM 4805 and Pan Am 1736 were cleared to taxi. In preparation for take off, KLM was leading the way on runway 30. To complicate matters, the weather on the tiny island had begun to deteriorate and visibility was minimal. Confusing instructions from the control tower allowed both aircraft to be on the same runway at the same time. KLM flight 4805 took off unaware that Pan Am Flight 1736 was still on the same runway. The flight crew of the Pan Am flight only became aware of the KLM flight when the lights of the approaching aircraft became visible. At this point, Captain Grubb of Pan Am 1736 tried to take evasive action and turned his aircraft sharply to the left, and the crew of KLM also attempted evasive by pulling back on the throttle in a futile attempt at clearing the runway. Only the nose of the KLM jet cleared the runway, the undercarriage of the jet slammed into Pan Am 1736 ripping through the center section of the plane. KLM then lost control, slammed into the ground, and burst into flames, 500 feet past the initial point of collision. All 248 passengers and crew aboard KLM 4805 were killed, and only 61 passengers and crew on board Pan Am 1736 survived out of 396. Total fatalities for the crash were 583. This was the single worst airline disaster of the twentieth century, and the shear number of deaths was only surpassed by the terrorist attacks of September 11, 2001.[59]

The majority of passengers on both flights had been headed for a Mediterranean cruise when the crash occurred; many on board Pan Am 1736 were from Leisure World in Laguna Hills, California. One hundred and fourteen individually unidentified and three identified bodies were flown to Orange County for burial at Westminster Memorial Park (the cemetery had donated the grave plots). The caskets containing the remains of the victims were flown to the El Toro Marine Corp Air Station, and then transported by a fleet of hearses to the cemetery.[60]

A graveside memorial service was conducted by Catholic, Protestant, and Jewish clergy, all 117 victims were buried in identical burial vaults with a metallic tag number (in case of later identification) in a 10,000 square foot plot.

❧ Their mass grave is topped with a large bronze memorial plaque that bears the names of each victim.[61] The burial plot of the victims of the Canary Islands air tragedy is found in the Meditation lawn, block 19F. It is located a short distance northwest of the grave of Jerry Avritt.

CHARLES DWIGHT "RED" DORMAN

Driving around the west side of the Meditation lawn is the final resting place of two noteworthy people. First, is professional baseball player, Charles Dwight "Red" Dorman (October 3, 1905 to December 7, 1974). He was a right-hand hitting outfielder who played for the Cleveland Indians in 1923 and 1928. He appeared in 26 games, had 79 at bats, 29 hits with a career batting average of .367.[62]

❧ His grave is found in the Meditation lawn, block 19C, lot 49, space 1. At the intersection of Carlyle, Burns, and Whitman Drives find the grave of Joseph Crossley on the west curb; three rows east is Dormans burial plot.

NEAL LESLIE FREDRICKS

Interred nearby is cinematographer Neal Leslie Fredricks (July 24, 1969 to August 14, 2004). Fredricks, a native of Newport Beach, California, is best known as the director of photography on the ground-breaking horror film, *The Blair Witch Project* (1999). Other major film credits include sequels to The Blair Witch Project:

⤐ *The Burkittsville 7* (2000)

⤐ *Shadow of the Blair Witch* (2000)

⤐ *Killer Me* (2001)

⤐ *Out of Sync* (2002)

⤐ *The Legend of Diablo* (2004)

⤐ *The Stone Cutter* (2007)

He was married to writer/director Ann Lu in 1999, but the couple divorced in June of 2003. Fredricks died on August 14, 2004, off the coast of the Florida Keys, while filming the movie *Cross Bones*. The small plane in which he was filming developed engine trouble, crashing into the ocean, and all aboard the plane except Fredricks (who was strapped in with his camera) were able to escape the plane before it sank.[63]

❧ His grave is found in the Meditation lawn, block 19C, lot 250, space 4. Thirteen rows east of Red Dorman, locate the grave of Oliver and Norma Stepp; three marker north is Fredricks final resting place. His grave marker is very hard to read, and his epitaph is simply "Movie Maker."

CHARLES FORREST CURRY, JR.

Just across the street and northwest of the lawn of Meditation is the flag-shaped Armed Forces lawn area, which is bordered by Carlyle, Arnold, and Whitman Drives. Buried here is U.S. Congressman Charles Forrest Curry, Jr. (August 13, 1893 to October 7, 1972). Curry, a Republican, was a member of the U.S. House of Representatives from California's 3rd congressional district from March 4, 1931 to March 3, 1933. He succeeded his father Charles F. Curry, Sr. (who had died on October 10, 1930), as the representative of California's 3rd district. In the November 1931 election, Charles Curry, Jr. handily defeated his three opponents in a write-in campaign for the vacant congressional seat.[64]

He only served one uneventful term in the House of Representatives. In 1932, The Great Depression was in full swing, and Republican approval ratings were at a low point. The General Election of 1932 ushered in a wave of Democrat candidates to elected office, including Franklin D. Roosevelt to the presidency. Curry was conveniently defeated by his Democratic rival, Frank H. Buck.

After his defeat, Curry settled into a quiet life in Southern California, engaging in the practice of law, and other businesses. He died on October 7, 1972 in Long Beach, California at age seventy-nine.

&&& Congressman Curry is buried in the Armed Forces lawn, block 17, lot 36, space 4. Locate the grave marker of Minnie L. Lonaker on the east curb; sixteen rows west is Curry's burial plot.

KENNETH L. WORLEY

Southwest of the Armed Forces lawn is the Four Seasons lawn area. Interred on the west side of the section are three persons of note. First, is Medal of Honor recipient, Kenneth L. Worley (April 4, 1948 to August 12, 1968). Marine Corp Lance Corporal Kenneth Worley was posthumously awarded the Congressional Medal of Honor by President Richard Nixon in 1970. His Medal of Honor Citation reads;

> *"For conspicuous gallantry and intrepidity at the risk of his life above and beyond the call of duty while serving as a Machine Gunner with Company L, Third Battalion, Seventh Marines, First Marine Division in action against enemy forces in the Republic of Vietnam. After establishing a night ambush position in a house in the Bo Ban Hamlet of Quang Nam Province, security was set up and the remainder of the patrol members retired until their respective watch. During the early morning hours of 12 August 1968, the Marines were abruptly awakened by the platoon leader's warning that "Grenades" had landed in the house. Fully realizing the inevitable result of his actions, Lance Corporal Worley, in a valiant act of heroism, instantly threw himself upon the grenade nearest him and his comrades, absorbing with his own body, the full and tremendous force of the explosion. Through his extraordinary initiative and inspiring valor in the face of almost certain death, he saved his comrades from serious injury and possible loss of life although five of his fellow Marines incurred minor wounds as the other grenades exploded. Lance Corporal Worley's gallant actions upheld the highest traditions of the Marine Corps and the United States navy. He gallantly gave his life for his country.*
>
> *Richard Nixon."*[65]

Vietnam War hero and Medal of Honor recipient Kenneth Worley's grave.

Although Orange County has been home to numerous Medal of Honor recipients, Kenneth Worley is the only award winner to be interred within the county. He is buried in the Four Seasons lawn, block 29, lot 784, space 4. From the west curb, across the street from the Last Supper Mausoleum, find the grave marker of Michael W. Pinder; ten rows east is the Vietnam War hero's unassuming final resting place.

DANIEL J. "DANNY" LOCKIN

A short distance from the grave of Kenneth Worley, in the southwest corner of the lawn section, is actor Daniel J. "Danny" Lockin (July 13, 1943 to August 21, 1977). Lockin was an actor and dancer who appeared on Broadway and in several film musicals in the 1960s. His Broadway credits include:

- *West Side Story*
- *The Sound of Music*
- *The Music Man*
- *Take Me Away*
- *Hello, Dolly*

It was in *Hello, Dolly* when he caught the eye of actor Gene Kelly, who cast Lockin in the role of Barnaby in the 1967 film version of the musical. Following the filming of this movie, he headed back to Broadway to reprise the same role with Ethel Merman in the lead. Other film credits include an appearance in the film musical *Gypsy* (1962).[66]

On August 21, 1977, Lockin was found stabbed to death in the apartment of Charles Hopkins in Anaheim, California. Hopkins originally told police investigators that he believed Lockin was an intruder and that he was just protecting himself.[67] This proved to be a lie, due to the amount of stab wounds Lockin had received (over 100), and the fact that witnesses stated they saw the two men at a Garden Grove bar frequented by homosexuals the night of the slaying. His story again changed when Hopkins stated that he awoke that evening to find Lockin's body in his apartment, but did not know how it got there.

During the initial investigation, police had found a book of pornographic images that detailed scripts of murder by torture. This evidence was later ruled inadmissible because police had failed to obtain a search warrant before procuring the evidence. Because of these developments, the prosecution was unable to secure a first degree murder conviction; instead they settled on voluntary manslaughter. Charles Hopkins was sentenced to only four years in state prison.[68]

❧ Daniel Lockin's grave is located in the Four Season's lawn, block 29, lot 219, space 4, on the southwest curb.

JESSE BARNES

Buried not far from Danny Lockin is professional baseball player Jesse Barnes (August 26, 1892 to September 9, 1961). Barnes was a hard throwing right-hand pitcher who played thirteen seasons for the Boston Braves, New York Giants, and Brooklyn Dodgers from 1915 to 1927. He was a main stay of John McGraw's New York Giants pitching staff during the early 1920s. Barnes was a member of the 1921 and 1922 New York Giants World Championship teams. In 1921, he won two World Series games. He was on the mound in the tenth inning of game two of the 1922 World Series, when umpire George Hildebrand controversially called the game because of darkness. On May 7, 1922, Barnes threw a no hitter against the Philadelphia Phillies, winning the game 6-0. His career statistics of 422 games played, 2569.2 innings pitched, 153 wins against 149 losses, 180 complete games, with a career earned run average of 3.22, rank him near the top of all-time pitchers. He is also the only National League pitcher to walk twice in one inning; this was accomplished on October 2, 1917. His brother, Virgil Barnes, also played professional baseball for the New York Giants and Boston Braves from 1919 to 1928.[69] Jesse Barnes died on September 9, 1961 in Santa Rosa, New Mexico of a heart attack, while on a road trip with his family.[70]

❧ His grave is located in the Four Season's lawn, block 29, lot 224, space 1. From Daniel Lockin's grave, walk one row north, and five graves east.

BRADLEY JAMES NOWELL

Buried in the Ivy lawn area is rock singer Bradley James Nowell (February 22, 1968 to May 25, 1996). Nowell was the lead singer and a founding member of the alternative rock band Sublime. The ska-punk-reggae trio was founded in Long Beach, California, in 1988. Nowell was on vocals and lead guitar, with Eric Wilson on bass guitar, and Bud Gaugh on drums. The band released four albums:

⇛ *Jah Won't Pay the Bills* (1991)

⇛ *40 Oz. to Freedom* (1992)

⇛ *Robbin' the Hood* (1994)

⇛ *Sublime* (1996)

The album *40 Oz. to Freedom*, and the hit single "Date Rape," appeared at number one on the Billboard Music Charts for five weeks in 1995. Nowell had a soulful voice, which had great emotion. He reminded people of other great reggae singers like Bob Marley and Jimmy Cliff.

Nowell struggled for many years with his inner demons. He battled addiction to a wide variety of drugs, especially heroin. In the early morning hours of May 25, 1996, while on tour with the band in San Francisco, Nowell was found dead from an overdose of heroin in an area motel room.[71]

His final resting place is hard to miss and is found in the Ivy lawn, block 31, section 114, space 4. The grave can be found along the west side of Shakespeare Lane, in the center of the section, two rows from the curb. Nowell's grave is often adorned with notes and flowers from fans. The nearby curbs and trees are littered with graffiti, and are etched with tributes to their fallen rock hero. The simple epitaph of his marker reads: "Now at Peace."

Bradley Nowell was the lead singer of the 1990's alternative rock band Sublime, who tragically overdosed on heroin.

George F. Blaeholder

The final noteworthy burial at the cemetery is professional baseball player George F. Blaeholder (January 26, 1904 to December 29, 1947). Blaeholder a right-handed starting pitcher who played eleven seasons mostly for the St. Louis Browns, Philadelphia Athletics, and Cleveland Indians, from 1925 to 1936. He was credited by Hall of Fame pitcher Bob Feller with originating the slider, but more than likely, he was the first to popularize the pitch. (The slider is a pitch that is a cross between a fastball and a curveball. It breaks down with more speed than a curveball and less than a fastball.)

Blaeholder's career statistics are 338 games played, 1,914.1 innings pitched, 104 wins and 125 losses, 106 complete games, with an earned run average of 4.54. He died on December 29, 1947 in Garden Grove; California.[72]

He is buried in the Oaks lawn section 34, block AA, lot 49. This section is along the western border of the cemetery, nearest Beach Boulevard. Find the grave marker of Maria F. Vega on the east curb, and two rows west is Blaeholder's final resting place.

LOMA VISTA MEMORIAL PARK

This cemetery was established in 1914 by Argus Brutus Adams. The original thirty-seven acres of land was purchased from the Bastanchury family for $15,000 In 1934, the mausoleum was crafted from imported Italian marble. It also has beautiful stained-glass windows, hand-painted murals, and a small chapel area. This cemetery has the distinction of holding the oldest Memorial Day celebrations in Orange County, started in 1938.

The grounds of the cemetery are not easy to maneuver; the lawn areas and roads are not well marked and many of the lot plugs are missing or covered over. As a main point of reference, the mausoleum is found in the center of the grounds, and the oldest part of the cemetery is located in the northeast section. Buried within the grounds are numerous local pioneers and military veterans from the Civil War to the present day. Although, Loma Vista is not brimming with famous graves, there are still a handful of noteworthy people to discuss.

SAMUEL LAFORT COLLINS

The first famous grave within the cemetery is Congressman Samuel Lafort Collins (August 6, 1895 to June 26, 1965). Collins was a Republican politician from Orange County. He was the Orange County District Attorney from 1928 to 1932, and served in the U.S. House of Representatives, representing the 19th District of California from 1932 to 1936. He lost a re-election bid in 1936 to Democrat Samuel R. Sheppard. Returning to California state politics, Collins was elected to the state assembly in 1940, representing Orange County's 75th District, a seat that was previously held by Thomas Kuchel (see Anaheim Cemetery). During his tenure in the assembly, Collins was elected Speaker of the Assembly (1947 to 1952). In 1952, he ran unsuccessfully for the California State Senate, after which he retired to the private practice of law in Fullerton. Collins died on June 26, 1965, from a heart failure at age sixty-nine.[73]

He is buried in the West Lawn 4 area, lot 815, space 6. On the west side of the lawn, near the bend in the road between West Road and West Drive, find the small grave marker of Brent Pearce Crossley, and three rows east is the Congressman's final resting place.

ANDY RUSSELL

Following West Drive to the north side of the cemetery, and the West lawn number one area, interred here is singer and actor Andy Russell (September 16, 1919 to April 16, 1992). Born Andres Rabago in East Los Angeles, California, Russell was a bilingual crooner, who was a contemporary of Frank Sinatra in the 1940s. Throughout the decade, he had chart topping hits such as:

- "What a Difference a Day Makes" (1944)
- "Amor" (1944)
- "I Dream of You" (1944)

+─♦ "Laughing on the Outside" (1946)

+─♦ "Anniversary Song" (1947)

+─♦ "Underneath the Arches" (1948)

Russell replaced Sinatra on the popular radio show, *Your Hit Parade*, in 1947. Despite his successes in the United States, Russell chose to launch his film career south of the border in Mexico and Argentina. There he appeared in numerous film and television shows, which included *The Andy Russell Show* in Argentina from 1956 to 1965. In the late 1960s, he returned to the United States, and made a comeback as a headliner at the Sahara Hotel in Las Vegas, but this was not very successful. Russell retired to Sun City, Arizona, and on April 16, 1992, died from complications of a stroke.[74]

❦ His final resting place is located in the West Lawn 1 area, lot 24, space 5, in the northwest side of the section, and is on the curb.

AL CAMPANIS

After viewing Russell's grave, drive to the mausoleum; interred within the complex is legendary baseball executive Al Campanis (November 2, 1916 to June 21, 1998). Campanis spent forty-four years in the Brooklyn and Los Angeles Dodgers organization, as a player, scout, and executive. As a player, he appeared in seven games for the 1943 Brooklyn Dodgers. In 1947, he was assigned to the Dodgers minor league team in Montreal, to help groom Jackie Robinson for his major league debut. As a scout, he discovered future hall of famers Sandy Koufax, and Roberto Clemente. As a general manager, he moved both Bill Russell and Davey Lopes to the infield from the outfield. They joined Steve Garvey, and Ron Cey, in a group that played together for eleven years, winning the 1981 World Series. Campanis was also a close friend of Tommy Lasorda and helped the future hall of fame manager rise in the ranks of the organization. He championed the development of scouting in the Dominican Republic in the 1960s and 1970s.

But he is best known for racially insensitive comments he made on *Nightline* in 1987. In an interview, Campanis was asked by host Ted Koppel, why he thought there were no black managers in the major leagues, and if there was still prejudice in the game? Campanis answered, "You have to pay your dues, you generally have to go to the minors, and the pay is low; it's just that they may not have some of the necessities to be a field manager or general manager, I don't know, how many quarterbacks are there, how many pitchers, why aren't blacks good swimmers, they don't have buoyancy." In the aftermath of the comments, Campanis issued an apology for his remarks but this was not enough to save his job. Mounting pressure from civic leaders and civil rights groups left Dodger owner Peter O'Malley with no choice but to fire Campanis. In the aftermath of the incident, Major League Baseball reexamined its minority hiring practices, which led to improvements.

Campanis lived the remainder of his life in quiet seclusion, never having been formally recognized by the team or the sport for his career accomplishments. He died on June 21, 1998 in Fullerton, California, of coronary artery disease at age eighty-one.[75]

❧ He is buried in the main mausoleum, alcove 7, crypt 520. After entering the doors on the west side of the mausoleum, walk straight through the chapel area; the first hallway on the left, after the chapel is alcove 7. On the left wall, two rows from the top, and two from the left is Campanis' final resting place.

CECIL SCOTT "C.S." FORESTER

After leaving the mausoleum, proceed directly across the street to the small Coronita lawn section. This is the area with the flag pole and Civil War memorial in the center. Interred here are three noteworthy people.

First, is famed novelist Cecil Scott "C.S." Forester (August 27, 1899 to April 2, 1966). He was a prolific English writer who penned numerous books, novels, and short stories. Forester had early success as an author with his first novel, *Payment Deferred* (1926) at the age of twenty-six. He is best known for his Horatio Hornblower series of sea adventure books that started with *Beat to Quarters* (1937). He wrote many notable books, such as:

+→❧ *The African Queen* (1936) made into an Academy Award winning movie starring Humphrey Bogart and Katharine Hepburn in 1951

+→❧ *The General* (1936)

+→❧ *The Gun* (1933)

+→❧ *The Ship* (1943)

+→❧ *Hunting the Bismark* (1959) made into the movie *Sink the Bismark* (1960)

Famed author of the Horatio Hornblower series of books, C.S Forester's final resting place at Loma Vista Memorial Park, Fullerton.

After World War II, he settled in Berkeley, California, but in 1964, suffered a series of strokes that left him partially paralyzed. He moved to Fullerton, California, shortly after his condition worsened to be closer to his two sons. Forester died on April 2, 1966 in Fullerton, California, after suffering a heart attack. Prior to the stroke in 1964, Forester had been working on the final Hornblower adventure novel, *Hornblower and the Crisis*, but the stroke left him unable to write and the book was left unfinished. After his death, the final chapters of the book were pieced together using notes that he had left behind, and the novel was posthumously published in 1967.[76]

Forester is buried in the Cornoita Lawn, lot 22, space 12. It is found on the south side of the lawn, six rows from the east curb, under the shade of a large oak tree.

WALTER AND CORDELIA KNOTT

On the opposite side of the lawn is interred amusement park pioneers Walter and Cordelia Knott (December 11, 1887 to December 3, 1981), (January 23, 1890 to April 12, 1974). The Knotts turned a small berry stand in Buena Park, California, into a multi-million dollar amusement park. In 1920, the Knotts purchased a twenty acres farm, and sold berries along side the road for five cents a basket. The farm and the fortunes of the Knotts changed in the early 1930s, when they met Rudolph Boysen (see Melrose Abbey). Boysen had developed a new hybrid berry, the boysen berry. It was a cross between a blackberry, red raspberry, and logan berry. Walter began to cultivate the berry at his farm, and it became wildly popular at the road side stand. People came from all over the region to buy the new berry. The crowds were so large that Cordelia opened a small fried chicken restaurant next to the stand to feed the masses. With the crowds continuing to expand, Walter built a replica ghost town adjacent to the restaurant to entertain people while they waited for their dinners.

For the next few decades, the Knott's restaurant and ghost town complex attracted thousands of tourists. Only Disneyland Park, a few miles south, in Anaheim, drew bigger crowds.

In 1968, the Knotts fenced off the farm area, and began to charge admission. This was the beginning of the modern Knott's Berry Farm Amusement Park. Over the next few decades, the park expanded, adding new rides and exhibits. Walter was active in the administration of the amusement park complex until the death of Cordelia on April 12, 1974. After her death, Walter lost interest, and turned over management of the park to his children. For the next seven years, Walter took an interest in local political issues, and lived in a small mobile home located behind the Knott's restaurant. He died on December 3, 1981 at age ninety-one from complications of Parkinson's disease.[77] The Knott family no longer owns the amusement park or the Knott's Berry Farm brand of jams and jellies but their legacy is still felt. The amusement park that Walter and Cordelia started from a small berry stand still attracts millions of visitors each year, and the Knott's Berry brand of food products is a staple of grocery stores all over the world.

Theme park pioneers, Walter and Cordelia Knott's burial plot.

✿ The Knotts are buried side by side in the Cornoita lawn, lot 15, spaces 21, and 22. Their graves are found on the north side of the lawn, several rows from the east curb, and four graves north of the heart-shaped sidewalk in the center of the lawn.

MICHAEL EDWARD SIMON

From the Cornoita lawn, take Circle Drive to the Cypress lawn area, which is located in the northeast section of the cemetery. The lawns in the northeast side of the park are part of the original cemetery. Interred here is professional baseball player Michael Edward Simon (April 13, 1883 to June 10, 1963). Simon, a catcher, played seven years in professional baseball, first for the Pittsburgh Pirates (1909-1913), then in the Federal League for the St. Louis Terriers (1914), and Brooklyn Tip-Tops (1915). Primarily a back up catcher, he appeared in 378 games, had 1,069 at bats, with 241 hits, and career batting average of .225. Simon was a member of the 1909 Pittsburgh Pirates World Championship team.[78] He died on June 10, 1963 in Los Angeles, California.

✿ Simon is buried in the Cypress lawn, lot 529, space 2. His grave is found five rows from the south curb and two graves east of the border of the baby lawn section (on the west side of Cypress lawn).

LON NOL

Directly south and across the street from the grave of Mike Simon is the Rose lawn. Buried on the north curb is the former President of Cambodia Lon Nol (November 11, 1913 to November 17, 1985). Nol was President of Cambodia during the later stages of the Vietnam War. He was an army general who in a coup overthrew the 1,100-year-old royal monarchy of Prince Norodom Sihanouk in March of 1970. He had been unhappy with the government's neutral stance against the communists in the region. He was a staunch anti-communist and ally of the United States. At the outset of the take-over, Communist rebel guerrilla groups fought the

Cambodian government. The government army led by Nol was no match for the rebels, even with aid from the U.S. military. By April 1975, the communists controlled over seventy-five percent of the country. With inflation and internal political corruption out of control, Nol was forced to flee the country. The Communists led by Pol Pot, then took over the country and created the Khymer Rouge regime. This regime implemented severe agrarian reforms that led to the killing of millions of Cambodian citizens. The Khymer Rouge was over thrown in 1979.

Lon Nol was forced into exile, moved to Fullerton, California, were he led a quiet life until his death on November 17, 1985 from heart failure.[79]

Former Cambodian President Lon Nol's grave.

He is buried in the Rose lawn on the north curb. His ornate black marble tombstone is adorned with a picture of the former President, and reads: "President, Lon Nol, 1913-1985, Cambodia."

GEORGE BENN KEY

The oldest section of Loma Vista Memorial Park is the Northeast lawn. Interred here are many pioneers of the area that include George Benn Key (1854 to 1916), a prominent Placentia area rancher. He was the superintendent of California's first commercial Valencia orange grove (near present day Cal State University, Fullerton).

He developed twenty acres of citrus trees on his own ranch land. Today, Key's ranch is listed on the National Registry of Historic Landmarks. The house was built in 1898, and the grounds consist of two acres of well-manicured gardens. It is located at 625 W. Bastancury Road, Placentia, a short drive from the Loma Vista Memorial Park.

George Key's grave is located on the curb in the Northeast lawn, near the old cemetery office.

DONALD R. WRIGHT

Buried a few yards away from Key is former Chief Justice of the California State Supreme Court, Donald R. Wright (February 2, 1907 to March 21, 1985). Wright, a conservative, was the 24th Chief Justice of the California Supreme Court from 1970 to 1977. A graduate of Stanford University, and Harvard Law School, he was first appointed a judge by Governor Earl Warren in 1953. Wright moved swiftly up the ranks, and in 1968, he was appointed by Governor Ronald Reagan to the State Court of Appeals. In 1970, he moved up to the states highest court. In 1972, Wright, an ardent death penalty foe, along with a majority of other justices of the high court, struck down the controversial law. This saved hundreds of death row inmates from execution, including Charles Manson, and Robert F. Kennedy's assassin Sirhan Sirhan. Other controversial rulings included the allowing of lawsuits to be filed against bartenders who serve drinks to obviously intoxicated patrons, who then caused injury to others. This was eventually overturned by the California State legislature.

Justice Wright retired from the bench in 1977, and was succeeded as Chief Justice by Rose Elizabeth Bird. Wright died on March 21, 1985 in Pasadena, California, from a heart attack.[80]

He is buried in the Northeast lawn, lot 454, space 6. His grave is found on the west curb, a few steps away from George Key. Wright's small flat grave marker reads: "Donald R. Wright, 1907-1985, 24th Chief Justice of California."

JOHN T. "JACK" SALVERSON

The final noteworthy grave in Loma Vista Memorial Park in located in the Buena Vista lawn 2 area. Interred here is professional baseball player John T. "Jack" Salverson, (January 5, 1914 to December 28, 1974). Salverson was a right-handed relief pitcher who played five seasons for the New York Giants (1933-1934), Pittsburgh Pirates (1935), Chicago White Sox (1935), and Cleveland Indians (1943 and 1945). He appeared in 87 games, winning 9 and losing 9, with an earned run average of 3.99. He was a member of the 1933 New York Giants World Championship team.[81]

He is buried in the Buena Vista lawn, lot 604, space 4, from the south curb of the lawn. Locate the grave of Frances Dyer Bogart, thirteen rows north is Salverson's final resting place.

STEPHEN BECKER & SETH FESSENDEN

Also buried at Loma Vista are Stephen Becker and Seth Fessenden, who were victims of the shooting at the Cal State Fullerton library on July 12, 1976. Their story, along with other victims of the tragedy, will be discussed in Chapter Eight, "Murder and Mayhem."

THE CRYSTAL CATHEDRAL
MEMORY GARDENS

12141 Lewis Street
Garden Grove, California 92840

Open everyday from sunrise to sunset.

The origins of the Crystal Cathedral, Memorial Gardens cemetery, begin in 1955 with the Reverend Robert Schuller. Reverend Schuller began his ministry preaching from the top of a local Orange drive-in theater. In 1957, a chapel was built on the location of the present day Crystal Cathedral complex. It is from these humble beginnings that the congregation grew to the millions of worshippers of today.

In 1970, Reverend Schuller launched the weekly *Hour of Power* television show, and by the middle of the decade the show was being seen in all fifty states. The popularity of the ministry helped the complex grow to what it is today. In 1991, Reverend Schuller had an idea of creating a world-class cemetery on the grounds of the Crystal Cathedral, and the Memorial Gardens were dedicated later that same year. The cemetery is located at the base of the 236-foot Crystal Cathedral spire, which stands as the grand entrance to the burial grounds. The

The grand entrance into the Crystal Cathedral Memory Garden. The empty crypts pictured in the center are the future burial spot for Reverend Schuller and his wife.

cemetery is self-referred to as the "Westminster Abbey of America." There are only a handful of noteworthy interments on the premises. The Memorial Garden is a tranquil place for peaceful meditation and reflection.

JOHN CREAN

The entrance to the cemetery is flanked on both sides by large waterfalls and fountains. At the bottom of the grand staircase stands a large empty crypt; this will one day hold the remains of Reverend Robert Schuller and his wife. To the right of the Schuller tomb is a private family estate that holds the remains of businessman and philanthropist John Crean (July 4, 1925 to January 11, 2007).

Crean was a multi-millionaire Orange County businessman who was the founder of Fleetwood Enterprises in 1950. Fleetwood would become a three billion dollar a year, Fortune 500 Company, that operated numerous recreational vehicle manufacturing plants through the United States and Canada. Crean and his wife, Donna, were devout Lutherans and believed in tithing at least ten percent of their income to worthy causes. Among the recipients of their generosity were Hoag Memorial Hospital, The Orange County Philharmonic Society, The Crystal Cathedral, The Santa Ana Zoo, The Orange County Republican Party, and the Lutheran High School of South Orange County.

In addition, Crean was an avid cook, and from 1992-1998 and he co-hosted a cable cooking show, *At Home on the Range*, with his good friend, Barbara Venezia. In 1998, Crean sold his interest in Fleetwood Enterprises and retired to a quiet life.

He died on January 11, 2007, at his Santa Ana Heights home of heart disease.[81] His funeral was held at the Crystal Cathedral and was attended by over 1,000 mourners. The services were officiated by Reverend Schuller, and in his eulogy stated that:

> *"The church you're sitting in, the Crystal Cathedral,*
> *would not be here without John Crean."*

Crean is buried in a private family estate just to the right of the future crypt of Reverend Schuller and the lawn area. His simple grave maker reads: "on the road again."[83]

RICHARD ARTHUR "DICK" KLEINER
HORTENSIA "CHICKI" KLEINER

To the immediate left of the empty Schuller crypt, on the main lawn area, is a wall of niches that contain the cremated remains of Hollywood columnist and biographer Richard Arthur "Dick" Kleiner (March 9, 1921 to February 13, 2002). Kleiner was a popular syndicated celebrity columnist for numerous newspapers and magazines throughout the country. He began his career in 1964, covering Hollywood related subjects. His popular "Ask Dick Kleiner," a question and answer column, covered a wide range of Hollywood celebrity news and gossip. He was also a prolific author who penned several books, including:

- *The Ghost That Danced with Kim Novak and Other True Tales of the Supernatural* (1969)
- *The World's Worst Wisher* (1969)
- *E.S.P. and the Stars* (1970)
- *Index of Initials and Acronyms* (1971)
- *Mervyn Leroy:Take One* (1974)
- *The Two of Us* (1976)
- *Please Don't Shoot My Dog* (1981)

In addition to being an author and columnist, Kleiner also dabbled in song writing, penning the lyrics to the campy ode to baseball superstar Willie Mays, "Say Hey—The Willie Mays Song," that was recorded by The Treniers.

Richard's father, Israel S. Kleiner was a biochemist who, in 1915, co-discovered the causes of diabetes. Ironically, his son Richard would die from complications of diabetes and heart disease on February 13, 2002, at his home in San Juan Capistrano, California.[84]

Kleiner's cremated remains are found along side his wife Hortensia "Chicki" Kleiner (a Hollywood publicist who died in 2004), in the Garden of Eternity, niche J-5, 11A. The Kleiner's niches are located in the lawn area, to the immediate left of the Schuller crypt, on the bottom right corner of the wall.

THURL RAVENSCROFT

Proceed back up the stairs, turning right and walking down the sidewalk until you find a wall with a colorful mosaic that resembles an outreaching hand. Interred within the wall are the ashes of famed animation voice actor Thurl Ravenscroft (February 6, 1914 to May 22, 2005). Ravenscroft was not a recognizable face, but his booming baritone voice was unmistakable. He was best known as the original voice of Tony the Tiger, whose catch phrase "they're g-r-r-r-eat" became an iconic catchphrase on Kellogg's Frosted Flakes commercials. In addition to Tony the Tiger, he was the voice of different characters in numerous Disney films such as:

- *One Hundred and One Dalmations*
- *The Sword and the Stone*
- *The Aristocats*
- *Dumbo*
- *Peter Pan*
- *Sleeping Beauty*
- *The Jungle Book*

At Disneyland Park and Disneyworld, he is the voice for many characters on rides such as:

 Country Bear Jamboree

 The Haunted Mansion

 Disneyland Railroad

 Pirates of the Caribbean

For twenty years, beginning in 1974, he was the voice of the Pageant of the Masters, a summer tradition in Laguna Beach, California. He died on May 22, 2005, from prostate cancer.[85]

Voice actor Thurl Ravenscroft's cremation niche, he was best known as the voice of Tony the Tiger for Frosted Flakes.

 His cremated remains are found in a niche in the bottom left hand corner of the mosaic wall.

JOHNNIE WAYNE CARL

Retrace your path north along the sidewalk. Crossing over the entrance staircase, proceed along the path, just before the cemetery office. On the right are two private glassed-in rooms. The first room contains the ashes of Johnnie Wayne Carl (January 15, 1947 to December 17, 2004). He was the musical director of the Crystal Cathedral for thirty years, and was a prolific arranger and composer.

Carl wrote over 3,500 musical arrangements that included 200 hymns. He was a good friend of pianist Roger Williams, and John Tesh, with whom he collaborated on several albums. He also performed with Celine Dion, Michael Crawford, and the London Philharmonic Orchestra.

Carl suffered from bipolar depression for most of his life, and was hospitalized for the illness several times. On the afternoon of December 16, 2004, Carl got into an argument with a fellow employee of the Crystal Cathedral. This argument seemed to unhinge Carl, who retreated to his office. Shortly after returning to his office, employees heard gunshots. The police were called, and Carl barricaded himself in the office. For several tense hours, police negotiators attempted to resolve the standoff. At around 1:58 a.m. on the morning of December 17, 2004, a single gunshot was heard, police broke down the door to Carl's office and found the music director dead from a self-inflicted gunshot wound to the head.[86]

☬ Carl was cremated and his remains are found in the private Miller Room, just inside the glass doors on the right side. The door to the room is often locked, but if you peer through the glass, his urn (that resembles a musical note) is clearly visible.

MARIE A. CALLENDER

From the Miller room, follow the sidewalk around to the back of the cemetery. In the northwest corner is a room for cremated remains; it has a large multi-colored stained-glass window in it. Inside this room are the ashes of restaurant namesake Marie A. Callender (1907 to November 11, 1995). Marie Callender, along with her husband, Cal, and son, Donald, opened their first pie shop in Long Beach, California, in 1948. In early 1962, the operation and menu was expanded to include more than pie and baked goods. A coffee shop designed prototype bearing the name Marie Callender's was opened on Tustin Avenue in Orange, California. The restaurant sold soup and sandwiches, along with homemade pies.

Marie had left the family business by this time to open a small retail store in Orange, California, and Donald took over control of the operation. The successful restaurant chain was sold in 1990 to the Wilshire Restaurant Group, and is currently owned and operated by Castle Harlan Enterprises. There are currently, 139 restaurant locations throughout the western United States. The chain also has a line of frozen food products that are sold in grocery stores throughout the country.

Marie Callender, the name sake of the restaurant chain, died on November 11, 1995, at her home in Laguna Hills, after a long battle with cancer.[87]

☬ Her ashes are found in the Sanctuary of Praise, niche E2N, B4. Standing in the doorway of the room, her niche is found on the forward wall, two from the bottom and four from the left.

LONNIE RAY FRISBEE

From the Sanctuary of Peace room, walk right to the back lawn area. Buried here is the final famous internee of the Crystal Cathedral grounds: 1960's hippie minister, Lonnie Ray Frisbee (1949 to March 14, 1997). Frisbee began his preaching career at age sixteen in the Haight-Asbury district of San Francisco in the late 1960s. In the early 1970s, he, along with Chuck Smith, were instrumental in establishing the first Calvary Chapel in Costa Mesa, California. Frisbee died of a brain tumor at age forty-three on March 14, 1997.[88]

☬ He is buried in the back lawn area. Follow the sidewalk right down the ramp from the Alcove where Marie Callender's ashes are interred. At the end of the sidewalk, on the grass, locate the grave of Marie Donlan, and four makers south is Frisbee's final resting place. His grave marker reads: "minister-missionary-evangelist"

MAGNOLIA MEMORIAL PARK

12241 Magnolia Street
Garden Grove, California 92841
Telephone: 714-539-1771

The cemetery was established in 1874, by the Everett family. The family owned ten acres that also included land on which the nearby Lutheran church stood. The cemetery was placed where it is today because it was the driest place in the area. The most of Garden Grove and Westminster was swamp with the water table at five feet. In 1882, half of the property was sold to William Lamson, including the cemetery, and the burial ground was named Westminster Cemetery. The cemetery remained in the hands of the Lamson family until the early 1950s. The cemetery was then purchased by the nearby Lutheran Church and was renamed Magnolia Memorial Park, not to be confused with Westminster Memorial Park, located a few miles away.

Today, the cemetery is owned and operated by the Tapestry Christian Fellowship Church. The cemetery is small by modern standards, and encompasses less than six acres. Interred here are many local pioneers and numerous Civil War veterans.

DIMITRIOS SPEROS "JIM" BAXES

There is only one noteworthy burial at this cemetery, professional baseball player Dimitrios Speros "Jim" Baxes (July 5, 1928 to November 14, 1996). Baxes played second and third bases for the Los Angeles Dodgers and Cleveland Indians in 1959. He started 1959 playing in eleven games with the Dodgers (who went on to become the eventual World Champions), but was released midway through the season; he was then signed by the Indians. He appeared in a total of 88 games, had 280 at bats, with 69 hits, and a career batting average of .246.[89]

He is buried in the Northeast Garden lawn, lot 136A, space 11. After entering the cemetery, the lawn is on the immediate right; find curb maker 136A, and eighteen graves north is Baxes final resting place. His marker reads: "you've left our lives but not our hearts."

HARBOR LAWN
MT. OLIVE MEMORIAL PARK

1625 Gisler Avenue
Costa Mesa, California 92626
Telephone: 714-540-5554

This cemetery was established in 1952 and was originally named Harbor Rest Memorial Park. It serves a large Jewish community and was renamed Harbor Lawn: Mt. Olive Memorial Park at an unknown date. The exact number of acres of the cemetery is unknown, but it is fairly large. It has well-maintained grounds and friendly employees.

ALBERT WENTWORTH DEMAREE

There are only three noteworthy interments here at Harbor Lawn; first is professional baseball player and cartoonist Albert Wentworth Demaree (September 8, 1884 to April 30, 1962). Demaree, a right-handed starting pitcher, played eight seasons for the New York Giants, Philadelphia Phillies, Chicago Cubs, and Boston Braves from 1912 to 1919.He was a member of four pennant winning ball clubs, 1912, 1913, and 1917 New York Giants, and the 1915 Philadelphia Phillies. He started game four of the 1913 World Series against the Philadelphia Athletics, lasting four innings, giving up four runs in an eventual 6-5 loss. He was a teammate of Gavy Cravath (see Melrose Abbey) on the 1915 Philadelphia Phillies.

In his career, he appeared in 232 games, winning 80 and losing 72, with 84 complete games, and an earned run average of 2.77.[90] After retiring from baseball in 1919, Albert became a syndicated sports cartoonist for over 200 newspapers, and was also employed by the *Sporting News* for thirty years. Demaree died on April 30, 1962, in Los Angeles, California, of an undisclosed lengthy illness at age seventy-eight.

He is buried in the North Memory Garden lawn, lot 147, space C. On the north curb, locate the marker of Otis W. Woodward; fourteen rows south is Demaree's unmarked grave.

KATHRYN CARD

Directly across the street and north of the North Memory Garden lawn is the Cypress Garden lawn area. Buried here are two noteworthy people, including actress Kathryn Card (October 4, 1892 to March 1, 1964). Card was a character actress who appeared in numerous television shows and films from the mid-1940s until the mid-1960s. She is best known for her role as Lucy's mother (Mrs. McGillicuddy) on I Love Lucy (1954-1956). Film credits include:

- *Kiss and Tell* (1945)
- *Undercurrent* (1946)
- *The Dark Past* (1948)
- *A Kiss for Corliss* (1949)

She appearred in dozens of television shows. Major credits include:

- *Perry Mason*
- *Rawhide*
- *Dennis the Menace*
- *The Red Skelton Show*

Card died on March 1, 1964 in Costa Mesa, California.[91]

❀ She is buried in the Cypress Garden lawn, lot 207, space E. Locate the marker of Eston and Violet Rose on the south curb; sixteen rows north, and just in front of the Memory Garden hedge is the Card grave. Her marker reads: "loving memories never die, as the years roll on and days pass by."

RON JESSIE

The final famous internee of the cemetery is buried in the Memory Garden, a squared-off area bordered by a hedge of bushes in the center of the Cypress Garden lawn. Interred here are the cremated remains of professional football player Ron Jessie (February 4, 1948 to January 13, 2006). Jessie was a wide receiver who played eleven seasons in the National Football League for the Detroit Lions, Los Angeles Rams, and Buffalo Bills from 1971 to 1981. Jessie was a standout football player at the University of Kansas, where he also participated in track and field. He was an All-American long jumper including the indoor long jump champion and a member of the 1969 U.S. Track and Field Federation national champions. Jessie was drafted in the eighth round of the 1971 NFL draft by the Dallas Cowboys; Jessie was traded that same year during training camp to the Detroit Lions. He was a solid number two receiver in his playing days, amassing career totals of 138 games played, with 265 receptions, 4,276 total yards, and 16.1 yards per catch average. He was a member of the Los Angeles Rams 1980, Super Bowl team, but did not play because of injury. Jessie died of a heart attack at his home in Huntington Beach on January 13, 2006.[92]

❀ His cremated remains are interred in the Memory Garden, 253-H3. Find the square hedge area in the center of the Cypress Garden lawn, enter the area from the south, walk to the northeast section of the area. Along the north hedge is the final resting spot of the NFL great. His small marker a rendering of a football player on the left, and a football on the bottom.

ST. ANDREW'S BY THE SEA
SAN CLEMENTE

2001 Calle Frontera
San Clemente, California 92673
Telephone: 949-492-2537

St. Andrew's by the Sea Methodist Church is perched on the bluffs overlooking the Pacific Ocean. In the tradition of the old churchyard burials, the Memorial Chapel Garden is located next to the church sanctuary. The garden cemetery is a place for the internment of cremated remains only; it is walled off and gated. A place of great beauty and peace, it has spectacular views of the Pacific Ocean and the city of San Clemente.

Robert C. Mardian

There is only one famous internee at this cemetery, Robert C. Mardian (October 23, 1923 to July 17, 2006). Mardian was a former assistant attorney general, and was also one of the Watergate Seven conspirators who were indicted and tried in connection with the scandal that led to the resignation of President Richard Nixon. Mardian was a leading Republican official during the Nixon presidency, and was considered one of the most powerful figures in Washington. He was a staunch Republican and supporter of Richard Nixon. Mardian was the attorney for President Nixon's Committee to Re-Elect the President in 1972, and was Chief of the Internal Security Division at the White House. He was implicated in the Watergate scandal along with John Mitchell, H.R. Haldeman, John Ehrlichman, Charles Colson, Gordon Strachan, and Kenneth Parkinson. Mardian was the Chief of Security, in charge of tapping phone lines of reporters, and subversives. He led the probe into the leak and publication of the top secret history of the Vietnam War, known as the Pentagon Papers. Mardian denied any knowledge or involvement of the break in at the Democratic National Headquarters office at the Watergate complex. He was tied to the investigation for attempting to force Attorney General Richard Kleindienst to release the Watergate burglars from jail. Mardian was convicted on one count of conspiracy to hinder the Watergate investigation. He was sentenced to ten months to three years in prison. The verdict was appealed and over-turned. It was argued that Mardian should have been tried separately from the other defendants due to his alleged limited role. The Watergate Special prosecutor declined to retry the case. In the aftermath, only Mitchell, Haldeman, and Ehrlichman were convicted and served jail time for the scandal. The other defendants including Mardian were either acquitted or the charges were dropped.

President Richard Nixon resigned the Presidency on August 9, 1974. After this ordeal, Mardian retired to private life, and running the family construction business in Phoenix, Arizona. For many years after, it was alleged that Mardian was the famous "deep throat" informant. Mardian denied these allegations, and in 2005, he was vindicated, when it was finally revealed that W. Mark Felt was indeed the infamous informant. Robert C. Mardian died from lung cancer on July 17, 2006, in San Clemente, California, while vacationing at his summer home.[93]

🙢🙠 His ashes are interred in the Memory Chapel Garden in the "Love" niche wall. The garden is located to the right of the main church sanctuary building. Enter through the large steel gates, and once inside, find the large steel cross in the right corner. To the right of the cross is the "Love" niche wall section. On the top row, and thirteen niches from the left, is Mardian's unassuming final resting place.

CATHOLIC CEMETERIES

The greatest use of life is to spend it for something that will last.

~William James
pioneering psychologist and philosopher (1842 to 1910)

The roots of Catholicism in Southern California run very deep. The history of the region is steeped in church traditions. California began as a Spanish colony, and the influence of Catholicism on the region is enormous. The Spanish explorers and early missionaries of the late seventeenth and early eighteenth centuries cemented the legacy of Spain, Mexico, and the church in the area. This chapter will discuss the significance of the four modern Catholic Archdiocese administered cemeteries.

HOLY SEPULCHER CEMETERY

7845 Santiago Canyon Road
Orange, California 92869
Telephone: 714-532-6551

Open daily from 8 a.m. until 5 p.m.

Holy Sepulcher is the largest of the Orange County Catholic Archdiocese administered cemeteries and was established in 1930. It is nestled in the rolling hills of rural Orange County. Within its twenty-six acres of well manicured lawns are the mortal remains of handful of sports heroes, Hollywood celebrities, inventors, business giants, and Orange County pioneers. It is also the final resting place to many of the diocese priests and nuns.

HARRY GASPAR

Located in lawn section D is professional baseball player Harry Gaspar (April 28, 1883 to May 14, 1940). Gaspar was primarily a right-handed starting pitcher who played during the "dead ball" era for the Cincinnati Reds from 1909 to 1912. He appeared in 143 games, winning 44 and losing 48, with career innings pitched and an earned run average of 825 and 2.69, respectively. His rookie season in 1909 was by far his best statistically, winning 18 games and losing 11, with an earned run average of 2.01.[1] After being reassigned to the minors in 1912, Gaspar refused to report to Toronto and was suspended.

In 1915, he was appointed player-manager for Sioux City in the Western League. His final year in professional baseball came in 1919.[2] After his playing days were over, Gaspar came to Santa Ana, California, and opened a bowling alley.

❧ Harry died on May 14, 1940, after a two-year battle with an undisclosed illness; he was fifty-seven.[3] His grave can be found in lawn D, Saint Dominic, tier 32, space 33. Locate the water stump nearest to the northwest corner of the lawn; six rows east from the curb is Gaspar's final resting place.

Marion Traversino

Marion Traversino (September 16, 1933 to April 6, 2004) was a professional ice skater. Marion was born in Chicago and moved with her family to Los Angeles in 1942. In her early teens she took dancing, acting, and ice skating lessons. She excelled at ice skating. At the age of fifteen, she joined Sonya Henie's ice skating show (a forerunner of today's Ice Capades), and later toured with Barbara Ann Scott's show. In 1948, her father, Mark Traversino Sr., produced the Ice Classics Show, starring Marion Traversino and Buddy Schroff. This show toured the United States and the South Pacific until 1951.

Following this exhausting tour, she moved on to television, performing on the local Los Angeles station KTLA's Frosty Frolics, 1951 to 1955. At the conclusion of the show, Marion retired from professional skating; she got married and settled in Orange County. She died on April 6, 2004 from complication of emphysema.[4]

❧ Her grave is found in the lawn H, St. Helena, tier 1, space 94. Traversino's grave marker is found in the middle of the section on the west curb, next to her father, Mark Traversino Sr.

Edward Roman "Ed" Sadowski

Buried in lawn G are several professional baseball players, first is a member of the original Los Angeles Angels, Edward Roman "Ed" Sadowski (January 19, 1931 to November 6, 1993). He was one of three brothers (Bob and Ted) who played in the major leagues.[5] Ed was primarily a back-up catcher, with limited offensive prowess. He played for the Boston Red Sox, Los Angeles Angels, and Milwaukee Braves from 1960 to 1966. He was an original member of the Los Angeles Angels in 1961.

His career highlights include 217 games played, had 495 at bats, 100 hits, 39 runs batted in, with a career average of .202. After his playing career, he was briefly employed as the pitching coach for the Montreal Expos.[6] He left baseball in 1970, and taught physical education at St. Anne, and St. Columban schools in Santa Ana. He held this position until his death on November 6, 1993, due to complications of amyotrophic lateral sclerosis (Lou Gehrig's disease); he was sixty-two.[7]

❦ Ed Sadowski's final resting place can be found in lawn section G, St. Jude, tier 20, space 207. Locate the grave of Ruben Gomez on the curb in the northeast part of the lawn; eleven markers south, under a small pine tree is his grave.

JOSEPH CHESTER STEPHENSON

The second ball player interred within the lawn is Joseph Chester Stephenson (June 30, 1921 to September 20, 2001). Stephenson, a catcher, played for the San Francisco Giants, Chicago Cubs, and Chicago White Sox from 1943 to 1947. He appeared in 29 games, had 12 hits in 67 at bats with a batting average of .179.[8]

After his playing days, he was hired as a scout for the Boston Red Sox, and was instrumental in discovering numerous star players such as Fred Lynn, Ken Brett, Glenn Hoffman, Bill Lee, Rick Burleson, and Dwight Evans. His son, Jerry Stephenson, was a relief pitcher for Boston Red Sox in the 1960s.[9] Stephenson was eighty when he died on September 20, 2000.

❦ His burial location is lawn G, tier 32, space 143. Find curb marker 145 on eastern side of the lawn. Five rows west is the grave of the legendary scout. His marker is inscribed with musical script and reads: "take me out to the ball game."

JENNY RICHARDS

Country singer Jenny Richards (d. June 1, 2005) is buried in lawn Z. She is the daughter of country recording artist Rusty Richards. Rusty is a former vocalist with the Sons of the Pioneers, a group founded by Roy Rogers, and the Frontiersmen. Rusty has recorded several solo albums including 2007's *American Cowboy*. His daughter, Jenny, was a local singer and songwriter who often performed at the Crazy Horse Saloon, as well as other music venues. Jenny Richards died on June 1, 2005 from cancer. At Irvine Valley College, she has been honored to have a music scholarship funded in her name.[10]

❦ Richards grave is found in lawn Z, St. Vincent DePaul, tier D, space 50. Her grave is unmarked and is found two rows from the eastern fence.

CARL N. KARCHER
MARGARET KARCHER

Lawn N is the final resting place to three very distinct and noteworthy people, Carl N. Karcher (January 16, 1917 to January 11, 2008) was an innovative businessman, entrepreneur, civic leader, and philanthropist. He was a shrewd businessman who parlayed a $326 hotdog stand investment into the multimillion dollar Carl's Jr. fast food kingdom. Karcher was born in Ohio in 1917, and was only formally educated through the eighth grade. What he lacked in formal education, Karcher made up with hard work, tenacity, and common sense.

In 1937, he moved from Ohio to Los Angeles and landed odd jobs. As a bakery deliveryman, he noticed many hotdog stands along his delivery route that were doing a good business. He and his wife, Margaret, decided that they would invest in a hotdog stand. Using their car as collateral, and putting up fifteen dollars of their own money, they scraped together enough to buy a stand. The Karcher's hotdog stand was a great success, and seeing this, they purchased several other locations.

In the mid-1940s the Karcher's moved to Anaheim and opened Carl's Drive-in Barbeque. In 1956, with continued success, Karcher opened the first Carl's Jr. restaurant, located in Anaheim. The chain that he founded would eventually encompass over 3,000 restaurants, located in forty-two states and in thirteen countries.[11]

Karcher was an innovator and pioneer in the fast food industry. His concepts, such as salad bars, self-service beverage bars, and indoor dining put him and his company Carl Karcher Enterprises at the forefront of the fast

The Karcher burial plot with statue of Francis of Assisi in background, Holy Sepulcher, Orange.

food industry. Not only was he a good businessman, but he was a supporter of charities and a vocal proponent of many political causes. A devote Catholic, he was a controversial opponent of gay rights and abortion, for which he was knighted into the Royal Order of Malta by Pope John Paul II. He was close friends with Presidents Nixon and Reagan and also had close ties with the entertainment industry, associating with such stars as Bob Hope.

Karcher was well liked and was frequently seen mingling with employees and customers at his restaurants. Late in life, Karcher rarely made public appearances, due to several strokes and the onset of Parkinson's disease. On New Year's Day 2008, he was admitted to St. Jude Medical Center with pneumonia. He slowly faded away and on Friday afternoon January 11, 2008, he died. Carl was preceded in death by his wife, Margaret (July 17, 2006).[12] His funeral mass was held at St. Boniface Catholic Church in Anaheim on the 18th of January. In attendance were over two thousand mourners.[13]

🌺 The Karcher's graves can be found in lawn section N, St. Francis, spaces 39 and 40. Locate the large statue of Saint Francis of Assisi in the middle of the lawn; the Karcher's marker is directly in front and is adorned with a lovely picture of the couple.

RUBY KEELER-LOWE

Also interred in lawn N and just steps away from the Karcher's is legendary stage and film actress Ruby Keeler-Lowe (August 25, 1910 to February 28, 1993). Keeler was an actress who was famous for a string of successful Warner Bros. musicals in the 1930s. Keeler was born in Dartmouth, Nova Scotia, Canada. At an early age her family moved to New York City. In her early teenage years, Ruby took up dance lessons. Her first taste of show business came in 1923 at the age of thirteen in George M. Cohen's The Rise of Rosie O'Reilly. An up-and-coming star in the making, she was noticed by Broadway producer Charles Dillingham and others. It was during this time that she met Al Jolson, and on September 21, 1928, after a brief courtship, they were married. Their relationship was difficult from the start, and in 1940, it ended in divorce.[14]

Keeler's stardom was cemented when, in 1933, producer Darryl Zanuck cast her in the Warner Bros. musical *42nd Street*, in which she co-starred with Dick Powell and Bebe Daniels. Other screen credits include:

- *Gold Diggers of 1933*
- *Dames* (1934)
- *Flirtation Walk* (1934)
- *Shipmates Forever* (1935)
- *Collen* (1936)
- *Ready, Willing, and Able* (1937)

In 1937, Keller left Hollywood, only appearing in two other films, the last being *Sweetheart of the Campus* (1941).[15]

She married John Lowe, an Orange County land developer in 1941, and settled into a life as a wife and mother. In 1971, show business again called out to Keller, and at the age of seventy-one, she came out of retirement to perform in the Broadway stage production of *No, No, Nanette*. After the show's conclusion, she again returned to a leisurely private life in Rancho Mirage, California.

Late in life, she suffered several strokes and was in a coma for a period of time. After recovering, she became the spokeswoman for the National Stroke Association. On Sunday morning, February 28, 1993, Ruby Keller died of kidney cancer at her home in Rancho Mirage. Her second husband John Lowe had preceded her in death in 1969.[16]

Ruby's grave can be found to the left of the St. Francis statue in lawn section N, St. Francis, tier 21, space 46.

Actress Ruby Keeler and husband John Lowe's grave.

JOSEPH E. PLEASANTS

The final noteworthy internee we will talk about now at Holy Sepulcher is Joseph E. Pleasants (1839 to 1934), an Orange County pioneer and rancher. In 1861, William Wolfskill, purchased the Rancho Lomas de Santiago from Teodocio Yorba. He entrusted the management of the rancho to Pleasants. The rancho encompassed what is today Santiago and Modjeska Canyons. Pleasants built a house near what is now Irvine Regional Park. Until his death in 1934, Pleasants acted as the unofficial custodian of the park.[17]

His final resting place is poetically situated so that it looks over the rolling hills for the former rancho. The grave is located in lawn section F, old St. Francis section, lot 20, space 4. On the west curb, locate number 17, and the grave of Katherine Gilman. Six rows east is the simple grave marker of Pleasants.

FRANK G. TEPLANSKY

Also interred at Holy Sepulcher is Frank G. Teplansky (1925 to July 12, 1976). He was one of the seven victims, who were shot and killed by Edward Charles Allaway in the 1976 Cal State Fullerton Library shooting rampage. His story will be told in Chapter Eight, "Murder and Mayhem."

ASCENSION CEMETERY

24754 Trabuco Road
Lake Forest, California 92630
Telephone: 949-837-1331

This cemetery was established by the Archdiocese in 1965. Located within the community of Lake Forest, Ascension is set on fifteen acres of park like grounds. It is surrounded by a quiet residential neighborhood. The guardian angel mausoleum located in the center of the cemetery is the newest such building in the diocese cemetery system. The grounds are easy to navigate with only one road; graves are laid out in a grid system with grave numbers clearly marked on the curb. Locating graves within the cemetery is quite easy.

NICOLE BROWN-SIMPSON

Ascension Cemetery is the final resting place to several noteworthy individuals. The most famous internment is that of murder victim Nicole Brown-Simpson (May 19, 1959 to June 12, 1994). She was born in Frankfurt, Germany, but raised in Orange County. In 1985, Nicole married football legend, actor, and television sports commentator O.J. Simpson. The Simpsons had two children, Sydney and Justin. Their married was rocky from the start with reports of domestic abuse, a precursor of events to come. In 1992, their relationship ended in divorced. In the months leading up to her murder, Nicole and O.J. had attempted to reconcile, but the couple continued to argue.

Murder victim Nicole Brown Simpson's final resting place at Ascension Cemetery, Lake Forest.

On the night of June 12, 1994, Nicole and a friend, Ron Goldman, were found stabbed to death near the front gate of Nicole's Brentwood-area townhouse. As the events unfolded and evidence mounted, many began to suspect O.J. Simpson as the killer.[18]

On June 7, 1994, Nicole's funeral service was held at St. Marin's Catholic Church in Brentwood. In attendance were over 200 mourners, including O.J., their two children, Nicole's family, and many others. After the church service, a long line of cars followed the white hearse on its fifty-mile trek south from Los Angeles to Ascension Cemetery in Lake Forest. At the cemetery, mourners huddled under two giant tents that encircled the gravesite. The Reverend Bruce Lavery offered a final blessing that lasted twenty-five minutes.[19]

The days , weeks, and months that followed Nicole's murder were filled with surreal and unimaginable events. Evidence mounted, and O.J. Simpson was arrested and charged with the murders. Prior to his arrest, he and friend Al Cowlings led police on the infamous slow speed chase in a white Ford Bronco from the gravesite of Nicole to his home in Brentwood.

The trial of O.J. Simpson, and the television events that surrounded the trial, forever changed the way future judicial proceedings are viewed. The so called "trial of the century" pitted high-powered attorney Johnnie Cochran against Los Angeles County Prosecutor Marcia Clarke. The often theatrical proceedings ended on October 3, 1995, with a verdict of not guilty. The televised reading of the verdict was seen by millions, making it one of the most watched television events in history.

Following his acquittal, Simpson continued to assert his innocence, and has stated his intent to find the "real" killers. Today, he is doing his search from behind bars at a Nevada State prison, where he is incarcerated for armed robbery, and kidnapping.

❀ Nicole's grave is located behind the guardian angel mausoleum in lawn A, tier 18, space 87. Along the south mausoleum wall, locate the grave of Stanley Szajner; three rows south is Nicole's simple grave marker that reads "always in our hearts."

WILLIAM HANNA

A few steps away from Simpson is the grave of famous cartoon mogul William Hanna (July 14, 1910 to March 22, 2001). Hanna began his cartoon career with the Harman-Ishing Studios in 1930 as a lyricist and composer for the Looney Tunes, and Merry Melodies cartoon series. In 1937, he moved to Metro-Goldwyn-Mayer and met Joseph Barbera. The team of Hanna and Barbera created the famous cat and mouse cartoon duo of Tom and Jerry. The *Tom and Jerry* series won the Academy Award for best animated short seven times, beginning with:

- "The Yankee Doodle Mouse" (1943)
- "Mouse Trouble" (1944)
- "Quiet Please" (1945)
- "The Cat Concerto: (1946)
- "The Little Orphan" (1947)
- "The Two Mouseketeers" (1951)
- "Johann Mouse" (1952)[20]

In 1957, Hanna and Barbera left MGM to form their own production company. Together they pioneered the use of inexpensive animation techniques for television. They produced over 3,000 cartoons, creating some of the most famous cartoon characters of all time, such as Huckleberry Hound, Casper the friendly ghost, Yogi Bear, The Flintstones, and Scooby Doo.

Hanna-Barbera Productions won eight Emmy awards for their cartoons. On March 22, 2001, William Hanna died at his home in Woodland Hills, California, at age ninety. He had continued to work producing cartoons up until his death.[21]

The cartoon pioneer is buried in lawn A, tier 16, space 81, fourteen graves to left and one row south from Nicole Simpson.

LOUIS BERNARD "LOU" STRINGER

A short walk and across the street from the mausoleum is lawn BB. Here is the final resting place of professional baseball player Louis Bernard "Lou" Stringer (May 13, 1917 to October 19, 2008). Stringer, a utility infielder, played six years from 1941 to 1950, for the Chicago Cubs, and Boston Red Sox. In 1941, his rookie season with the Cubs, Stringer replaced future Hall of Famer Billy Herman at second base. Statistically, this was his best season, leading the National League in assists with 462.[22] Over his career Stringer appeared in 409 games, had 1,196 at bats, 290 hits, with a career batting average of .242.[23]

Stringer also acted in several films; among them, *The Stratton Story* (1949), and *Three Little Words* (1950).[24] Lou Stringer died on October 19, 2008, in Lake Forest, California; he was ninety-one.

❧ His cremated remains are interred within lawn section BB, tier TJ, space 23. Find the curb markings for graves 95 and 100; then locate the marker of Tony and Joan Pascale. Eleven rows west from that point is Lou Stringer's grave.

GAIL DA CORSI-JOHNSON

Gail Da Corsi-Johnson (November 3, 1942 to February 5, 1999) was a singer, actress, and television personality. Gail began her career in show business appearing in several television episodes of *Mr. Ed*, (1963-65).[25] As a singer, she appeared with Bob Hope in his USO tour during the Vietnam War.

In 1967, her musical career took off when she replaced Kim Carnes as lead singer of the Grammy award-winning musical group, the New Christy Minstrels. After two years of touring with the minstrels, Gail formed her own group, New Kick, which released several albums.

The years of endless touring took a toll on Johnson. She began a new career path, taking a job as a news anchor at Orange County's public television station, KDOC.[26] She also appeared in numerous episodes of the daytime soap opera, *Days of Our Lives*, as the character Mimi Grosset (1979-80).[27]

❧ Gail Johnson died on February 5, 1999, in Mission Viejo; she had battled lymphoma for twelve years.[28] Her grave is located in lawn section A, tier 32, space 250. Locate the 250 grave marker on the south curb. Johnson's final resting place is directly in front, in the first row.

ROBERT T. HUNTER

Another noteworthy burial in lawn A is Robert T. Hunter (September 29, 1907 to September 17, 2000). He was a former chief justice of the Washington State Supreme Court. Hunter was born in Oklahoma, and was a graduate of the University of Washington Law School (1934). In 1935, he began his law practice in Grand Coulee, Washington, and later served as the city attorney, and justice of the peace. He was elected Superior Court Judge from Grant and Douglas counties, 1946-1957. Judge Hunter was appointed to the Washington State Supreme Court in 1957, and served on the high court until 1977. In 1969, he was appointed chief justice, and was the driving force behind Washington's establishment of a state appeals court.

Justice Robert T. Hunter retired from the court in 1977, and moved to southern California.[29] He died on September 17, 2000.

❧ His grave is located in lawn A, tier 24, space 277. Find curb marker 275; eight rows southwest is Judge Hunter's final resting place.

THOMAS J. FEARS

Also interred within the grounds of Ascension Cemetery, opposite lawn A on the other side of the street, is legendary wide receiver, and National Football League Hall of Famer Thomas J. Fears (December 3, 1922 to January 4, 2000). Fears was born in Guadalajara, Mexico, but was raised in Los Angeles. He was a graduate of the University of California, Los Angeles, where he played football

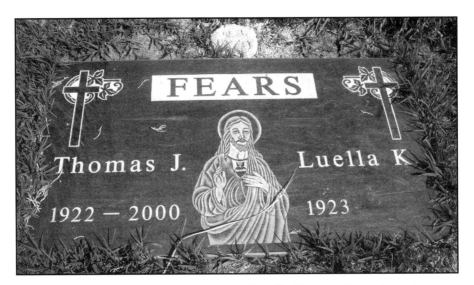

Los Angeles Rams wide receiver and Football Hall of Famer Thomas Fears grave.

and won All-American honors. During his senior year, controversy erupted when allegations arose of his being paid for appearing in a local sports store advertisement. The matter was later dropped. Fears and other UCLA players were cleared of the allegations.

Fears was drafted as a defensive back and played nine seasons for the Los Angeles Rams 1948 to 1956. In his first season with the Rams, Fears played both offense and defense, but made his biggest impact on offense as a receiver. Among his career accomplishments, he is credited with being the first receiver to line up on the line of scrimmage away from the tackle. He held many records throughout his playing days. In his first three seasons; he led the league in receptions. In 1950, he caught 84 passes, surpassing his own record of 77 set the prior year. During the 1950 season, in a game versus the Green Bay Packers, Fears caught a record 18 passes. He was always the "go to" guy when a big play was needed. Fears biggest moment came in the 1951 NFL Championship game versus the Cleveland Browns. In that game, with the score tied and time running out in the fourth quarter, Fears nabbed a short 13 yard pass from quarterback Norm Van Brocklin and raced 60 yards for the game-winning touchdown. This was the first and only championship the Rams won while in Los Angeles. Fears career statistics of 87 games played, 400 receptions, 5,397 yards, and 38 touchdowns, made him one of the leaders of his era.[30]

After ending his playing career in 1956, he was an assistant coach for the Green Bay Packers (1958, 1962-65), and the Los Angeles Rams (1959-61), and Atlanta Falcons (1966). In 1967, Fears became the first head coach of the expansion New Orleans Saints (1967-71). He was fired at the midway point of the 1970 season, having complied an underwhelming mark of 13 wins, 34 losses, with 2 ties in just less than 4 seasons. In 1970, Fears garnered the highest honor a football player could achieve when he was elected to the professional Football Hall of Fame.

During the 1970s, Fears also worked as a consultant on several football related movies:

- *Two Minute Warning* (1976) starring Charlton Heston
- *North Dallas Forty* (1979) with Nick Nolte

They later got him allegedly blacklisted from coaching in the NFL because of his role as technical advisor on the controversial film. He also appeared as an actor in a handful of movies such as:

- *Easy Living* (1949)
- *Crazy Legs* (1953)
- *Two Minute Warning* (1976)

Television credits include programs such as :

- *Warm Hearts, Cold Feet* (1987)
- *Mancuso, FBI* (1990).[31]

As the years past, Fears remained on the fringes of professional football but never again coached in the NFL. In 1990, he was named head football coach for the Milan football franchise of the International League of American Football.

In 1994, Fears was diagnosed with Alzheimer's disease, and spent the last six years of his life battling the illness. On January 4, 2000, he succumbed to the ravages of the disease.[32]

To locate Tom Fears grave, find the 270 marker on the east curb of lawn B. It is near a large palm tree, and two rows from the curb.

JOSEPH AMBROSE MURRAY

Joseph Ambrose Murray (November 11, 1920 to October 19, 2001) was a professional baseball player. Murray played briefly for the Philadelphia Athletics in 1950. He was a left-hand starting pitcher, who was called up from the minor leagues to the majors late in the season. Murray appeared in 8 games, with a record of 0 wins and 3 losses, in 30 innings, with an earned run average of 5.70.[33] Murray died on October 19, 2001 in San Clemente, California.

He is buried in lawn section A, tier 18, space 308. Locate the large tree stump waste receptacle on the bend in the road near the office. Seventeen rows south is Murray's grave. There will be a small tree with a memorial bench in memory of Fred Krinkel a few rows directly in front.

JEAN VANDER PYL

The final famous internment at Ascension is that of famed cartoon voice actress Jean Vander Pyl (October 11, 1919 to April 11, 1999). Vander Pyl was not a well-known face but her voice was always recognizable. She is best known as the voice of Wilma Flintstone in the popular 1960s television series, *The Flintstones*. This program was the first cartoon to run in prime time. It was also

Voice actress Jean Vander Pyl's grave. Note the small rendering of Wilma Flintstone on the marker.

the longest running prime-time cartoon program until it was surpassed by *The Simpsons* several decades later.

Jean appeared in all 167 episodes of the original series. After the original *Flintstones* went off the air in 1966, she continued to work as the voice of Wilma in dozens of additional cartoons. Vander Pyl was the voice for many other cartoon characters such as: Rosie the Robot and Mrs. Spacely on *The Jetsons*.[34] In 1994, she was awarded the Annie Award for life time achievement in the field of animation.[35]

On April 10, 1999 in Dana Point, California, she died from lung cancer. Ironically, all four main characters of the original *Flintstones* series, Alan Reed (Fred), Mel Blanc (Barney), and Bea Benaderet (Betty) all died from smoking related illnesses.[36]

Jean Vander Pyl is buried in lawn A, tier 34, space 350 on the south side of the office. Locate the St. Anne statue, and fifteen rows to the right is her final resting place.

GOOD SHEPHERD CEMETERY

8301 Talbert Avenue
Huntington Beach, California 92646
Telephone: 714-847-8546

The cemetery is open daily from 8 a.m. until 5 p.m. The office is open Monday through Friday from 8:30 a.m. to 5 p.m. and Saturday from 8:30 a.m. to 4:30 p.m.

Good Shepherd Cemetery was originally known as the Huntington Beach Cemetery and then as Roselawn Cemetery. In 1952, it was purchased by the Los Angeles Arch Diocese. Administration of the cemetery passed to the Arch Diocese of Orange in 1967, and was renamed Good Shepherd. The cemetery is situated on twenty acres of land that is only three miles from the Pacific Ocean.

Navigating the grounds is fairly easy, and locating graves is also very simple with lot numbers clearly marked on all curbs.

Most of the famous graves are located in the old sections of the cemetery that border Beach Boulevard.

There are only a handful of notable burials at this cemetery, the majority of which are professional baseball players.

CORNELIUS STEPHEN "CONNIE" CREEDEN

The first noteworthy internment at Good Shepherd Cemetery is professional baseball player Cornelius Stephen "Connie" Creeden (July 21, 1915 to November 30, 1969). Creeden was a utility infielder who played five games for the 1943 Boston Braves. After his brief baseball career ended, Creeden changed his name to Lee Burton, and began a career in the music industry that lasted thirty years. He died on November 30, 1969 in Santa Ana, California.[37]

❧ He is buried in lawn H, lot 1950, space 1. On the east curb, locate marker 1951, and the grave is two rows west. Cemetery records have him buried under the name Lee Burton, the death certificate has both names listed, but his actual grave marker reads Cornelius Creeden.

ROBIN CHRISTINE SAMSOE

At rest in lawn G is Robin Christine Samsoe (December 13, 1966 to June 20, 1979) who was allegedly murdered by accused serial killer Rodney James Alcala. On June 20, 1979, twelve-year-old Robin and several friends had gone to the beach for a day of fun. At some point during the afternoon, the girls were approached by a man, later indentified as Alcala. He wanted to take pictures, but was scared off by an adult friend of the girls. In the late afternoon, Robin had to leave for dance practice; she had forgotten her dance outfit at home, and fearing that it would take too much time to walk, asked to borrow a friend's bicycle. As she pedaled off for home, this was the last time Robin would be seen alive. For several weeks police conducted an intensive search for the young girl, and on July 6, 1979, a body was discovered by a state forestry employee in the foothills near Sierra Madre. At the Chantry Flat campgrounds north of Los Angeles County, police officials identified the skeletal remains as that of Robin Samsoe.[38]

On July 24, 1979, Rodney Alcala was arrested for Samsoe's murder based on composite drawings, and tips provided by four informants. Alcala, 35, a 1968 graduate of UCLA's theater arts department was a part-time photographer, was unemployed, and living with his parents at the time of his arrest.[39] After a lengthy trial on June 20, 1980, Alcala was found guilty of first degree murder with special circumstances, and sentenced to death.[40]

In a shocking turn of events on August 23, 1984, Alcala's murder conviction was overturned by the California State Supreme Court. The court ruled that the jury had been improperly told about Alcala's prior sex crimes.[41] In the second trial, new physical evidence surfaced that showed Alcala had been present at Sunset Beach, and had taken pictures at the location the day Samsoe disappeared. On May 28, 1986, his second trial ended with another first degree murder conviction, and was again sentenced to death.[42]

Murder victim Robin Samsoe's grave at Good Shepherd Cemetery, Huntington Beach.

On April 2, 2001, the unthinkable happened again, the California States Appeals Court overturned the second conviction and death sentence of Rodney Alcala. This time, "the defense had been precluded from developing and presenting evidence material to significant issues in the case."[43]

In other developments Los Angeles police detectives linked Alcala though DNA evidence to the sexual assault murders of four L.A. area women. In June of 2008, it was agreed that Alcala would be tried again for Samsoe's murder, and would also at the same time stand trial for the other four homicides. At the time of this printing, a trial date has been set for late 2009, and will take place in Orange County.[44] Rodney James Alcala alleged serial killer has spent the better part of the last three decades behind bars. It is hoped that one day justice will prevail.

🎗 Robin Samsoe's grave is located in lawn G, lot 1611, space 4. On the southwest curb, locate the 1601 marker. Eleven rows north, near the center of the lawn, is Robin's final resting place.

JESSE ROBERT "JIM" BUCKLES

Jesse Robert "Jim" Buckles (May 20, 1890 to August 2, 1975), professional baseball player. Jesse Buckles was a left-handed pitcher who played for the New York Yankees, appearing in two games during the 1916 season.[45]

🎗 He is buried in lawn E, lot 1311, space 1. Locate the 1324 marker on the east curb, fourteen rows near the middle of the lawn under a large pine tree is Buckles' grave.

PATRICK HOWARD MCNULTY

Patrick Howard McNulty (February 27, 1899 to May 4, 1963) was a professional baseball player. McNulty attended Ohio State University and was a start athlete in multiple sports. He was an outfielder who played five seasons for the Cleveland Indians from 1922 to 1927. His best year statistically was 1925; he appeared in 118 games, and had a career batting average of .314.[46]

✤ McNulty's grave is located in lawn E, lot 2321, space 4. Locate the 2328 marker on the northeast curb and follow the in-ground markers eight rows west to McNulty's gravesite.

ROBERT BURKS

Robert Burks (July 4, 1909 to May 13, 1968), was an award-winning cinematographer and a very successful cameraman who started out as a special effects specialist for Warner Studios. He went on to become one of the finest directors of cinematography. Burks worked for both Warner Brothers and Paramount Studious, during the 1950s and 1960s. Burks was Alfred Hitchcock's favorite cameraman, and worked on most of the director's films during this period. In 1956, he won the Academy Award for best cinematography for Hitchcock's *To Catch a Thief* (1955). Other famous film credits include:

- *Strangers on a Train* (nominated for an Academy Award in 1951)
- *Hondo* (1953)
- *Dial M for Murder* (1954)
- *Rear Window* (nominated for an Academy Award in 1954)
- *Vertigo* (1958)
- *North by Northwest* (1959)
- *The Music Man* (1962)
- *The Birds* (1963)
- *Patch of Blue* (nominated for an Academy Award in 1965)[47]

Academy award winning cinematographer Robert Burks final resting place.

On May 13, 1968, Burks and his wife, Elizabeth, were killed in a house fire at their Newport Beach, California home. Robert Burks is buried in lawn D, lot 1409, space 5. Locate 115 on the west curb of lawn D. Eight rows east, under a pine tree, is the Burks final resting place.

KIRT OBER

Not far from Robert Burks is the grave of actor Kirt Ober (1875 to June 1, 1939). Ober was a screen, stage, and vaudeville actor, whose film credits are unknown.[48] He once worked as a jockey.[49] Ober died on June 1, 1939 of a heart attack in Huntington Beach, California.[50]

His grave is located in lawn D, lot 179, space 10. From Robert Burks grave, walk about forty feet north and one row east.

FRANK BENJAMIN MANUSH

Also interred within lawn D is professional baseball player Frank Benjamin Manush (September 18, 1883 to January 5, 1965). Frank played third base for the Philadelphia Athletics in 1908. He appeared in 23 games, with 12 hits, and a batting average of .156.[51] Frank is the older brother of baseball hall of famer Henry "Heinie" Manush.[52] Frank Manush died on January 5, 1965, in Laguna Beach, California.

His grave is found in lawn D, lot 1211, space 3. From Robert Burk's grave, walk about twenty feet south, and one row east to Manush's final resting place.

DONALD J. "DON" MCMAHON

The final noteworthy internment at Good Shepherd is Donald J. "Don" McMahon (January 4, 1930 to July 22, 1987) who was a professional baseball player. McMahon was a right-handed relief pitcher who played eighteen seasons in the major leagues from 1957 to 1974 for the Milwaukee Braves, Houston Colt 45's, Cleveland Indians, Boston Red Sox, Chicago White Sox, Detroit Tigers, and San Francisco Giants. He was a dominant pitcher who played before the "closer" position was created. McMahon's statistics of 874 games played (27th all-time), record of 90 wins and 68 losses, 153 saves (64th all-time), and earned run average of 2.96 (155th all-time), were among the league leaders of his era. In 1958, he was selected to represent the Milwaukee Braves in the All-Star Game. He was a member of the 1957 World Series Champion Milwaukee Braves, and also appeared with the Braves in the 1958 World Series. In 1968, he again won a World Series Championship with the Detroit Tigers.[53]

After retiring from playing, he was the pitching coach for the San Francisco Giants, Minnesota Twins, and Cleveland Indians. In 1986, he was hired by the Los Angeles Dodgers as a scout and coach. He was a good friend and childhood companion of Oakland Raiders owner Al Davis.[54] On July 22, 1987, while pitching batting practice before a game at Dodgers Stadium, he had a fatal heart attack.

Don McMahon is buried in lawn A, lot 192, space 4. Find the 192 grave marker on the east curb; his grave is on the curb in the first row.

MURDER AND MAYHEM

Indeed, history is nothing more than tableau of crimes and misfortunes.

~Voltaire
writer and philosopher (1694 to 1778)

The following chapter discusses five radically different historical events that did not necessarily occur in Orange County but end tragically. Most of the participants are buried in different graveyards throughout the county. Topics of discussion will include:

- the Juan Flores Gang,

- the Center Street Shoot out,

- the Battle of Tomato Springs,

- the Crash of Pan Am Flight 103,

- the mass shooting at Cal State Fullerton, and

- the unsolved murders of the original night stalker.

THE JUAN FLORES GANG

Orange County in the 1850s was a lawless and ruthless place. Roving bands of criminal groups roamed the countryside of the region. With powerful leaders such as Poncho Daniel, Manuel Marquez, and Joaquin Murrieta, these gangs of bandidos terrorized the settlers of the area. One of the most powerful and deadly bandit gangs to develop was led by Juan Flores.

Flores was born into a prominent area family, but by his teen years, he'd turned to a life of crime. While in prison, Flores befriended other youths, and formed the "los manilas" gang. This bandit gang, whose numbers varied from fifty to one hundred, gained a cult-like following in the region. Under his leadership, the gang was able to steal and terrorize at will for almost two years. Flores was seen by many as a vigilante folk hero, akin to the likes of Jesse James.

One of the most famous incidents involving the "los manilas" occurred in January of 1857, when the Flores gang raided the little town of San Juan Capistrano. This incident would leave a wide path of death and destruction in its wake. It would also be the beginning of the demise of the criminal group. On Sunday, January 25, 1857, a local teamster named Garnet Hardy of San Juan Capistrano was advised that the Flores gang was hiding out in the local hills, and were waiting to rob unsuspecting wagon trains. Hardy sent word to his brother Alfred Hardy (a prominent citizen) in Los Angeles of the pending bandit trouble. The message was passed on to Los Angeles County Sheriff James Barton. He organized a posse of six men that included constables William Little, Charles Baker, Charles Daly, Frank Alexander, and an unknown scout. The posse, led by Barton, soon left Los Angeles in pursuit of the bandits.[1]

On Thursday morning, January 29, 1857, the Flores gang, impatient and needing supplies, raided the town of San Juan Capistrano. While Flores visited his girlfriend, a local girl named Martina "Chola" Burruel, other members of the gang attacked and robbed the store of merchant Michael Krazewski. What the gang could not carry out, they destroyed.

Later that day, the gang return to the town and looted the stores of Henry Charles, Manuel Garcia, and Charles Pfugardt. Charles and Garcia were lucky and fled unharmed; Pfugardt was not as fortunate. He attempted to stop the looting and was shot and killed. The gang members then ordered the shop clerk to make them dinner, while the body of Pfugardt lay on the floor nearby. Securing all the supplies they would need, the Flores gang then fled to the local foothills.[2]

On Friday morning, January 29, 1857, Sherriff Barton and his group arrived at the Sepulveda Ranch. A local man told Barton that the Flores gang was hiding in the local foothills and there were at least fifty bandidos in the group.

Returning to the road to San Juan Capistrano, the posse was about twelve miles north of the Sepulveda Ranch near present day Laguna Canyon when they were overrun and ambushed by members of the Flores gang. Twenty bandits rode from the hills and suddenly swooped down on the tiny posse. Barton, realizing that his group was out manned and out gunned, fired fruitlessly on the advancing bandits. In quick order, Barton, Little, Baker, and Daly were shot dead. Alexander and the unknown scout were able to escape unharmed. After removing

The rendezvous tree (located on Junipero Serra Road). Legend states that the Flores gang met here before the raid on San Juan Capistrano.

The Garcia adobe (present day). The first floor was used by merchant Michael Krazewski and was the scene of the Flores gangs first raid.

valuables from the bodies of the slain lawmen, the bandidos rode off into the distant Santa Ana Mountains.[3]

When word of the tragic massacre of Barton's posse reached Los Angeles, three large posses were formed, one under the leadership of Andres Pico. These groups left Los Angeles in pursuit of the killer bandits. The Flores gang hearing that a large company of men were in hot pursuit, dispersed into small groups throughout the mountains.

Juan Flores and several members of his gang including Juan Catabo, and Francisco Ardillero were surrounded and captured near present day Silverado Canyon. The three gang members were taken into custody after a short gun battle, and then taken to the home of Theodocio Yorba. During the night, Flores was able to overpower his guards and escape, Catabo and Ardillero were not as lucky. The next morning, Pico, not wanting the two remaining criminals to escape, ordered their immediate execution. Catabo and Ardillero were unceremoniously hung from a large sycamore tree near the road (present day, 1/2 mile south of the entrance to Irvine Lake on the right side of Santiago Canyon Road).[4] The bodies of the dead bandidos were left hanging, while the posse rode off in pursuit of the gang leader. Juan Flores was recaptured a few days later near the Simi Pass. He was taken into custody and brought to Los Angeles. He stood trial for the murder of Sheriff Barton and the others, and was found guilty. He was sentenced to death, and on February 14, 1857, was hung on a hill near what is present day downtown Los Angeles.[5]

In the aftermath of the carnage, many members of the Flores gang fled and dispersed throughout the region, and never again regrouped. Most of the prominent members were hunted down and executed. Many of the prominent participants in the incident are allegedly buried at the old Mission Cemetery in San Juan Capistrano. They include :

- George Pfugardt

- Michael Krazewski

+→❦ Martina Burreal

+→❦ Garnet Hardy

+→❦ Henry Charles

+→❦ Mr. Buckner (he was a member of the second posse, who shot himself accidentally, while in pursuit of the bandits)

There was a third cemetery in San Juan Capistrano. This burial ground was for Protestants. The Capistrano Cemetery for Protestants was located near the present day Marco Forster Middle School on Camino del Avion, south of downtown. When the land was developed, the remains were supposedly dug up and reburied. There is no record of where the bodies were reburied or who was actually interred at the site. Legend states that five bodies were left in the original cemetery location. Who these five people are is a mystery. It is possible that some of the participants listed above were buried in this cemetery but there is no proof.[6]

❦ Interred elsewhere are Juan Catabo (aka Juan Silvas, Juan Sauripa) and Francisco Ardillero (aka Guerro Ardillero). They are presumed buried in an unmarked grave near the place of their execution, off of Santiago Canyon Road, south of Irvine Lake.

Look for a small grove of sycamore trees, half a mile south of the entrance to Irvine Lake. Near the road is a large, menacing tree, looming large above the other smaller trees. It is alleged that from one of its branches the two bandidos

The Old Mission Cemetery, San Juan Capistrano.

Legend states that this large sycamore tree is the tree in which the bandidos Juan Catabo and Francisco Ardillero were executed. The bandits are both presumed to be buried nearby in unmarked graves.

were hung. Their unmarked graves are also assumed to be nearby. The bodies of Sheriff Barton, Little, Baker, and Daly were returned to Los Angeles for burial. Juan Flores is also presumed to be buried in Los Angeles and other participants have unknown burial locations.

THE SHOOT OUT ON CENTER STREET

CHARLES F. LEHMAN

The first Anaheim law enforcement officer to be killed in the line of duty was Anaheim town marshal Charles F. Lehman (d. July 23, 1872). Gunfights between gamblers, gunslingers, and lawmen in the old west were common. But such events were unheard of in the quiet vine-growing colony of Anaheim.

The tragic details of Marshal Lehman's murder play out like an old west movie. On Sunday evening, July 21, 1872, ex-city Marshal David Davis (a political rival of Lehman's), and a man named Horton were engaged in a spirited game of poker at Goldstein's Brewery-Saloon, located on Center Street (renamed Lincoln Avenue).

Around 6 p.m., a dispute arose between the two card players, words were exchanged, tempers flared, and guns were drawn. Davis allegedly drew his revolver first, which prompted Horton to flee the saloon through the rear of the building. Davies followed and the gunfight continued in a vacant lot adjacent to

Marshal Lehman's grave at Anaheim Cemetery.

the saloon. Both Davis and Horton fired at each other from close range, both failing to injury the other.

From his office, Marshal Lehman heard the shots and rushed to investigate the disturbance.[7] Attempting to quell the fight and arrest Horton, Lehman was shot in the abdomen.[8] Horton immediately leaped onto a horse and rode away, while Lehman lay mortally wounded. The Marshal was carried a short distance to Higgin's Drugstore and administered first aid.[9] Horton was pursued by an angry mob and was captured a short distance away, hiding in a vineyard. After receiving first aid, Lehman was transferred to Mrs. Brown's Boarding House where he died two days later. On his deathbed, Lehman insisted that he was shot by Davis not Horton. These statements led to the arrest of Davis, who was charged with manslaughter.[10]

At the trial in Los Angeles, Davis was defended by Frank Ganahl, the leading criminal defense attorney in the county. After a brief trial, Davis was acquitted of all charges.[11] As for Horton, he was detained for a short period of time, eventually gaining his release from jail. After his discharge, Horton left Anaheim, faded into history, and was never seen or heard from again.[12]

Charles Lehman's funeral was one of the largest ever attended in the early days of the Anaheim colony.[13]

His final resting place lay unmarked for over 100 years. In 1995, Anaheim historical preservationists placed a memorial plaque at his grave in Anaheim Cemetery, lawn ACP, section 1, lot 34, space 1. His flush-to-the-ground marker is found west of the pioneer gate and near the south wall.

DAVID S. DAVIS

The other famous character of the shootout on Center Street was David S. Davis (1835 to April 17, 1918) and he is also interred at Anaheim Cemetery. Davis was a colorful character, frontier gunfighter, gambler, and lawman. His arrival in Anaheim and prior whereabouts are sketchy. What *is* known is that he was elected Anaheim town Marshal in 1870, and his short career in law enforcement was quite controversial.

Early in 1870, an incident involving some citizens and the marshal developed. Davis was determined to disrupt a celebration of the French capitulation to the Germans in the Franco-Prussian war. This was due to Davis' allegiance to France. Apparently, some German citizens were planning to use some sort of fire torches to celebrate, but Davis forbade this in the public streets. The mayor of Anaheim, Max Strobel, was appealed to and overrode Davis' order, granting a permit for use of fire in the public streets. This angered Davis, who stated, "the first man who touches a match to that kindling is my prisoner." A man by the name of Fritz struck a match and was instantly hit on the head by Davis and rendered unconscious. Tempers arose, but cooler heads prevailed, and the celebrations were moved to private lots.[14]

Another incident involving Davis also occurred in 1870, and this resulted in the use of deadly force. Apparently, a woman had been severely beaten and mistreated by a male Indian acquaintance. At some point, several weeks after the attack, the woman had fully recovered from her injuries, and was able to indentify her attacker. Marshal Davis was summoned; he went to the saloon where the Indian man was known to hangout. While attempting to arrest the culprit, a scuffle ensued. The Indian attempted to flee and was shot by Davis. The Indian man died of his wounds several days after the incident.

Davis was involved in yet another shooting incident, where an alleged horse thief was shot and killed. The alleged thief was rumored to be holding up in Soquel Canyon. A posse led by Davis tracked the thief and corned him in the canyon. Shots were fired and the horse thief was killed.[15]

David Davis' career as a peace officer was short. He lost re-election to Charles F. Lehman in early 1872. This caused much animosity between the two men which might have led to the shootout and death of Lehman at Goldstein's saloon on July 21, 1872.[16] Despite his rough demeanor, Davis had many friends, and continued to live in Anaheim until his death on April 17, 1917.[17]

His burial location is in lawn AAD1, lot 63, space 5. The grave is found across the street from the mausoleum. Locate the grave marker of Angeline Sonneman on the east curb; four rows west is Davis' burial site.

David Davis' burial plot at Anaheim Cemetery.

THE BATTLE OF TOMATO SPRINGS

JOE MATLOCK

Almost fifty-six years to the day, four miles from where Sheriff Barton and his posse were gunned down by the Juan Flores gang, another bandit shot it out with law enforcement. On December 15, 1912, Joe Matlock (also known as Ira Jones) an out-of-work drifter, assaulted seventeen-year-old, Myrtle Huff, on her uncle's (William A. Cook) Irvine area ranch. Matlock then escaped into the foothills near Tomato Springs. The sheriff's department was contacted and a posse consisting of Sherriff C.E. Ruddock, Santa Ana city Marshall Samuel Jernigan, Constable Calvin E. Jackson, Deputy Sheriffs Robert Squires and James Stacy, Jailer Theo Lacy, Leonard A. West, William Culver, and Al Prather, all made their way to the Tomato Springs area. By the time the posse had arrived, Matlock was hold up in a hideout in the western hills. As Deputy Sheriff Squires and Stacy led the posse, and were making their way up the steep ridge, Matlock suddenly appeared and opened fire. Deputy Stacy was shot through the shoulder, leg, and wrist, while Deputy Squires sustained a mortal gunshot wound to the head. The remaining members of the posse returned fire and encircled the bandit to ensure he would not escape.

Feeling the posse was out gunned, Sheriff Ruddock sent for reinforcements. Meanwhile members of the posse made their way to the injured officers. Stacy and the body of Squires were found in a ravine and were carried to safety. As the party made their way down the hillside, shots again rang out. This time Al Prather sustained a gunshot wound to the head and William Culver was shot in the left knee.

At around 12 p.m., reinforcements arrived on the scene: Captain Nathan Ulm, and 150 men of company L of the California National Guard. The unit proceeded carefully up the steep hillside, creeping closer and closer to Matlock position. Seeing that his position was hopeless, Matlock burst from the brush, rushing forward, and firing his rifle. The men of company L opened fire, hitting Matlock, who fell dead from a wound to the head.[18] The Battle of Tomato Springs was over. It was the last great manhunt, Western style, to take place in Orange County.

Who was the bandit? Questions about the true identity of the gunman arose immediately after the battle. Was his name really Ira Jones, or was it Joe Matlock? J.D. Matlock, of Eugene, Oregon, alleged father of the deceased publicly denied that the gunman was his son. But according to some sources, he privately told Sheriff Ruddock that the dead man was, indeed his son, Joe Matlock. According to this same source, the body of the bandit was secretly shipped back to Eugene, Oregon with his father.[19] There are no public records of this ever happening. The burial lists at the Santa Ana Cemetery show that Joe Matlock was indeed interred in an unmarked pauper's grave in the cemetery. Could there have been a cover-up? Could the supposed grave containing the remains of the bandit, Joe Matlock, be empty? After almost 100 years, there are no living participants of the incident, and there is no actual written proof of a cover-up. The only thing that is certain is that Joe

Matlock is dead, and was buried some place, and that some place points to the Santa Ana Cemetery.

❧ The Tomato Springs bandit, Joe Matlock, is buried in an unmarked, paupers grave in lawn CO, lot 33, space 1. The lawn is just north of the cemetery office and is filled with unmarked graves. The burial plots in this section are laid out haphazardly, in no particular order, and this makes finding exact burial locations impossible.

ROBERT SQUIRES

Deputy Sheriff Robert Squires (1870 to 1912) was the first Orange County Deputy Sheriff killed in the line of duty. His funeral on December 18, 1912, was the largest ever held in the city of Santa Ana. Pallbearers included Orange County Sheriff Ruddock, Los Angeles County Sheriff Hammel, Superior Court Judge Z.B. West, and Marshal Jernigan.[20]

❧ Robert Squires is buried at Fairhaven Memorial Park, lawn L, lot 36, space 1. From the south curb locate the grave of Isabelle Tucker, and four rows north is his final resting place.

SAMUEL JERNIGAN

Other participants of the battle that are buried in Orange County Cemetery's are Marshal Samuel Jernigan (November 3, 1876 to October 25, 1966). He is interred at Melrose Abbey in Anaheim, Acacia mausoleum hallway, crypt 8F. Upon entering the mausoleum area, turn right at the first hallway, immediately on the left, two rows from the bottom, and three crypts from the left is Jernigan's crypt.

Deputy Squires final resting place at Fairhaven Memorial Park.

The Following are Buried at Fairhaven Memorial Park

Calvin E. Jackson

✿ Constable Calvin E. Jackson (1868 to 1938) is buried in lawn K, lot 11, space 1. Locate the grave marker of Mae Foster Jackson on the east curb, and two rows west is his final resting place.

Leonard A. West

✿ Posse member, Leonard A. West (1872 to 1955) is buried in lawn R, lot 82, space 4. Locate the grave marker of Lillian E. Felder on the east curb, and three rows west is West's burial plot.

Captain Nathan Ulm

✿ Interred at Santa Ana Cemetery are Captain Nathan Ulm (August 10, 1869 to November 19, 1913), lawn D, section 14, lot 4, space 2. Find the grave marker of Anna L. Eyman on the east curb; seven rows west is his final resting place.

James F. "Tex" Stacy

✿ Deputy Sheriff James F. "Tex" Stacy (d.1922), is buried in lawn L, lot 51, space 6. Find the grave of Gertie M. Newcomb on the south curb, and nine rows north is Stacy's burial spot.

Tex Stacy's grave site at Santa Ana Cemetery.

THEO LACY

❧ Orange County Jailer, Theo Lacy, is buried in lawn Z. Locate the marker of Fred Bitticks on the south curb, and eight rows north is Lacy's burial plot.

Other prominent people involved in this incident are either buried outside of Orange County or their burial locations were unable to be determined.

THE TERRORIST BOMBING
OF PAN AM FLIGHT 103

On the evening of December 21, 1988, over Lockerbie, Scotland, Pan Am Flight 103 was blown up and it crashed. On board the Boeing 747 were 259 passengers and crew members; all passengers and 11 people on the ground perished. A terrorist bomb had been stored in luggage beneath the aircraft and exploded 38 minutes after taking off from London's Heathrow Airport.

In 2001, a trial of the suspected terrorists, Lamin Khalifah Fhimah, and Abdel Basset Ali-al Megrahi took place in Scotland. Megrahi was found guilty of murder and sentenced to 27 years in prison. The other defendant, Fhimah, was acquitted.

THREE CREW MEMBERS OF PAN AM 103
ARE BURIED IN ORANGE COUNTY

LILIBETH MACALOLOOY

Flight attendant Lilibeth Tobila Macalolooy (November 2, 1961 to December 21, 1988) is buried at Forest Law, Cypress.

❧ Her final resting place is found in the Garden of Protection, lot 3970, space 1, two rows in front of the statue of Jesus with the little children (Westside). Follow the sidewalk from the west curb of the lawn to the enclosed area near the statue. Lilibeth's large bronze marker (shared with her grandmother Natividad) is hard to miss. The grave is most often adorned with large bouquets of colorful flowers, and is well maintained.

Flight attendant Lilibeth Macalolooy's grave at Forest Lawn-Cypress.

Flight attendant Jocelyn Reina's final resting place at Forest Lawn.

JOCELYN REINA

❦ A fellow Pan Am flight attendant, (May 26, 1962 to December 21, 1988) is also interred at Forest Lawn, Cypress in the Garden of Memory, lot 166, space 1. Her grave is found near the intersection of Cypress Drive and Memory Lane. Locate John T. Reina's (Jocelyn's grandfather) grave marker on the south curb. One row north, near the corner of the brick wall, is Jocelyn's final resting place.

JERRY D. AVRITT

Flight engineer Jerry Avritt's grave at Westminster Memorial Park.

A third victim of the crash with Orange County roots is the flight engineer of Pan Am 103, Jerry D. Avritt. He is buried at Westminster Memorial Park in the Meditation lawn, block 19F, lot 424, space 4. Locate marker G183 on the south curb (kind of worn and hard to read), and then find the grave of Merle and Ethel Horner. Twelve rows north is the Avritt grave. The epitaph of his marker reads "On Eagles Wings," and is also adorned with a rendering of a 747 jet plane. Ironically, Avritt is buried only yards away from the mass gravesite of victims of the Canary Islands air collision of March 27, 1977.

SHOOTING RAMPAGE AT CAL STATE, FULLERTON

On the morning of July 12, 1976, California State University, Fullerton custodian Edward Charles Allaway shot and killed seven school employees, and wounded two at the campus library. Allaway had been employed at the university for a year, when desponent over the recent break-up of his marriage, blamed co-workers for the demise, then went on a shooting rampage at the school.

At 9 a.m., Allaway entered the university library and made his way to the basement. He entered the Instructional Media Center, and with no warning, opened fire with a .22 caliber rifle.

The first victim, Paul Herzberg (an IMC technician), was shot and killed at his desk. Second victim, Bruce Jacobsen (another IMC technician), was shot and killed while attempting to take cover in a nearby conference room. In an adjacent office, Frank Teplansky (grahic artist) and professor Seth Fessenden were talking when shots rangout. Allaway burst into the office. With no place to hide, Teplansky and Fessenden were both shot and killed. The gunman then left the media center, headed to the outdoor hallway on the south side of the library. Here he was confronted by fellow custodians Deborah Paulsen and Donald Karges. Allaway fired several shots but missed. Paulsen and Karges both fled and were pursued by Allaway. Both were eventually caught, and they were also shot and killed. Allaway then left the basement area and headed to the first floor lobby area of the library. Here he was confronted by Donald Keran (associate librarian), Stephen Becker (library assistant), and Maynard Hoffman (custodial supervisor). Hoffman was shot and wounded as he stood near the elevators, Keran was shot and also wounded while sitting at his desk, and Becker was shot and killed, while attempting to flee through the main doors to the library. Allaway then fled the library, retracing his steps to the east side of the library, where he had left his car.[21]

The bloody rampage had taken less then ten minutes. In the carnage were left seven people dead or dying, and two seriously wounded. At the time, it was only the second such mass school shooting. (The first had taken place ten years earlier at the University of Texas, Austin. On August 1, 1966, gunman Charles Whitman, shot and killed fourteen people, while wounding thirty-two at the university campus.)

After getting in his car, Allaway drove to a local motel, called police indentifying himself as the shooter, and calmly waitied for them to arrive. He was taken into custody without incident.[22] At his murder trial a year later, Allaway testified that homosexual men were using the school's library for sexual liasons and were plotting to kill him. He was found not guilty by reason of insanity, and was reprimanded to the care of the Patton State Mental Hospital in San Berbardino, California.[23] It was later found that he suffered from severe paranoia and schizophrenia. Today, he is still incarcerated at the hospital. An attempt at freedom was denied in 2003, when public outcry and media attention, along with a determination that he still possed a threat, deprived him of release.[24]

Five of the seven victims of this tragedy are buried within Orange County.

BRUCE JACOBSEN
DEBORAH PAULSEN

Two of the fatalities, Paul Herzberg and Donald Karges, are interred outside of the county. At Forest Lawn, Cypress are custodians Bruce Jacobsen and Deborah Paulsen are at rest in the Ascension Mausolem, Sanctuary of Faithful Memory, crypts 6793 and 2794. Enter the mausoleum to the left of the large mural of the "Ascension." After entering the building, turn left at the first hallway. At the end of the hallway is the empty crypt that once held the remains of singer Karen Carpenter. Turn right into the Sanctuary of Faithful Memory hallway. On the right wall, seven crypts from the right, and two from the bottom is Deborah Paulsen's crypt. Bruce Jacobsen is interred on the same wall, eight crypts from the right, and two from the top.

FRANK TEPLANSKY

Buried at Holy Sepulcher Catholic Cemetery in Orange is graphic artist, Frank Teplansky. His grave is located in lawn F, tier 6, space 9. Locate marker number ten on the east curb, and six rows west is Teplanky's final resting place.

SETH A. FESSENDEN

The final two victims of the shooting are interred at Loma Vista Memorial Park in Fullerton. Professor Seth A. Fessenden (1903 to 1976) is buried in West Lawn #5, lot 103, space 6. Locate the grave marker of Robert L. Sebbo on the south curb, and ten rows north under a large tree is the professors grave.

STEPHEN L. BECKER

Library employee, Stephen L. Becker (1944 to 1976) is interred in the Buena Vista Lawn #2, lot 502, space 1. From the east curb, locate the marker of Jay and Virginia Powell; twenty-six rows west, also under a tree, is Becker's burial plot.

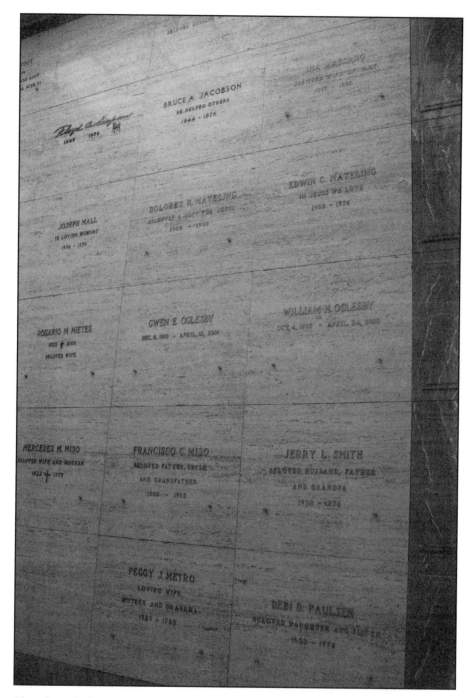

Shooting victims Deborah Paulsen's crypt pictured on bottom right with
Bruce Jacobsen's second row from the top center, Ascension mausoleum,
Forest Lawn-Cypress.

THE ORIGINAL NIGHT STALKER MURDERS

From 1979 to 1986, a serial killer stalked the bedroom communities of Southern California. The Original Night Stalker (not to be confused with serial killer Richard Ramirez) has been linked through DNA evidence to ten murders, four of which occurred in Orange County. He also has been linked to the "East Bay Rapists," a series of crimes (1976 to 1979) in which nearly fifty burglaries and rapes were committed in the San Francisco Bay and Sacramento areas. This killer is considered to be one of the worst unapprehended serial criminals in American history.

On December 30, 1979, the crimes turned to murder when, in the early morning hours, Robert Offerman and his girlfriend, Debra Manning, of Goleta, California, were shot to death in their home.[25] The killer struck again, this time in Ventura, California. On March 16, 1980, he bludgeoned to death prominent attorney, Lyman Smith, 43, and his wife, Charlene Smith, 33, in their home.[26]

The serial killer struck in Laguna Niguel on August 21, 1980. The victims Keith and Patty Harrington had been married only four months, when they were found bludgeoned to death in their gated community home of Laguna Shores. Keith, 24, was in his fourth year of medical school at the University of California, Irvine, and Patty, 27, was a pediatric nurse.[27] On February 5, 1981, Manuela Witthuhn, 28, was also found raped and bludgeoned to death in her Irvine home. Witthuhn was married but her husband was not home. He was in a local hospital recuperating from a recent illness.[28]

The killing spree continued later that same year, when another couple Cheri Domingo and Gregory Sanchez were found shot to death in their home in Goleta, California. This murder took place just a few blocks away from where the original killings occurred.[29]

The final murder linked to the Original Night Stalker case occurred on May 4, 1986. Eighteen-year-old Janelle Cruz was also found raped and bludgeoned to death in her parent's home in Irvine, California. The teenager was left home alone while her parents vacationed in Mexico. The single story home had also been listed for sale.[30] A suspect, Gregory Jesus Gonzalez, the girl's boyfriend, was briefly detained by police. He was soon released for lack of evidence. Apparently, the boy had visited Janelle earlier in the evening and soon after he left, she was attacked, raped, and killed by the unknown intruder.[31]

After the murder of Janelle Cruz, the killing spree abruptly ended. There is no further DNA evidence linking the killer to additional crimes. Police investigators have no suspects and the case remains unsolved. It is speculated that either the killer is in prison, has died, or just stopped killing. Recent news coverage, and a television program entitled "True Hollywood Stories Investigates: The Original Night Stalker," which aired in mid May 2009 on the "E" Entertainment channel, will hopefully bring new interest and clues to the twenty-plus year unsolved murder cases.[32]

In recent news, a Ventura area couple was found brutally stabbed to death by an unknown intruder. The May 20, 2009, murders of Brock and Davina Husted at their seaside, single-story home, in a gated community of Ventura, California, bears eerie similarities to the Original Night Stalker crimes. The Husted's home had also recently been for sale.[33]

Police say there was no motive for the killings and they appear to be random crimes. Is the Original Night Stalker back after twenty-four years, and has the recent publicity into the earlier killings awoken a murder? No one knows for sure. What is known is that the killer's motus operandi has changed little over the years. He has mainly stalked middle class couples, who live in single story homes, and often the homes had been for sale. He enters quietly through unlocked windows or doors in the middle of the night, subdues his victims, often killing the man first, then rapes and kills the woman.

✿ The Orange County victims of these crimes are buried in several cemeteries.

KEITH ELI HARRINGTON
PATRICE "PATTY" BRISCOE HARRINGTON

✿ Three of the victims are interred at Pacific View Memorial Park. They are Keith Eli Harrington (1955 to 1980) and Patrice "Patty" Briscoe Harrington (1951 to 1980). Their dual burial plot is located in the Lakeside lawn, lot 132, space E. Find curb marker 123, and nine rows north is their grave.

JANELLE LISA CRUZ

✿ Also buried at Pacific View is Janelle Lisa Cruz (1967 to 1986). Her final resting place is found in the Vista del Mar lawn, lot 888, space A, five rows north of General Quilter's grave.

MANUELA WITTHUHN

✿ The final Orange County victim is Manuela Witthuhn (d. 1981) and she is buried at El Toro Memorial Park. Her grave is found in the Live Oak lawn, block 7, lot 4, space 9. On the southeast curb find the marker of Jo Sherman Hein, and eleven rows northeast is Witthuhn's burial plot.

Original Night Stalker murder victim's Keith and Patty Harrington's final resting place at Pacific View Memorial Park.

CONCLUSION

The cult of celebrity in which many people propel themselves today, has become a new form of religion. The searching out and visitation of the graves of famous people has developed into a growing pastime for a large number of fans. Whatever the reason for visiting the graves of the rich, famous, infamous, and noteworthy, the main enjoyment is being as close to our heroes as possible. As noted historian Gerda Lerner writes:

> "What we do about history matters. The often repeated saying those who forget the lessons of history are doomed to repeat them has a lot of truth in it. But what are the lessons of history? The very attempt at definition furnishes ground for new conflicts. History is not a recipe book; past events are never replicated in the present in quite the same way. Historical events are infinitely variable and their interpretations are constantly shifting process. There are no certainties to be found in the past."

> Lerner continues, "We can learn from history how past generations thought and acted, how they responded to demands of their time and how they solved their problems. We can learn by analogy, not by example, for our circumstances will always be different than theirs were. The main thing history can teach us is that human actions have consequences and that certain choices, once made, cannot be undone. They foreclose the possibility of making other choices and thus they determine future events."

As Lerner stated above, history can be learned from and the actions of the past have consequences on the future. Thus, by our presence in these cemeteries, there is an announcement of our unbroken chain to the past, a link that stretches back to the roots of our county, state, and nation; the acts and deeds of our forbearers links us to the future. We can learn from their lives thus making our lives in the present better.

In this book, I have attempted to include as many of the famous graves of Orange County's most illustrious inhabitants as possible. The history of Orange County's famous dead was a journey of immense undertaking. No such study had ever been attempted. The road to completing this work was arduous and filled with many dead ends (no pun intended). The final product was a volume of work that I believe complements any history of the region. It has been an all-encompassing adventure, covering the lives of numerous entertainment celebrities, sports stars, politicians, historical figures, and infamous scoundrels. The sheer number of famous and noteworthy people that have called Orange County home over the past 200 years was amazing. Their stories of triumph and tragedy had never been told and finally this sad fact has been rectified.

My intention is simply to celebrate the history and culture of Orange County through its noteworthy citizens. It is not just about death, dying, and cemeteries. In contrast, it is a book written about the celebration of life. Then why are we drawn to the graves of the famous? Simply put, we may be fascinated by lives that we do not have. The paradox is that, in reality, these people are just like us, they have had joys, loves, triumphs, and defeats. Their lives were much like our own and their destiny is our destiny. These people are more than just granite, marble, and bronze markers that adorn their graves. They were people like you and I, with dreams and aspirations. The lesson is simple and the answer is quite mundane, but in the end, all we really want is to be remembered.

BIBLIOGRAPHY

Books:

Asinof, Eliot. Eight Men Out: The Black Sox and the 1919 World Series. New York: Henry Holt and Company, 1987.

Barrier, Michael. Hollywood Cartoons: American Animation in its Golden Age. New York: Oxford Press, 1999.

Bricken, Gordon. The Civil War Legacy in Santa Ana. Tustin, California: Wilson Barnett Publishing, 2002.

Butler, Patricia. "Angels Dance and Angels Die: The Tragic Romance of Pamela and Jim Morrison." New York: Omnibus Press, 1998.

DeBarthe, Joe. "The Life and Adventures of Frank Grouard, Chief of Scouts, U.S.A." St. Joseph, Missouri: Cumbe Printing Company, 1894.

Ellsworth, S. George. The Journals of Addison Pratt. Salt Lake City, Utah: University of Utah Press, 1990.

Fraser, Chelsea. Famous American Flyers. New York: Thomas Y. Cromwell Company, 1944.

Friis, Leo. Orange County Through Four Centuries. Santa Ana, California: Pioneer Press, 1982.

Garden Grove Historical Society. Images of America: Garden Grove. Charleston, South Carolina: Arcadia Publishing, 2005.

Hafran, Ann W., and Leroy R. Hafran. Journals of Forty-Niners: Salt Lake to Los Angeles. Lincoln, Nebraska: University of Nebraska Press, 1998.

Hallan-Gibson, Pamela. "Ghosts and Legends of San Juan Capistrano." San Juan Capistrano: The San Juan Capistrano Historical Society, 1983.

Hallan-Gibson, Pamela. The Golden Promise: An Illustrated History of Orange County. Northridge, California: Windsor Publishing, Inc., 1986.

Hallan-Gibson, Pamela. Images of America: San Juan Capistrano. San Francisco, California, Arcadia Publishing, 2005.

Henke, James. The Jim Morrison Scrapbook. San Francisco: Chronicle Books, 2007.

Kaplan, Mike. Variety: Who's Who in Show Business. New York: Garland Publishing, Inc., 1983.

Karst, Gene, and Martin J. Jones, Jr. Who's Who in Professional Baseball. New York: Arlington House, 1973.

Katz, Ephrain. The Film Encyclopedia. 2nd ed. New York: Harper Collins, Inc., 1994.

Marquis, Albert Nelson. Who's Who in America: 1934-1935. Chicago: A.N. Marquis Company, 1934.

Marsh, Diann. Santa Ana: An Illustrated History. 2nd ed. Encinitas, California: Heritage Publishing Company, 1994.

MacLean, Angus, The Legends of the California Bandidos. Arroyo Grande, California: Bear Flag Books, 1977.

Morgan, Warren F. "Reflections in Orange of Merle and Mabel Ramsey." Laguna Beach, California: Mission Printing Company, 1973.

Orange County Historical Society. Orange County History Series. Vol.1. Santa Ana, California: Pioneer Press, 1931.

Reichler, Jospeh L., ed. The Baseball Encyclopedia: The Complete and Official Record of Major League Baseball. New York: MacMillan Publishing Company, 1988.

Romanowski, Patricia, Holly George Warren, and John Pareles, eds. The New Encyclopedia of Rock and Roll. New York: The Rollingstone Press, 1995.

Shatzkin, Mike. The Ballplayers: Baseball's Ultimate Biographical Reference. New York: William Morrow and Company, Inc., 1990.

Smith, Richard R. Fender: The Sound Heard 'Round the World. Fullerton, California: Garfish Publishing Company, 1995.

Still, Henry. To Ride the Wild Wind: A Biography of Glenn L. Martin. New York: Julian Messner, Inc., 1964.

Talbert, Thomas B., ed. Historical Volume and Reference Works: Covering Garden Grove, Santa Ana, and Tustin. Vol.1. Whittier, California: Historical Publications, 1963.

Taylor, John. Airfacts and Feats. New York: Sterling Publishing Company, 1980.

Ten Boom, Corrie. The Hiding Place. 25th anniversary ed. Grand Rapids, Michigan: Chosen Books, 1984.

Truitt, Evelyn Mack. Who was Who on Screen. 2nd ed. New York: R.R. Bowker Company, 1977.

Ward, Robert, and Cynthia Ward. The Anaheim Cemetery. Anaheim, California: The Anaheim Historical Society, Inc., 2002.

Wayne, Pilar, with Alex Thorleifson. John Wayne: My Life with the Duke. New York: McGraw Hill, 1987.

On the Web:

Find a Grave, www.findagrave.com by various contributors.

Internet Movie Database, www.imdb.com by various contributors.

Wikipedia, www.wikipedia.org by various contributors.

Newspapers:

The Los Angeles Star, various years and contributors.

The Los Angeles Times, various years and contributors.

The News Post (Laguna Beach), various contributors.

The Orange County Register, various years and contributors

The Register (Santa Ana), various years and contributors.

The San Francisco Chronicle, various years and contributors.

The Santa Ana Daily Register, various years and contributors.

The Southern Californian, various contributors.

The Weekly Gazette (Anaheim), various contributors.

Note: Materials sited by Wikipedia are a part of a full compilation of information and may or may not be the lone source.

ENDNOTES

CHAPTER 1 – THE HISTORIC CEMETERIES

1. Gary A. Warner, "Nixon Dies," *The Orange County Register*, April 23, 1994, 1.

2. Ibid.

3. Ibid.

4. Ibid.

5. Gary A. Warner, "The Final Farewell," *The Orange County Register*, April 28, 1994, 1.

6. MSNBC.com, "List of Presidential Rankings," http://msnbc.com/id/29216774/ (accessed May 29, 2009).

7. Warner, "The Final Farewell."

8. Leo J. Friis, *Orange County Through Four Centuries*, (Santa Ana, California: Pioneer Press, 1982), 11.

9. The San Juan Capistrano Historical Society, "Father John O'Sullivan," http://sjhistorysociety.com/osullivan.html (accessed May 26, 2009).

10. Pamela Hallan-Gibson, *Images of America: San Juan Capistrano*, (San Francisco, California: Arcadia Publishing, 2005), 83.

11. Jerry Nieblas, interview by Michael Barry, San Juan Capistrano, CA, June 5, 2009.

12. San Juan Capistrano Historical Society, "Don Juan Forster," http://sjchistoricalsociety.com/index.html (accessed June 5, 2009).

13. Pamela Hallan-Gibson, *The Golden Promise: An Illustrated History of Orange County*, (Northridge, California: Windsor Publications, Inc., 1986), 34.

14. Findagrave.com, "Bernardo Yorba," http://findagrave.com/bernardoyorba (accessed June 1, 2009).

15. Chris Jepsen, O.C. History Roundup.com, "The Pink Lady of Yorba Cemetery, Santa Ana, etc. October 28, 2007," http://ochistorical.blogspot.com/2007/10/pink-lady-of-yorba-cemetery-santa-ana.html (accessed June 9, 2009).

CHAPTER 2 – THE ORANGE COUNTY PUBLIC CEMETERIES

1. Jean O. Pasco, "Here Lies History at Anaheim Cemetery," *The Los Angeles Times*, July 11, 2005, B-3.

2. Orange County Historical Society, *Orange County History Series*, vol. 1 (1931; repri., Santa Ana, California: Pioneer Press, 1968), 33-36.

3. Warren F. Morgan, *Reflections in Orange of Merle and Mabel Ramsey*, (Laguna Beach, California: Mission Printing Company, 1973), 53.

4. Leo J. Friis, *Orange County Through Four Centuries*, (Santa Ana, California: Pioneer Press, 1982), 24.

5. Richard D. Curtiss, "Maria Petra Jesus Ontiveros" (proposal, Mother Colony Household, Inc., general meeting, Anaheim, California, January 13, 1975).

6. "Ceremony to Honor Pioneer," *The Register* (Santa Ana), Friday, May 28, 1976, B2.

7. "Death of A. Langenberger," *The Weekly Gazette* (Anaheim, California), Thursday, April 11, 1895, 1.

8. Anaheim Colony Historic District Links, "Anaheim's First Cemetery," http://anaheimcolony.com/cemetery.htm. (accessed October 21, 2008).

9. "Married," *Southern Californian*, (Anaheim, California), April 18, 1874, 3.

10. "Death of A. Langenberger."

11. "Last Pioneer Laid To Rest Saturday," *Anaheim Gazette*, October 16, 1913.

12. Friis, 49.

13. Morgan, 101.

14. Friis, 52.

15. Morgan, 58.

16. Friis 79.

17. Hallan-Gibson, 135.

18. Friis, 53-54.

19. Morgan, 144-145.

20. Ibid.

21. Friis, 67.

22. Morgan, 145.

23. S. George Ellsworth, *The Journals of Addison Pratt*, (Salt Lake City, Utah: University of Utah Press, 1990), 3.

24. Ibid., 12-13.

25. Ibid., 105-110.

26. Ibid., 112-115.

27. Ibid., 116-121.

28. Jolyn Hunting and Julia Kenyon, Manuscript Registers, "Addison Pratt Family Papers (1830-1931)," Utah State University Library/ Special Collections, http://library.usu.edu/specol/manuscript/collms228b.html (accessed October 7, 2008).

29. Ibid.

30. Ellsworth, 334-335.

31. Ann W. Hafen and Leroy R. Hafen, *Journals of Forty-Niners: Salt Lake to Los Angeles*, (1954; repr., Lincoln, Nebraska: University of Nebraska Press, 1998), 67.

32. Ellsworth, 520-522.

33. Wikipedia Foundation, Inc., "Addison Pratt," http://en.wikipedia.org/wiki/addison_pratt (accessed, October 21, 2008).

34. The Obituary of Thomas Kuchel, The Orange County Register, November 23, 1994, Metro 7.

35. Ibid.

36. Wikipedia Foundation, Inc., "Thomas Kuchel," http://en.wikipedia.org/wiki/thomas_kuchel. (accessed, October 21, 2008).

37. Obituary of Thomas Kuchel.

38. Anaheim Gazette, February 2, 1888, 1.

39. Ibid.

40. "Doomed Anschlag," Anaheim Gazette, February 23, 1888, 1.

41. Garden Grove Historical Society, *Images of America: Garden Grove*, (Charleston, South Carolina: Arcadia Publishing,2005), 15.

42. Robert and Cynthia Ward, *The Anaheim Cemetery*, (The Anaheim Historical Society, Inc., 2002), 18.

43. Wikipedia Foundation, Inc., "John Raitt," http://en.wikipedia.org/wiki/John_Raitt (accessed, November 19, 2008).

44. Los Angeles County Department of Health Services, *Certificate of Death for John Raitt*, January 29, 2005.

45. Southern California: Orange County, "Murdered on Mme. Modejeska's Mount Ami Ranch," *The Los Angeles Times*, Monday, August 1, 1892, 7.

46. Southern California: Orange County, "Murderer of Capt. McKelvey Still at Large," *The Los Angeles Times*, Wednesday, August 3, 1892, 7.

47. Southern California: Orange County, "Full Particulars of the McKelvey Murder," *The Los Angeles Times*, Tuesday, August 2, 1892, 7.

48. Ibid.

49. Torres Taken, "Arrest of the Santa Ana Murderer," *The Los Angeles Times*, Thursday, August 11, 1892, 1.

50. Southern California: Orange County, "Formal Arraignment of Torres the Murderer," *The Los Angeles Times*, Saturday, August 13, 1892, 7.

51. "Lynch Law At Santa Ana," *The Los Angeles Times*, Sunday, August 21, 1892, 14.

52. Pamela Hallan-Gibson, *The Golden Promise: An Illustrated History of Orange County*, (Northridge, California: Windsor Publications, Inc., 1986), 136.

53. "Horrible Double Murder," *Anaheim Gazette*, Thursday, October 17, 1889, 3.

54. "Tragedy in Tustin," *The Los Angeles Times*, October 17, 1889, 1.

55. Ibid.

56. Ibid.

57. "Mrs. Scholl Dead," *The Los Angeles Times*, November 3, 1889, 16.

58. Wikipedia, "Richard Cromwell," http://en.wikipedia.org/wiki/Richard_Cromwell (accessed July 9, 2008).

59. Katz, 305.

60. Wikipedia.

61. Obituary of Richard Cromwell, The Los Angeles Times, October 13, 1960.

62. CNET Networks, Inc., TV.com, "Justin Carmack," http://tv.com/justin-carmack/person/68220/summary.html (accessed June 16, 2008).

63. Obituary of Justin Carmack, The Orange County Register, July 26, 2000.

64. Diann Marsh, *Santa Ana: An Illustrated History*, 2nd ed. (Encinitas, California: Heritage Publishing Company, 1994), 36-39.

65. Ibid., 39.

66. Ibid., 37.

67. Shatzskin, 297.

68. Reichler, 922.

69. Thomas B. Talbert, ed., *Historical Volume and Reference Works: Covering Garden Grove, Santa Ana, and Tustin*, vol.1, (Whittier, California: Historical Publications, 1963), 871-872.

70. Obituary of James Boyd Utt, The Register [Santa Ana], March 2, 1970.

71. "Grave of Arbuckle's Mother is Neglected," *The Los Angeles Times*, September 13, 1921, 13.

72. Obituary of Robert McFadden, The Santa Ana Daily Register, May 9, 1923.

73. Bricken, 56-58.

74. Obituary of Dr. Henry Head, Santa Ana Daily Register, December 6, 1919.

75. Friis., 62.

76. Ibid., 53-54.

77. Ibid., 55.

78. Ibid., 55.

79. Joe DeBarthe, *The Life and Adventures of Frank Grouard, Chief of Scouts, U.S.A.*, (St. Jospeh, Missouri: Combe Printing Company, 1894), 21.

80. Ibid., 22.

81. Wikipedia, "The Battle of the Rosebud," http://en.wikipedia.org/wiki/Battle_of_The_Rosebud (accessed November 12, 2008).

82. Wikipedia, "Spiritualism," http://en.wikipedia.org/wiki/Spiritualism (accessed January 9, 2009).

83. Debarthe, 24-25.

84. Evelyn Mack Truitt, Who was Who on Screen, 2nd ed., (New York, New York: R.R. Bowker Company, 1977), 104.

85. County of Orange, Certificate of Death for Charles G. Perley, (Santa Ana, California: February, 1933).

86. Scott M. Reid, "Griffith Joyner a Master of Self-Motivation," The Orange County Register, September 22, 1998, News 1 and 18.

87. Phil Garlington, "Hundreds Bid FloJo Goodbye," The Orange County Register, September 26, 1998, Metro 2.

88. Gary W. Warner, "Leonard Fribourg, career Marine, dies," The Orange County Register, August 17, 1993, Metro 2.

89. Ibid.

90. Ibid.

91. The Internet Movie Data Base, "John Beck III," http://imdb.com/name/nm0065184/ (accessed February 19, 2009).

92. Katz, 129.

93. Ibid.

94. The Internet Encyclopedia of Cinematographers, "Joseph Biroc," http://cinimatographers.nl/GreatdoPh/biroc.htm (accessed February 19, 2009).

95. Reichler, 1256.

96. Shatzkin, 734.

97. Reichler, 1256.

98. Ibid, 2529.

99. The Internet Movie Data Base, "George Metkovich," http://imdb.com/name/nm0582566/ (accessed February 16, 2009).

100. Find a grave, "George Metkovich," http://findagrave.com/George_Metkovich (accessed February 16, 2009).

101. Nova Scotia Canada, Archives and Records Management, Government Administrative Histories, "Department of Provincial Secretary," http://gov.ns.ca/nsarm/gaho/authority.asp?ID=114 (accessed February 20, 2009).

102. Michael Barrier, Hollywood Cartoons: American Animation in its Golden Age, (New York, New York: Oxford University Press, 1999), 478.

103. The Internet Movie Data Base, "Warren Foster," http://imdb.com/name/nm0288111/ (accessed February 19, 2009).

104. Ibid.

105. The Intenet Movie Data Base, "Ralph Freeto," http://imdb.com/name/nm0293689/ (accessed February 16, 2009).

106. David Greenwald, "Christian Nelson Man invented Eskimo Pie ice cream bar," The Orange County Register, March 10, 1992, Metro 10.

107. Funding Universe, "Eskimo Pie Corporation," http://fundinguniverse.com/company-histories/Eskimo-Pie-Corporation-Company-History.html (accessed February 16, 2009).

108. Greenwald.

109. Lynn Elber, "Gordon Jump, 71, 'WKRP' actor," The Orange County Register, September 23, 2003, Local 7.

Chapter 3 – Fairhaven Memorial Park

1. Katz, 187.

2. "Bruckman Film Writer, Ends Life," *The Los Angeles Times*, January 5, 1955.

3. Larry Lytle, "The Command To Look," The Scream On-line, http://thescreamonline.com/photo/photo06-01/mortensen/commandtolook1.html (accessed June 16, 2008).

4. Unknown Author, "William Mortensen," Find A Grave. http://findagrave.com/cgi-bin/fg.cgi?page=gr&GRid=8914 (accessed June 16, 2008).

5. "Arthur E. Beaumont, Noted marine Artist, Dies at 87," *The Los Angeles Times*, January 24, 1978, D4.

6. Reichler, 1891.

7. Ibid., 1687.

8. "Rites Set for Artist Evylena Nunn Miller," *The Los Angeles Times*, March 1, 1966, B16.

9. IMDB.com, Inc., The Internet Movie Data Base, "Maryesther Denver," http://imdb.com/name/nm0219893/ (accessed June 16, 2008).

10. Unknown Author, "Mary Esther Denver," Find A Grave. http://findagrave.com/cgi-bin/fg.cgi?page=gr&GRid=9737 (accessed June 16, 2008).

11. "Fluor Funeral Set Tomorrow," *The Santa Ana Register*, July 31, 1944, p.1 and 2.

12. "J. Simon Fluor Dies At Age 72," *The Register* [Santa Ana, California], September 10, 1974, p. 1

13. Reichler, 1763.

14. Henry Still, *To Ride the Wind: A Biography of Glenn L. Martin*, (New York, New York: Julian Messner Inc., 1964), 19.

15. Still, 20.

16. Ibid., 43.

17. "Santa Ana Services Set For Famed 'Son' Who Flew First Plane Here," *The Register* [Santa Ana], December 5, 1955, A1-2, and 10.

18. Time, Inc., Time Magazine, "Kites to Bombers," http://time.com/magazine/article/0,9171,931281-1,00.html (accessed June 17, 2008).

19. Still, 116.

20. Wikipedia Foundation, Inc., "Glenn L. Martin Company," http://en.wikipedia.org/wiki/Glenn_L._Martin_Company (accessed June 16, 2008).

21. John Taylor, *Airfacts and Feats*, (New York, New York: Sterling Publishing Company, 1980), 210.

22. Stills, 89-94.

23. Wikipedia., "Glenn L. Martin, Company."

24. *The Register* [Santa Ana], December 5, 1955, A1-2, and 10.

25. "More Than 300 Attend Plane Pioneer's Rites," *The Register* [Santa Ana], December 10, 1955, A1-2.

26. IMDB.com, Inc., The Internet Movie Data Base, "Linda Cordova," http://imdb.com/name/nm01796521/ (accessed June 16, 2008).

27. "Obituary of Margaret Irving," *The Orange County Register* [Santa Ana] March 9, 1988, B9.

28. IMDB.com, Inc., The Internet Movie Data Base, "Margaret Irving," http://imdb.com/name/nm04103303/ (accessed June 16, 2008).

29. Ibid.

30. "Obituary of Margaret Irving."

31. Pamela Hallan-Gibson, *The Golden Promise: An Illustrated History of Orange County*, (Northridge, California: Windsor Publications, Inc., 1986), 201.

32. "James Irvine, Jr., Passes Away Sunday Afternoon at Hospital In Los Angeles," *The Santa Ana Daily Register*, June 24, 1935, p. 1 and 2.

33. "Sports Pioneer Boyd Ellis Dead," *The Register* [Santa Ana, California], July 8, 1974, Sports, C1.

34. Ibid.

35. Gene Ellis, interview by Michael Barry, Anaheim, CA, February 4, 2009.

36. "Sports Pioneer Boyd Ellis Dead."

37. Wikipedia, "Rollin R. Rees," http://en.wikipedia.org/wiki/Rollin_R._Rees (accessed June 16, 2008).

38. "Rollin R. Rees Dies Suddenly During Night," *The Santa Ana Register*, May 31, 1935, Friday evening edition,

39. Albert Nelson Marquis, *Who's Who in America: 1934-1935*, (Chicago, Illinois: The A.N. Marquis Company, 1934), 647.

40. Shatzkin, 532.

41. Reichler, 1106.

42. Friis, 175-76.

43. "Fender 'marketing genius' dies at 91," *The Orange County Register*, January 9, 2009, Local, 10.

44. Wikipedia, "Raymond C. Hoiles," http://en.wikipedia.org/wiki/Raymond_C._Hoiles (accessed June 16, 2008).

45. "R.C. Hoiles Funeral Set 2 PM Monday," *The Register* [Santa Ana], November 1, 1970, A1.

46. Chelsea Fraser, *Famous American Flyers*, (New York, New York: Thomas Y. Crowell Company, 1944), 332-336.

47. Wikipedia, "Douglas Corrigan," http://en.wikipedia.org/wiki/Douglas_Corrigan (accessed June 16, 2008).

48. Harry L. Graham, "Herbert Dunn, 87, First 'Cisco Kid,' Dies in CM," *The Register* [Santa Ana], April 15, 1979, A1.

49. Shatzkin, 808.

50. Reichler, 1308.

51. "Bob Nieman, .295 lifetime hitter in 12 major league seasons, dies at 58," *The Register* [Santa Ana], March 12, 1985, C3.

52. "Obituary of William Spurgeon," The Santa Ana Daily Register, June 21, 1915.

53. Ibid.

54. Thomas B. Talbert, ed., *Historical Volume and Reference Works: Covering Garden Grove, Santa Ana, and Tustin*, vol.1, (Whittier, California: Historical Publications, 1963), 81-83.

55. Friis, 96-97.

56. "The Obituary of James McFadden," *The Santa Ana Daily Register*, June 10, 1919, Tuesday evening edition, 4.

57. Friis, 96-97.

58. "The Obituary of James McFadden."

59. "John McFadden Drops Dead in Store As He Reads Paper," *The Santa Ana Daily Register*, June 24, 1915, Thursday evening edition, 1.

60. Ibid.

61. Hallan-Gibson, 320-321.

62. Ibid.

63. Paul Gillette, The Civil War Round Table of Orange County, "Civil War Grave Registration," http://cwrtoorangecounty-ca.org/victor%montgomery.htm.

64. "Victor Montgomery Met Sudden Death," *The Santa Ana Daily Register*, October 19, 1911, Thursday evening edition, 1.

65. Ibid.

66. Gordon Bricken, *The Civil War Legacy in Santa Ana*, (Tustin, California: Wilson/Barnett Publishing, 2002), 50-52.

67. Hallan-Gibson, 308.

68. Ibid.

69. Wikipedia, "Corrie Ten Boom," http://en.wikipedia.org/wiki/Corrie_Ten_Boom (accessed June 16, 2008).

70. Corrie Ten Boom, *The Hiding Place*, 25th anniversary ed. Grand Rapids, Michigan: Chosen Books, 1984), 117.

71. Wikipedia, "Corrie Ten Boom."

72. Ten Boom, 203.

73. Wikipedia, "Corrie Ten Boom."

74. Ten Boom, 218.

75. Wikipedia, "Corrie Ten Boom."

76. Ten Boom, 218-219.

77. Wikipedia, "Corrie Ten Boom."

78. Ten Boom, 12.

79. "Ex-Associate of Lucille Ball; Onetime Spanish Court Jester Dies," *The Los Angeles Times*, July 19, 1975, OC5.

80. IMDB.com, "Pepito Perez," http://imdb.com/name/nm0702332/ (accessed March 3, 2009).

81. Truitt, 367.

82. James Henke, *The Jim Morrison Scrapbook*, (San Francisco, California: Chronicle Books, 2007), 39-40.

83. Wikipedia, "Pamela Courson," http://en.wikipedia.org/Pamela_Courson (accessed June 16, 2008).

84. Patricia Butler, *Angels Dance and Angels Die: The Tragic Romance of Pamela and Jim Morrison*, (New York, New York: Omnibus Press, 1998), 157-164.

85. Ibid., 188-193.

86. Ibid., 202-211.

87. IMBD.com, William Brooks Ching," http://imbd.com/name/nm0157893/ (accessed June 16, 2008).

88. "The Obituary of William Ching," *The Orange County Register*, July 4, 1989, B5.

89. Ben Wener, "Champion of electric guitar, 90," *The Orange County Register*, August 28, 1999, Local news 6.

90. Wikipedia, "John Morrow," http://en.wikipedia.org/wiki/John_H._Morrow (accessed June 16, 2008).

91. Unknown Author, "John Howard Morrow," Find A Grave." http://findagrave.com/johnhowardmorrow (accessed June 16, 2008).

92. Chuck Anderson, The Old Corral, Villians, "Pierce Lyden," http://b-westerns.com/villians.htm (accessed June 16, 2008).

93. Richard R. Smith, *Fender: The Sound Heard 'Round the World*, (Fullerton, California: Garfish Publishing Company, 1995), 30.

94. Rock and Roll Hall of Fame and Museum, Inc., "Leo Fender," http://rockhall.com/inductee.Leo_Fender (accessed June 16, 2008).

95. Laura-Lynne Powell, "Guitar maker Fender dies at 81," *The Orange County Register*, March 22, 1991, 1 and 14.

96. Phil Burgess, National Hot Rod Association, "Pappy Hart," http://nhra.com/content/news.asp?articleid=2902&zoneid=8 (accessed June 16, 2008).

97. IMBD.com, "Bobby Nelson," http://imbd.com/name/nm0625190/ (accessed June 16, 2008).

98. "The Obituary of Robert Nelson," *The Orange County Register*, August 7, 1993, Metro 6.

99. Find A Grave.com, "W.T. Grace," http://findagrave.com/cgi-bin/fg.cgi?page=gr&GRid=8526 (accessed June 16, 2008).

100. Shatzkin, 307.

CHAPTER 4 – PACIFIC VIEW MEMORIAL PARK

1. Steve Bisheff, "George Harry Yardley III 1928-2004," *The Orange County Register*, August 14, 2004, Sports 1.

2. Evelyn Mack Truitt, *Who Was Who on Screen*, 2nd ed., (New York, New York: R.R. Bowker Company, 1977), 61.

3. IMDB.com, Inc., "Edmund Burns," http://imdb.com/name/nm0122652/ (accessed March 5, 2009).

4. Truitt, 456.

5. Mike Kaplan, *Variety: Who's Who in Show Business*, (New York, New York: Garland Publishing, Inc., 1983), 53.

6. Ibid.

7. Gene Karst and Martin J. Jones, Jr., *Who's Who in Professional Baseball*, (New Rochelle, New York: Arlington House, 1973), 903.

8. River Raisin Dodels, Inc., "UP Super Turbines," http://riverraisinmodels.com/up8500.html (accessed March 27, 2009).

9. "The Yankee Boomer," http://griffincunningham.net/Griffin/MAIN/yankeeboomer2/Ybaug21945pg1.pdf (accessed March 27, 2009).

10. Obituary of Arthur E. Stoddard, *The Los Angeles Times*, March 26, 1969, C4.

11. Joseph L. Reichler, ed. *The Baseball Encyclopedia: The Complete and Official Record of Major League Baseball*, 7th ed. (New York, New York: MacMillan Publishing Company, 1988), 857.

12. Lin Ezell, "File document of Major General Charles J. Quilter," U.S.M.C. Headquarters Museum.

13. Ibid.

14. "General's Last Rites Held," *The News Post* (Laguna Beach, California), March 22, 1978, 1-2.

15. YellowWorld.org, "Alfred Song," http://yellowworld.org/politics/30.html (accessed March 10, 2009).

16. Valarie J. Nelson, "Dave Freeman, 1961-2008; Co-wrote '100 Things to Do Before You Die,'" *The Los Angeles Times*, August 26, 2008, Metro-6.

17. "Myford Irvine Found Shot," *The Los Angeles Times*, January 12, 1959, 5.

18. "Myford Irvine Rites Conducted," *The Los Angeles Times*, January 16, 1959, 15.

19. IMDB.com, "Margaret Early," http://imdb.com/name/nm0247401/ (accessed March 10, 2009).

20. Ephrain Katz, *The Film Encyclopedia*, 2nd ed. (New York, New York: Harper Collins, Inc., 1994), 344.

21. Scott A. Thompson, "Frank Gifford Tallman Biography," Aero Vintage Books, http://www.aerovintage.com/tallman-bio.htm (accessed March 18, 2009).

22. Reichler, 899.

23. Katz, 890.

24. "Jack Faulkner, Executive Worked with Franchise in L.A., St. Louis," *The Los Angeles Times*, September 30, 2008, Metro B-7.

25. Matt Lait, "Robert C. Wian, Founder of Bob's Big Boy, Dies at 77," *The Los Angeles Times*, Metro 1.

26. IMDB.com, "Toni Wayne," http://imdb.com/name/nm0915649/ (accessed March 11, 2009).

27. Wikipedia Foundation, Inc., "Josephine Alicia Saenz," http://en.wikipedia.org/wiki/josephine_alicia_saenz (accessed March 11, 2009).

28. Pilar Wayne with Alex Thorleifson, *John Wayne: My Life with the Duke*, (New York, New York: McGraw-Hill, 1987), 8-10.

29. Ibid., 15.

30. Ibid., 15-19.

31. Ibid., 23-24.

32. Ibid., 36-37.

33. Katz, 1436.

34. Wayne, 177.

35. Dorothy Townsend, "John Wayne Buried in Quiet, Private Rite," *The Los Angeles Times*, June 15, 1979, A1.

36. Rick Vanderknyff, "Marion Mack; Keaton Co-Star in 'The General,'" *The Los Angeles Times*, May 14, 1989, Metro-36.

37. Chris Knapp, and Daniel Chang, "Theater magnate James Edwards Jr. dies," *The Orange County Register*, April 27, 1997, News-1.

38. Truitt, 298.

39. Scott A. Thompson, "Paul Mantz Biography," Aero Vintage Books, http://www.aerovintage.com/mantz-bio.htm (accessed March 18, 2009).

44. "Fulton; Big-Band Singer Wrote Hit Perry Como Song," *The Los Angeles Times*, November 21, 1993, Metro-28.

41. Wikipedia Foundation, Inc., "Ivory Tower (song)," http://en.wikipedia.org/wiki/Ivory_Tower_(song) (accessed March 20, 2009).

42. The Internet Movie Data Base.com, "Carried Away (Movie)," http://imdb.com/title/tt0115837/soundtrack (accessed March 20, 2009).

43. Wikipedia, Inc., "If You are but a Dream (Song)," http://en.wikipedia.org/wiki/If_You_Are_But_A_Dream (accessed March 20, 2009).

44. "Fulton; Big-Band Singer Wrote Hit Perry Como Song."

45. "Rites Set for Composer 'Country' Washburne," *The Los Angeles Times*, January 23, 1974, B2.

46. "Body of Salazar to Lie in State in East Los Angeles," *The Los Angeles Times*, September 1, 1970, 3.

47. Charles T. Powers and Jeff Perlman, "One Dead, 40 Hurt in East L.A. Riot," *The Los Angeles Times*, August 30, 1970, 1 and 18.

48. Paul Houston and Richard Vasquez, "Salazar was Killed by Tear-Gas Shell," *The Los Angeles Times*, August 31, 1970, 1 and 14.

49. "Body of Salazar to Lie in State in East Los Angeles."

50. The Internet Movie Data Base.com, "Harry F. Perry," http://imdb.com/name/nm0675091/ (accessed March 20, 2009).

51. Ibid., "William Austin," http://imdb.com/name/nm0042552/bio (accessed March 20, 2009).

52. "Toastmasters Founder, Dr. R.C. Smedley, Dies," *The Los Angeles Times*, September 12, 1965, B3.

53. The Internet Movie Data Base.com, "Harold Minjir," http://imdb.com/name/nm0591409/ (accessed March 20, 2009).

54. Ibid., "Al Clark," http://imdb.com/name/nm0163617/ (accessed March 20, 2009).

55. Ibid., "Ted J. Kent," http://imdb.com/name/nm0448867/ (accessed March 20, 2009).

56. Kristina Lindgren, "Retired Cal State Fullerton Professor, Nobel Nominee Loh Sen Tsai Dies at 91," *The Los Angeles Times*, January 5, 1993, Metro-4.

57. "Otto W. Timm, Pioneer of U.S. Aviation, Dies at 84," *The Los Angeles Times*, July 5, 1978, F-1.

58. Ibid., "John Gallaudet," http://imdb.com/name/nm0302664/ (accessed March 20, 2009).

59. Katz, 1183-1184.

60. The Internet Movie Data Base, "Clarence Upson Young," http://imdb.com/name/nm0949404/ (accessed March 21, 2009).

61. Katz, 1438-1439.

62. The Internet Movie Data Base, "Barbara McLean," http://imdb.com/name/nm0572492/bio (accessed March 21, 2009).

63. Katz, 875.

64. Nancy Wride, "Frieda Pushnik; Circus' 'Armless, Legless Girl Wonder," *The Los Angeles Times*, December 29, 2000, Metro-8.

65. Dorothy Townsend, "Big Band Leader Freddy Martin Dies in Newport," *The Los Angeles Times*, October 2, 1983, OC A1 and 18.

66. The Internet Movie Data Base, "Freddy Martin," http://imdb.com/name/nm05523031/ (accessed March 23, 2009).

67. Townsend.

68. Larry Welborn, "Man charged with murder, making daughter confess Teen's father, slain wife's sister held for allegedly planning 1985 killing," *The Los Angeles Times* September 23, 1988, A1.

69. Ibid.

70. Ibid.

71. Gregg Zoroya, "Parole board releases killer Cinnamon Brown," *The Los Angeles Times*, February 28, 1992, Metro-1.

72. Jeff Collins, "Stepmother's killer Cinnamon Brown appears on Orah, says she's anxious to return home," *The Los Angeles Times*, May 15, 1991, Metro-2.

73. Jeff Collins, "Convicted killer confesses to murder-for-hire scheme," *The Los Angeles Times*, July 24, 1990, Metro-4.

74. "NBC's 'Murder' ranked 3rd highest miniseries," *The Los Angeles Times*, February 20, 1991, Show-3.

75. The Internet Movie Data Base.com, "Niles Welch," http://imdb.com/name/nm0919624/ (accessed March 24, 2009).

76. "Peter Plotkin Artist," http://peterplotkinartist.com/ppbio.html (accessed March 23, 2009).

77. The Internet Movie Data Base, Inc., "Jeanne Carmen," http://imdb.com/name/nm0138384/ (accessed March 24, 2009).

78. Jeff Overley, "Good Looks, skill on links brought fame for Jeanne Carmen, 77," *The Orange County Register*, December 25, 2007, Local-2.

79. The Internet Movie Data Base, Inc., "Jeanne Carmen."

80. Overley.

81. "Les Baxter; Music Arranger, Composer," *The Los Angeles Times*, January 20, 1996, Metro-18.

82. The Internet Movie Data Base, Inc., "Les Baxter," http://imdb.com/name/nm0005958/ (accessed March 24, 2009).

83. "Helen Grace, 88; With Husband, Built Chocolate Empire Bearing Her Name," *The Los Angeles Times*, December 25, 2002, Metro-9.

84. Patricia Romanowski, Holly George-Warren, and Jon Pareles, eds., *The New Encyclopedia of Rock and Roll*, (New York: The Rollingstone Press, 1995), 834-835.

85. David Haldane, "Bobby Hatfield, 63; Singer Was Half of Righteous Brothers," *The Los Angeles Times*, November 6, 2003, B-14.

86. "Hatfield's death caused by cocaine," *The Los Angeles Times*, January 7, 2004, E-2.

87. Romanowski, 807-808.

88. Greg Burk, "Kevin Dubrow, 1955-2007; Singer for metal band Quiet Riot," *The Los Angeles Times*, November 27, 2007, Metro-8.

89. Romanowski, 808.

90. "Dubrow's death is ruled an overdose," *The Los Angeles Times*, December 12, 2007, Calendar-2.

91. Steve Springer, "Prominent Referee Halpern Dies in Apparent Suicide," *The Los Angeles Times*, August 22, 2000, Sports-6.

92. The Internet Movie Data Base, Inc., "Paul D. King," http://imdb.com/name/nm0455126/ (accessed March 25, 2009).

93. Myrna Oliver, "A. Melin; Introduced Frisbee and Hula Hoop," *The Los Angeles Times*, June 30, 2002, Metro-15.

94. Rich Roberts, "Malavasi, Ex-Coach of Rams, Dead at 57," *The Los Angeles Times*, December 16, 1987, Sports-1.

95. The Internet Movie Data Base, Inc., "Nan Leslie," http://imdb.com/name/nm0504160/ (accessed March 30, 2009).

96. Reichler, 2162.

97. Mike Shatzkin, ed. *The Ballplayers: Baseball's Ultimate Biographical Reference*, (New York, New York: William Morrow and Company, Inc., 1990), 1045.

98. Jeffrey A. Perlman, "James Roosevelt, Son of F.D.R., Dies at 83," *The Los Angeles Times*, August 14, 1991, Metro-1.

99. The Internet Movie Data Base, Inc., "James Roosevelt," http://imdb.com/name/nm0740484/ (accessed March 30, 2009).

100. Perlman.

101. Ibid.

102. Ibid.

103. Andi Atwater, "George Siposs, 64 developed medical devices, etc," *The Orange County Register*, November 27, 1995, Metro-2.

104. The Internet Movie Data Base, Inc., "June Storey," http://imdb.com/name/nm0832475/ (accessed March 31, 2009).

105. Ibid., "Wilfred Cline," http://imdb.com/name/nm0005668/ (accessed March 31, 2009).

106. Ibid., "Dorothy Dare," http://imdb.com/name/nm0201118/ (accessed March 31, 2009).

107. Ibid., "John Eldridge," http://imdb.com/name/nmo253141/ (accessed March 31, 2009).

108. Michael Barrier, *Hollywood Cartoons: American Animation in its Golden Age*, (New York: Oxford Press, 1999), 36-38.

109. Burt A. Folkart, "Rudolf Ishing; Founded Cartoon Studio," *The Los Angeles Times*, July 22, 1992, Metro-12.

110. Claire Noland, "John Gordy, 1935-2009; Ex-Detroit Lions lineman headed NFL players' union," *The Los Angeles Times*, February 1, 2009, Metro-8.

111. Dennis McLellan, "Jay Migliori, 70; Key member of Supersax," *The Los Angeles Times*, September 7, 2001, Metro-13.

CHAPTER 5 – FOREST LAWN MEMORIAL PARK

1. Romanowski, 163.

2. Ibid., 879.

3. "Danny Flores, 77; Musician Who Shouted 'Tequila' on 1950's Hit," *The Los Angeles Times*, September 24, 2006, Metro-12.

4. "Angel Florez," http://members.tripod.com/DM_One/angel.html (accessed April 29, 2009).

5. IMDB.com, "Lisa Whelchel," http://imdb.com/name/nm0924075/ (accessed April 29, 2009).

6. Ibid., "Kelly Parsons," http://imdb.com/name/nm0663856/ (accessed April 29, 2009).

7. "Angel Florez."

8. IMDB.com, "George Grandee," http"//imdb.com/name/nm0334831/ (accessed April 29, 2009).

9. "Angels' Dick Wantz Succumbs to Brain Tumor," *The Los Angeles Times*, A1.

10. IMDB.com, "Philip Ford," http://imdb.com/name/nm02285831/ (accessed April 29, 2009).

11. Romanowski, 857-858.

12. "Sandy West; Drummer for the influential all-female rock'n'roll band the Runaways," *The Los Angeles Times*, Metro-11.

13. "Runaways drummer Sandy West dies at 47," *The U.S.A. Today*, October 24, 2006.

14. Myrna Oliver, "Harold Wertz; 'Bouncy' in 'Our Gang' Films," *The Los Angeles Times*, December 5, 1999, B-8.

15. Black Pants, Inc., wrestler profiles, "Abe Kashey," http://onlineworldofwrestling.com/Profiles/a/abe-kashey.html (accessed April 29, 2009).

16. IMDB.com, "Abe Kashey," http://imdb.com/name/nm0440538/ (accessed April 29, 2009).

17. Dennis McLellan, "Glenn Quinn, 32; Actor was in TV series *Roseanne* And *Angel*," *The Los Angeles Times*, Metro-23.

18. IMDB.com, "Glenn Quinn," http://imdb.com/name/nam0703849/ (accessed April 30, 2009).

19. McLellan.

20. "Creator of Crashes Killed on Film Set," *The Los Angeles Times*, August 21, 1989, Metro-1.

21. Romanowski, 194-195.

22. "Taxi Crash Kills L.A. Rock 'n' Roll Singer," *The Los Angeles Times*, April 18, 1960, 20.

23. "Young Rock 'n' Roll Idol Buried in Satin Shroud," *The Los Angeles Times*, April 26, 1960, B9.

24. "Passings; Sharon Sheeley, 62; as teen, Wrote 1950's hit 'Poor Little Fool'," *The Los Angeles Times*, May 20, 2002, Metro 9.

25. Katz, 920.

26. "Ken Maynard's Funeral Rites Set Tuesday," *The Los Angeles Times*, March 25, 1973, 3.

27. Jerry Belcher and Charles P. Wallace, "Vic Morrow, 2 Children Die in Film Accident," *The Los Angeles Times*, July 24, 1982, A1.

28. Reichler, 820.

29. Harry Trimborn, "Two Woman Fliers Die in Plane Crash," *The Los Angeles Times*, February 18, 1965, 1.

30. "Two FBI Men and Indian Slain Near Wounded Knee," *The Los Angeles Times*, June 27, 1975, B1.

31. "Indians Not Guilty in FBI Slayings," *The Los Angeles Times*, July 17, 1976, A1.

32. James S. Granelli, "Sidney H. Kelley, 92; Sold Cars, Blue Book," *The Los Angeles Times*, December 7, 2001, B12.

33. Nicole Gaouette, "Juanita Millender-McDonald, 68; Southland congresswoman," *The Los Angeles Times*, April 23, 2007, B9.

CHAPTER 6 – OTHER PRIVATE CEMETERIES

1. Wikipedia Foundation, Inc., "Jimmy Austin," http://en.wikipedia.org/wiki/Jimmy_Austin (accessed July 17, 2008).

2. Gene Karst and Martin J. Jones, Who's Who in Professional Baseball, (New Rochell, New York: Arlington House Publishers, 1973), 35.

3. Joseph L. Reichler, ed. The Baseball Encyclopedia: The Complete and Official Record of Major League Baseball, 7th ed. (New York, New York: MacMillan Publishing Company, 1988), 718.

4. Ibid.

5. Ibid., 1854.

6. Mike Shatzkin, ed. The Ballplayers: Baseball's Ultimate Biographical Reference, (New York, New York: William Morrow and Company, Inc., 1990), 437.

7. The Obituary of Earl Hamilton, The Register [Santa Ana], (Section C, p.3), November 19, 1968.

8. Wikipedia, "John Mills Houston," http://en.wikipedia.org/wiki/John_Mills_Houston (accessed July 17, 2008).

9. Wikipedia, "Rudolph Boysen," http://en.wikipedia.org/wiki/Rudolph_Boysen (accessed February 9, 2009).

10. Knott's Berry Farm, "Historical Background," http://www.knotts.com/coinfo/history/index.shtml (accessed February 9, 2009).

11. "Developer of Boysenberry Dies in Anaheim," The Santa Ana Register, November 25, 1950, 1.

12. The Obituary of Dallas Bixler, The Orange County Register, August 18, 1990, Metro section B, 1.

13. IMDB.com, Inc., The Internet Movie Data Base, "Marshall Stedman," http://imdb.com/name/nm824331/ (accessed July 19, 2008).

14. The Obituary of Marshall Stedman, The Santa Ana Register, December 17, 1943, 17.

15. IMDB.com, Inc., The Internet Movie Data Base, "Barbara Read," http://imdb.com/.

16. Wikipedia, "Barbara Read," http://en.wikipedia.org/wiki/Barbara_Read (accessed February 9, 2009).

17. "Ex-Wife Of TV D.A. Suicide in Laguna," The Register [Santa Ana], December 12, 1963, 1.

18. The Obituary of Carolyn Jones, The Orange County Register, August 4, 1983, D9.

19. IMDB.com, Inc., "Carolyn Jones," http://imdb.com/name/nm0427700/ (accessed August 22, 2008).

20. Katz, 707.

21. The Obituary of Carolyn Jones.

22. Wikipedia, "Gavvy Cravath," http://en.wikipedia.org/wiki/Gavvy_Cravath (accessed August 22, 2008).

23. Karst, 205.

24. Reichler, 868.

25. Ibid., 650.

26. The Obituary of Gavvy Cravath, The Register [Santa Ana, California], 23 May 1963.

27. IMDB.com, Inc., "Robert Fellows," http://imdb.com/name/nm02715241 (accessed August 24, 2008).

28. Ibid., http://imdb.com/title/tt0045883/awards.

29. Ibid., http://imdb.com/title/tt0047086/awards.

30. Ibid., http://imdb.com/name/nm02715241.

31. Wikipedia, "Take Me Out to the Ballgame," http://en.wikipedia.org/wiki/Take_Me_Out_To_The_Ball_Game.

32. Jack O'Connell, "Take Me Out Celebrates 100th Birthday," The Baseball Hall of Fame, posted may 5, 2008, http://web.baseballhalloffame.org/news/article.jsp?ymd=20080505&content_id=7228&vkey=hof_news.

33. Wikipedia, "Jack Norworth," http://en.wikipedia.org/wiki/jacknorworth.

34. The Obituary of Jack Norworth, The Register [Santa Ana, California], Septermber 2, 1959.

35. Ibid.

36. Wikipedia, "Shine on Harvest Moon," http://en.wikipedia.org/wiki/Shine_On_Harvest_Moon.

37. The Obituary of Jack Norworth.

38. The Songwriters Hall of Fame, "Jack Norworth," http://songwritershalloffame.org/exhibits/C267, (accessed August 25, 2008).

39. Evelyn Mack Truitt, Who was Who on Screen, (New York, New York:R.R. Bowker Company, 1977), 347.

40. The Obituary of Jack Norworth.

41. Truitt, 131.

42. Reichler, 2227-2228.

43. Shatzkin, 1177.

44. Reichler, 2228.

45. Wikipedia, "Lefty Williams," http://en.wikipedia.org/wiki/lefty_williams

46. Eliot Asinof, Eight Men Out: The Black Sox and the 1919 World Series, (New York, New York: Henry Holt and Company, 1987), 116-118.

47. Ibid., 273.

48. J.M. Flagler, "Requiem for a Southpaw," The New Yorker, December 5, 1959, 230-235.

49. The Obituary of Claude Williams, The Register [Santa Ana, California] 6 November 1959, evening edition.

50. County of Orange, Certificate of Death for Claude Preston Williams, (Santa Ana, California: November 4, 1959).

51. "Harry Buffum, Longtime Civic and Business leader, Succumbs," The Los Angles Times, April 7, 1968, G1.

52. Reichler, 2062.

53. Ibid., 1721.

54. Reichler, 2146.

55. Jeffrey Perlman, "$128.5 Million Awarded Over Car Crash, Fire," The Los Angeles Times, February 7, 1978, C1.

56. "Rites Set for Stafford Repp," The Los Angeles Times, November 8, 1974, B4.

57. Shatzkin, 1057.

58. Katz, 565.

59. "304 Californians Aboard in Canary Islands Disaster," The Los Angeles Times, March 28, 1077, A8.

60. Don Smith, "Remains of Many Crash Victims Arrive," The Los Angeles Times, April 23, 1977, OC6.

61. Evan Maxwell, "Rites Held for 117 who Died in Jet Crash," The Los Angeles Times, April 28, 1977, A22.

62. Reichler, 914.

63. IMDB.com, Inc., "Neal Fredricks," http://imdb.com/name/nm0292864/ (accessed May 13, 2009).

64. "Son of Curry to be Named," The Los Angeles Times, October 12, 1930, 2.

65. C. Douglas Sterner, Home of Heroes.com," Recipient of the Medal of Honor, Vietnam War, U.S. Marine Corp, Kenneth Worley," http://homeofheroes.com/moh/citiation_1960_vn/Worley_kenneth.html (accessed May 13, 2009).

66. IMDB.com, Inc., "Danny Lockin," http://imdb.com/name/nm0516906/ (accessed May 14, 2009).

67. Steve Emmons, "Murder Suspect Pleads Innocent in Actor's Death," The Los Angeles Times, August 27, 1977, OC26.

68. "Man Gets 4-Year Prison Term in Death of Actor," The Los Angeles Times, September 29, 1978, OC-A5.

69. Reichler, 1655.

70. "Old Time Giants Pitcher Barnes Dies During Trip," The Los Angeles Times, September 11, 1961, C6.

71. Mike Boehm, "The Examined Life Ends for Brad Nowell," The Los Angeles Times, June 1, 1996, 1.

72. Karst, 79.

73. "Sam L. Collins, Ex-Assembly Speaker, Dies," The Los Angeles Times, June 27, 1965, 26.

74. Myrna Oliver, "Andy Russell, 72; Bilingual '40's Singer, Latin Film Star," The Los Angeles Times, April 20, 1992, 24.

75. Ross Newman, "Controversial Ex-Dodger Exec Camoanis Dies," The Los Angeles Times, June 22, 1998, 1.

76. Dave Felton, "C.S. Forester, Creator of Hornblower, Dies," The Los Angeles Times, April 3, 1966, 2.

77. David Shaw, "Walter Knott Dies at His Famed Berry Farm at 91," The Los Angeles Times, December 4, 1981, OC1.

78. Reichler, 1460.

79. Penelope McMillan, " Ex-Cambodian President Lon Nol Dies in Fullerton," The Los Angeles Times, November 18, 1985, 3.

80. Eric Malnic,"Ex-Chief Justice Wright, Foe of Death Penalty, Dies," The Los Angeles Times, March 22, 1985, 1.

81. Reichler, 2119 and 2120.

82. Robin Hinch, "Services announced for John Crean," The Orange County Register, January, 11 2007.

83. Jeff Overley, "1,000 mourners celebrate John Crean's life," The Orange County Register, January 19, 2007.

84. Myrna Oliver, "Dick Kleiner, 80; Boraodway and Hollywood Columnist, Biographer," The Los Angeles Times, February 27, 2002, B-11.

85. Valarie J. Nelson, "T. Ravenscroft, 91; Gave Voice to Tony the Tiger, Disney Movies," The Los Angeles Times, May 25, 2005, B-14.

86. Jeff Gottlieb, "Mental Illness Plagued Church Musical Director; The Crystal Cathedral's prominent composer had threatened suicide well before the standoff," The Los Angeles Times, December 18, 2004, A1.

87. Anna Cekola, "Restaurant Chain Founder Dies; Obituary: Laguna Hills resident, whose pie shop grew into a multimillion dollar business, succubs to cancer Saturday. She was 88," The Orange County Register, November 12, 1995, 1.

88. Bill Billiter, "Garden Grove Funeral Services for Hippie Preacher," The Los Angeles Times, March 18, 1993, 3.

89. Reichler, 737.

90. Shatzkin, 267.

91. IMDB.com, Inc., "Kathryn Card," http://imdb.com/name/nm013293/ (accessed May 22, 2009).

92. Mike Terry, "Ron Jessie, 57; Ex-Ram Reciever Played 11 Seasons in NFL," The Los Angeles Times, January 17, 2006, B11.

93. Patricia Sullivan, "Robert Mardian; Attorney Caught Up in Watergate Scandal," The Washington Post, July 21, 2006, B7.

Chapter 7 – The Catholic Cemeteries

1. Reichler, 1824.

2. Shatzkin, 380.

3. "Former Big League Ball Player Dead," The Register [Santa Ana], Wednesday, May 17, 1940, A1.

4. Mark Traversino, Jr., interview by Michael Barry, Anaheim, California, February 10, 2009.

5. Shatzkin, 956.

6. Sports Reference, L.L.C., "Ed Sadowski," www.baseball-reference.com/s/sadowed01.shtml (accessed January 12, 2009).

7. "Ex-Angel Sadowski dies of ALS at 62," The Orange County Register, Tuesday, November 9, 1993, Sports 3.

8. Reichler, 1495.

9. Peter Gammons, "Stephenson Dead at 80," The Boston Globe, Sports-5.

10. Amy Richards, "Recital Honors Late Canyon Resident," The Orange County Register, News 1.

11. Gwendolyn Driscoll, Tiffany Montgomery, Nancy Luna, and Barbara Giasone, "A Fast Food Pioneer Dies," The Orange County Register, Saturday, January 12, 2008, News 3.

12. Ibid.

13. Nancy Luna and Michael Mello, "A mentor to all," *The Orange County Register*, Saturday, January 19, 2008, News 1and 14.

14. Katz, 732.

15. Ibid.

16. The Obituary of Ruby Keller, *The Orange County Register*, Monday, March 1, 1993, Metro B4.

17. Leo J. Friis, *Orange County Through Four Centuries*, (Santa Ana, California: Pioneer Press, 1982), 51.

18. Tony Saavedra, Teri Sforza, and Barbara Diamon, "Nicole Brown Simpson Left lasting Mark," *The Orange County Register*, June 15, 1994, News 12.

19. Anne C. Mulkern, "O.J., Others Mourn Ex-Wife," *The Orange County Register*, June 17, 1994, News 1.

20. Michael Barrier, *Hollywood Cartoons: American Animation in its Golden Age*, (New York, New York: Oxford Press, 1999), 403-410.

21. Stephen Lynch, "William Hanna, half of carton conglomerate dies," *The Orange County Register*, March 23, 2001, News 1.

22. Shatzkin, 1055.

23. Reichler, 1502.

24. IMDB.com, The Internet Movie Data Base, "Lou Stringer," http://imdb.com/name/nm08345781/ (accessed February 25, 2009).

25. IMDB.com, "Gail De Cossi," http://imdb.com/name/nm1544142/ (accessed February 25, 2009).

26. Robin Hinch, "A Life Story, Gail Johnson a Singer with a Heart of Gold," *The Orange County Register*, February 11, 1999, Metro 5.

27. IMDB.com, "Gail Johnson," http://imdb.com/name/nm0425112/

28. Hinch. Metro 5.

29. "Robert T. Hunter; Washington State Judge," *The Los Angeles Times*, September 21, 2000, Metro-8.

30. Pro Football Hall of Fame.com, "Tom Fears," http://profootballhof.com/hof/member.jsp?player_id=66 (accessed February 25, 2009).

31. IMDB.com, "Tom Fears," http://imdb.com/name/nm0269916/ (accessed February 25, 2009).

32. Steve Bishoff, "Tom Fears: 1922-2000, Catch became Fears' Legacy," *The Orange County Register*, January 6, 2000, Sports 1.

33. Reichler, 2032.

34. Peter Larsen, "A Cartoon Voice Fades into the Past," *The Orange County Register*, April 13, 1999, News 1.

35. IMDB.com, "Jean Vander Pyl," http://imdb.com/name/nm0888717/ (accessed February 25, 2009).

36. Larsen, News 1.

37. Reichler, 870.

38. "Body of Missing Girl Found Near Campground," *The Los Angeles Times*, July 7, 1979, OC1.

39. Gary Jarlson, "Man Arrested in Girl's Murder," *The Los Angeles Times*, July 25, 1979, E4.

40. Doug Brown, "Jury Asks for Death Penalty in Alcala Case," *The Los Angeles Times*, May 9, 1980. OC1.

41. "State High Court Reverses Conviction in Girl's Death," *The Los Angeles Times*, August 23, 1984, A1.

42. David Reyes, "Alcala Found Guilty ar Retrialin Killing of 12-Year-Old Girl," *The Los Angeles Times*, May 29, 1986, OC-A1.

43. Jerry Hicks, "Federal Judge Overturns Alcala Conviction," *The Los Angeles Times*, Orange County Edition, April 3, 2001, Metro 1.

44. Larry Welborn, "Suspect in Serial Kiilings to be Tried in O.C.," *The Orange County Register*, June 13, 2008, Local 2.

45. Reichler, 1700.

46. Shatzkin, 723.

47. Katz, 194.

48. Truitt, 349.

49. "The Obituary of Kirt Ober," *The Los Angeles Times*, June 3, 1939, 15.

50. Truitt, 349.

51. Reichler, 1209.

52. Shatzkin, 664.

53. Ibid., 720.

54. Randy Youngman, "Dodgers Scout McMahon Dies After Pitching batting Practice," *The Orange County Register*, July 23, 1987, Sports 1.

CHAPTER EIGHT – MURDER AND MAYHEM

1. "The Late Murder of Sheriff Baron and Three of his Party," The Los Angeles Star, Saturday, January 31, 1857, 1.

2. Ibid.

3. Ibid.

4. "The Pursuit of the Robbers," The Los Angeles Star, Wednesday, February 3, 1857, 1.

5. Angus MacLean, The Legend of the California Bandidos, (Arroyo Grande, California: Bear Flag Books, 1977), 56-58.

6. Pamela Hallan-Gibson, Ghosts and Legends of San Juan Capistrano, 3rd ed. (The San Juan Capistrano Historical Society, 1983), 22.

7. "Killing of Charles F. Lehman," The Southern Californian (Anaheim, California), Saturday, July 27, 1872, 3.

8. "Murder At Anaheim," The San Francisco Chronicle, Wednesday, July 24, 1872, 2.

9. "Page From Early History, Razing of Building Recalls Shooting Affray," The Anaheim Gazette, April 8, 1909.

10. "Center Street shootout has place in city history," The Anaheim Bulletin, Thursday, November 24, 1983, A3.

11. "Page From Early History."

12. "Center street shootout."

13. "Page From Early History."

14. Ibid.

15. Ibid.

16. "Center street shootout."

17. "Page From Early History."

18. "Bandit Assaults Girl, Kills Bob Squires, Wounds Three Others," The Santa Ana Daily News, December 16, 1912, 1 and 5.

19. Morgan, 200.

20. "Hundreds Attending Brave Man's Funeral," The Santa Ana Daily News, December 18, 1912. 1.

21. Don Smith, "Five Minutes of Terror," The Los Angeles Times, July 14, 1976, 3.

22. Evan Maxwell, "7 Die in Fullerton Shooting Spree," The Los Angeles Times, July 13, 1976, 1.

23. Evan Maxwell, "Allaway Found Not Guilty in Sanity Phase of Murder Trial," The Los Angeles Times, November 3, 1977, OC1.

24. David Reyes, "Mass Killer's Bid for Release Denied," The Los Angeles Times, December 24, 2003, B3.

25. "2 Found Slain in Goleta," The Los Angeles Times, December 31, 1979, A1.

26. "Pair Fatally Bludgeoned," The Los Angeles Times, March 17, 1980, A1.

27. Jerry Hicks, "Young Couple Murdered in Niguel Shores," The Los Angeles Times, August 23, 1980, OC-B1.

28. "Irvine Police Task Force to probe Death of Woman," The Los Angeles Times, February 9, 1981, OC-A8.

29. DirectNIC.com, "The East Area Rapist/ Original Night Stalker," http://ear-ons.com/crimes.html (accessed June 1, 2009).

30. Maria La Ganga, "Investigation Continues in Murder of Woman," The Los Angeles Times, May 7, 1986, OC-A2.

31. "Arrest Made in Woman's Death," The Los Angeles Times, June 24, 1986, OC-A2.

32. Sean Emery, "Original Night Stalker focus of new cable special," The Orange County Register, May 7, 2009, Local 6.

33. Steve Chawkins, "Family Slaying a Mystery," The Los Angeles Times, May 22, 2009, A3.

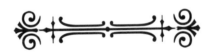

NAMES INDEX